The Laws of Yesterday's Wars 4

International Humanitarian Law Series

VOLUME 75

The International Humanitarian Law Series is a series of monographs and edited volumes which aims to promote scholarly analysis and discussion of both the theory and practice of the international legal regulation of armed conflict.

The series explores substantive issues of International Humanitarian Law, including:

- Protection for victims of armed conflict and regulation of the means and method of warfare
- Questions of application of the various legal regimes for the conduct of armed conflict
- Issues relating to the implementation of International Humanitarian Law obligations
- National and international approaches to the enforcement of the law and
- The interactions between International Humanitarian Law and other related areas of international law such as Human Rights, Refugee Law, Arms Control and Disarmament Law, and International Criminal Law.

The titles published in this series are listed at *brill.com/ihul*

The Laws of Yesterday's Wars 4

From Mesopotamia to Somalia

Edited by

Samuel White

BRILL | NIJHOFF

LEIDEN | BOSTON

Cover illustrations: © Medina Abdirashid Ali. Made by and printed with kind permission of Medina Abdirashid Ali.

Library of Congress Cataloging-in-Publication Data
Names: White, Samuel C. Duckett editor
Title: The laws of yesterday's wars 4 : from Mesopotamia to Somalia / edited by Samuel White.
Other titles: Laws of yesterday's wars four
Description: Leiden ; Boston : Brill/Nijhoff, 2026. | Series: International humanitarian law series, 1389-6776 ; volume 75 | Includes index.
Identifiers: LCCN 2025036434 (print) | LCCN 2025036435 (ebook) | ISBN 9789004703070 hardback | ISBN 9789004703094 ebook
Subjects: LCSH: War (International law)—History | War—History | Humanitarian law | War—Egypt—History | War—Somalia—History | War—Africa, West—History | LCGFT: Law materials
Classification: LCC KZ6385 .L398 2026 (print) | LCC KZ6385 (ebook) | DDC 341.6—dc23/eng/20250808
LC record available at https://lccn.loc.gov/2025036434
LC ebook record available at https://lccn.loc.gov/2025036435

Typeface for the Latin, Greek, and Cyrillic scripts: "Brill". See and download: brill.com/brill-typeface.

ISSN 1389-6776
ISBN 978-90-04-70307-0 (hardback)
ISBN 978-90-04-70309-4 (e-book)
DOI 10.1163/9789004703094

This book is printed on acid-free paper and produced in a sustainable manner.

Contents

Foreword

At its heart, international humanitarian law (IHL) is a normative framework that draws upon the universal idea that what unites us is deeper than what divides us. In the numerous obligations found in IHL, there are profound threads of what it means to be part of the human race in terms of survival during war; be it as a combatant, a prisoner/detainees or as part of the civilian population. As a collection of treaties, protocols, customary law and academic writings, the concept of reducing suffering in times of armed conflict inevitably spans cultures as sadly a collective experience throughout the ages and across the globe is use of force to resolve disputes between and within States.

This Volume of the Series is focused across roughly two geographical areas, although temporally they are quite separate. The first is of Mesopotamia, where Pharaonic Egypt, the Hittites and the Torah are all explored in-depth. The second geographic area is of sub-Saharan Africa, with two regional blocs (West Africa and Southern Africa) as well as one specific case study of the Somali.

The methodology of the chapters vary. Those papers that explore Mesopotamia do through a doctrinal approach, although Norman Solomon brings his lived experiences to bear when interpreting the Torah. The regional blocs of West and Southern Africa again rely on a mixed methodology of doctrine and qualitative studies, whilst the Somali research is ground-breaking in terms of its breadth and depth of qualitative field research.

Whilst the methodology varies, the Volume is consistent both internally and with the other Volumes of the series. So far, 30 chapters have been covered by the *Laws of Yesterday's Wars* series. With each of them, a deeper understanding of how societies have sought to restrict warfare becomes clearer.

Such understandings are increasingly precious today, as we navigate a world that often seems to be without the necessary adherence to basic IHL principles. Calls that claim IHL is no longer relevant to the modern battlefield require responses and reflections that are located in historical comprehension of how methods and means of fighting over the years have developed. In this sense this series has merit in not only giving us interesting knowledge about the past, but ideas and inspiration on how to move forward and continue to advocate for mitigation during the horrors of war. For organisations such as RedR Australia, where the experts we deploy into crisis and conflict need to combine their specific skill set with strong cultural competencies, '*Laws of Yesterday's Wars*' is valuable.

There is often a degree of skepticism, especially from academics, when it is proposed to look to historical, cultural and religious practices to find connections with current black letter international law. Indeed, the dangers of a 'cut and paste' approach do exist (ie correlating useful examples that connect to rules and ignoring those that don't). Anything that brings a fragmented and overly culturally relative reading of established and basic IHL obligations creates significant challenges. However, these warnings must be balance with the reality that in aiming for respect and application of IHL, finding methods to create traction with the idea that even wars have limits, is necessary and life-saving. In my early career as a Legal Adviser to the ICRC in the Pacific region, talking to authorities about 'the Geneva Conventions' did not always gain the impact that I was looking for, to move ratifications and implementation forward. Working with experts from the many countries in region, hearing the stories, songs, poems and other ways history about warring culture was handed down, resulted in the creation of *Protection Under the Palm*. This small booklet demonstrated the ideas and concepts embedded in IHL were not foreign notions and I have been delighted over the years to see the proliferation – from Africa to the Middle East – of books, documents and articles that highlight connections between what is understood and practiced locally to the universal ambitions of IHL. Furthermore, more recent research such as the ICRC's *Roots of Restraint*, highlighted that along with the formal trainings on IHL, informal structures and processes that socialize combat ethics (such as religion, business practices, cultural beliefs) also has influence on cultivating restraint during armed conflict.

Laws of Yesterday's Wars series is more than a fascinating read, with a scope and scale across geography and timeframes. It is a reminder that many of the wicked problems we face today have been carefully thought about and responded to in the past. It is a reminder that we need to find the connections, the commonality and build out from such a base to change the behaviors and actions of today. Finally, it is a reminder that whilst war has been a staple of history, so too is the aim to reduce the impact and suffering of armed conflict part of our complex human heritage.

Dr Helen Durham AO
CEO – RedR Australia

Acknowledgements

Like anything, these works do not just occur in isolation; thanks are required to the multiple individuals and teams that worked on the project.

To the contributors who saw the goal of the project, and who saw it through – thank you.

To Professor Tim McCormack and the Brill team, who assisted with the entire publishing process, and to Ms Helen Jeffcoat, who compiled the index – thank you.

Finally, and most importantly, to my wife & daughters – thank you for always making it balanced.

Contributors

Editor

Samuel White
is the Senior Research Fellow at the National University of Singapore's Centre for International Law. In 2025, he was made a Fellow of the Royal Historical Society for his work on cross-cultural approaches to warfare.

Concurrently to academia, Samuel has served as both a Royal Australian Infantry Corps and an Australian Army Legal Corps officer in a variety of tactical, operational and strategic level postings. In 2018, he served as Associate to the Honourable Justice John Logan of the Federal Court of Australia, Supreme & National Courts of Papua New Guinea, and President of the Defence Force Discipline Appeals Tribunal. He is admitted to practice as a Solicitor in the State of Queensland and before the High Court of Australia; as well as a Barrister and Solicitor in New Zealand.

Contributors

Anthony Spalinger
Emeritus Professor serves at the University of Auckland, New Zealand. He has been there for over 40 years, researching the intersection between Ancient Egypt and the concept of war. He has held multiple academic fellowships, including a Fulbright to Paris.

Ayan Abdirashid Ali
holds a Bachelors of Law and International Relations from the University of Adelaide. She works with the South Australian Attorney General's Department and is a researcher on various areas of International Law including, International Maritime, Customary, Humanitarian Law and Theory (TWAIL). Ayan also researches the relationship between Traditional Somali Literature and laws, governance, and peace and conflict resolution systems for which she has various forthcoming publications on. Ayan has regularly presented her research with the ICRC, the UNHCR, the Global Protection Cluster, the Geneva Graduate Institute of International and Development Studies, and with the Heritage Institute for Public Policy (Mogadishu, Somalia). She is of Somali background and has conducted all translations herself.

Godfree Matthew
is a law lecturer in the Department of International Law and Jurisprudence, with Adekunle Ajasin University, Akungba-Akoko, Ondo State, Nigeria. He is a scholar with sound academic backgrounds in sociology, theology, history and law. His areas of core competence include International Humanitarian Law and Military Law. Godfree Matthew has written about 60 Articles published in both national and international journals. He is currently a PhD student with University of Jos, Nigeria. He is also a legal practitioner with Pwajok, Ikowe & Co. NO. 28 Ahmadu Bello Way, Jos, Nigeria.

Norman Solomon
was born in Cardiff, S. Wales, in 1933, and educated there and at St. John's College, Cambridge. He served as rabbi to Orthodox Congregations in Manchester, Liverpool and London before founding, in 1983, the Centre for the Study of Judaism and Jewish/Christian Relations at the Selly Oak Colleges, Birmingham. Fellow in Modern Jewish Thought at the Oxford Centre for Hebrew and Jewish Studies from 1995–98, he is a member of Wolfson College, Oxford, and of the Oxford University Teaching and Research Unit in Hebrew and Jewish Studies. He is a Past President of the British Association for Jewish Studies, Vice President of the World Congress of Faiths, and a Patron of the International Interfaith Centre, and has participated in Interfaith Dialogue in over twenty countries on five continents. His publications include *Judaism and World Religion* (1991), *The Analytic Movement: Hayyim Soloveitchik and his School* (1993), *A Very Short Introduction to Judaism* (1996, 2025), *Historical Dictionary of Judaism* (1998, 2025), *The Talmud: A Selection* (2009), *Torah from Heaven* (2012), *Making Sense of "God"* (2023), as well as numerous articles and reviews.

Rory Cox
PhD, is a Professor in Medieval History at the University of St Andrews and a Fellow of the Royal Historical Society. His interdisciplinary research explores the history of violence and ethics from the ancient to the modern world. He has published extensively on the historical just war tradition, military history, uses of torture, and political theory. His latest book, *Origins of the Just War: Military Ethics and Culture in the Ancient Near East* (Princeton University Press, 2023) was awarded the 2024 Distinguished Book Award for Non-U.S. Military History by the Society for Military History.

Sarah Jean Mabeza
is the Regional Legal Advisor at the Pretoria Delegation of the International Committee of the Red Cross. She has an LLB degree from the University of KwaZulu-Natal, and an LLM degree in Human Rights and Democratisation in Africa from the Centre for Human Rights at the University of Pretoria.

Tamalin Bolus
is a Legal Advisor at the Pretoria Delegation of the International Committee of the Red Cross. She has an LLB degree from the University of Sussex, and an LLM degree in International Humanitarian Law and Human Rights from the Geneva Academy of International Humanitarian Law and Human Rights.

Introduction

These volumes find their origin in a rather odd place. On one rather unexceptional evening, I was watching the HBO show, *Vikings*. The eponymously named show follows the mythic origins of Scandinavian raiders, who as they expand to find new land and new resources, come up against 'civilised' European society. For the most part, these Scandinavian men and women maintain their culture of warbands, raiding and looting. Yet, some do not – Rollo assimilates and becomes a Francophile, adopting the culture and the warfighting of the Franks in return for land and titles. This is all to say that after a few seasons of slowly less and less violence, by the time we come across a scene where a warband of Vikings defile and destroy a small French homestead, we are reminded of the brutality of the times. Outraged that these raiders would do such a thing to some innocent peasants, I said to myself 'surely that was a war crime even under Viking law.'

This series started in trying to address that question – which I did not even answer (Andrew Butler did).[1] Yet it catalysed a wider research question of: how international is international humanitarian law? Such a question was posited by Prof. Anthea Roberts in her work, and I have humbly tried to follow in her footsteps. I have also tried, as Editor, to respond to the implicit challenge laid down by Jean Pictet when he suggested that:

> humanitarian principles are common to all human communities wherever they may be. When different customs, ethics and philosophies are gathered for comparison, and when they are melted down, their particularities eliminated and only what is general extracted, one is left with a pure substance which is the heritage of all mankind.[2]

To distil this substance is a difficult challenge, and causes friction amongst those scholars who study comparative methodologies. Should one rely upon functionalism or contextualism? Both have their benefits and challenges. I am not quite sure the choice is as binary as it is made to seem.

1 Andrew Butler, 'Viking Laws of War' in Samuel White (ed.) *The Laws of Yesterday's Wars* (Brill Nijhoff, 2021) 150–171.

2 Jean Pictet, "Humanitarian Ideas Shared by Different Schools of Thought and Cultural Traditions", in Jean Pictet (ed.) *International Dimensions of Humanitarian Law*, Henry Dunant Institute, M. Nijhoff, Switzerland 1988 pp. 3–4.

 | DOI:10.1163/9789004703094_002

This series seeks to collect a wide set of cultural understandings of systems that control and mitigate violence (as of course, the concept of 'war' is not one that translates across all cultures)[3] to try to uncover what is the heritage of all mankind (with that gendered language to be taken from Pictet). At its heart, the comparative approach is as much about discovering idiosyncrasies as it is about highlighting commonalities.[4] This can be difficult and requires a great deal of introspection, as the great poet Burns reflected on in 1786:

> Oh, would some Power give us the gift
> To see ourselves as other see us!

One point that I have reflected on, and come to the uncomfortable conclusion of, is that the European model of warfare is ultimately incompatible with the protection of civilians. It is a system of law grounded in classism (from its medieval roots prioritising the chivalric class) and chauvinism. Mégret made this point decades ago,[5] although it has taken me some time to come to the same conclusion after seeing the plethora of models other cultures and civilisations have created over millennia: from the duels of Malabar, to the public control of violence in Indigenous Australia, all the way through to the overarching concept of *adat* in South East Asia. This Volume has highlighted the pan-African concept of *Ubuntu* – a polylinguistic term that can be roughly translated as "the belief in a universal bond of sharing that connects all humanity".[6] It further highlights the tension between divine right and the inverse relationship it has with humanitarian perspectives.

Now this is not to say that other systems of law have not evolved with the strict class-based rules (just look at Zuzana Špicová *Ancient Indian Laws of War* chapter in Volume II) nor that other systems do not internalise chauvinism (see again *Indigenous Australian Laws of War* in Volume I, or *Mongol Laws of War* in Volume III). In this Volume, we see class-ism built into Egypt, Israel, the

3 See the discussion of the term in Samuel White, 'Introduction' *Laws of Yesterday's Wars: Volume III*.

4 Bloch, 'Toward a Comparative History', 507; Geertz, *Interpretation of Cultures*, 43; Émile Durkheim, *The Division of Labor in Society*, trans. George Simpson, cited in Neil J. Smelser, *Comparative Methods in the Social Sciences* (Eaglewood Cliffs, NJ: Prentice-Hall, 1976), 2. Smelser, *Comparative Methods*, 1.

5 Frédéric Mégret, 'From "Savages" to "Unlawful Combatants": A Postcolonial Look at International Humanitarian Law's "Other"' in Anne Orford (ed), *International Law and its 'Others'* (Cambridge University Press, 2006) 265, 283.

6 Kenneth Mutuma and Eve Massingham, 'East African Laws of War' in Samuel White (ed.) *The Laws of Yesterday's Wars Volume II* (Brill Nijhoff, 2022) 214, 214–220.

Hitties and the Persians. But there is a difference I might reflect on between those systems, and modern international humanitarian law as embodied in the *Geneva Conventions*.

The European model on which modern IHL is based upon is one that balances civilian protection and military necessity. I might simply call it 'winning at a proportionate cost', although in many instances the act of winning allows for retrospective justification of what was proportionate. It is a system that some believe prioritises civilians and others believe prioritises the military.[7] Notwithstanding strong arguments for the former, personal experience suggests that the laws of war are there to legitimise the conduct of the military. It is a system of law, I would suggest, that is about legitimising victory and the steps taken for it. Chris Bailey made this excellent point in Volume I of the series, where he remarks that:

> While there is no denying that both Dunant and Lieber have had a tremendous impact on the development of LOAC, Lieber's real contribution was the fusing of these competing views. As Karl Chang articulates, the real impact of LOAC is the complimentary role it plays in conflict, "But just as the law functions as a restraint or shield to protect the defenseless, it also can serve as a sword – a justification for legitimate military action." In fact, the distinction drawn between the work of Dunant and Lieber create a false dichotomy over how armed conflict can and should be managed.[8]

Therefore, the comparative model allows us to not only see the similarities and differences between different systems of law, but critically question our own models and assess whether they are fit-for-purpose (if we are so open). As I noted in the Introduction to Volume I, the chapters are intended to be read alone. Yet, whilst standalone, all follow the same structural format, first exploring the culture in question and their system of governance, before addressing the key question: what was their specific goal of warfare? Not one is the same – Indigenous Australian warfare (as it related to the capture of women for marriage, and the protection of sacred land from sacrilege) is distinct from Aztec warfare (which was concerned with capturing individuals for sacrifice). The chapters then, in turn, look to address what was *prohibited* by that culture.

---

7 See Anne Quintin, *The Nature of International Humanitarian Law: A Permissive or Restrictive Regime* (Elgar Internationa, 2020).

8 Chris Bailey, 'Code of Necessity – Assessing the Lieber Code as a Form of Strategic Lawfare' in Samuel White, *The Laws of Yesterday's Wars* (Brill, 2021) 186.

In the past three volumes, I have belaboured the necessity for both good individual studies, and good comparisons, because scholars practicing one approach too often belittle the contributions of the other approach. Specialists in the history of one society tend to dismiss the comparisons as superficial, whilst those who tend to compare tend to dismiss the studies of single societies as hopelessly myopic and of limited value in the study of other societies. But it is necessary to have both if we wish to acquire reliable knowledge. In particular, it would be danger to generalise from just one society, or even to be confident about the interpretation of just one regulation of warfare.

Of course, there is risk when comparing and contrasting the different chapters in the series that the basic principle distilled, if it is to be common across all, is to be found within the most abstract of rules. I have written, relying upon the results of Volumes 1–3, of what I think is the most pure substance of the laws of war: that they exist.[9] Such a revelation might be critiqued for being too abstract, but I think it an important point. So far, no culture canvassed has existed in a 'sharp war' construct – belief that warfare should be fought without rules. This Volume is no different. The cultures canvassed here are thematically from Mesopotamia and Africa, but join the large geographic spread of cultures researched in preceding volumes. All chapters found within this Volume reflect that there has always been a general concept of 'right' and 'wrong' in warfare. I do not believe that to be an abstract concept, but one that is perhaps the most fundamental in existence.

Continuing the issue of methodology, then, it is important to reflect on some lessons learnt. There is a tendency to dismiss the sources and history of those that are not written. A personal account can perhaps reflect this, more than an academic source. At a garden party in 2023 at Windsor Castle, to which I was particularly underdressed, an archivist from the College of Arms teasingly commented that he never understood why Australians studied archival history when we had such little of it to research. When I observed that Indigenous Australian history is the oldest continuing culture in the world, he replied in all sincerity: but it is not written; it cannot be history. It is true. Indigenous Australian society was not a literate society. Yet that is not to say that the history is not there. It is – in the artwork, the land, the mythology and oral history of the First Nations.[10]

As Rory Cox, a contributor to this Volume, has written elsewhere:

9 See Samuel White, 'War Without Limits: A Historical Critique of Sharp War Theory' (2024) *International Review of the Red Cross* 1–20.

10 See Marica Langton & Aaron Corn, *Law* (Thames & Hudson, 2023).

> Prayers, poetry, literary tales, and material evidence can tell us much about ethical norms and attitudes towards war and death. Such sources might even provide a more realistic – or at least more emotional – rendering of societal attitudes than, for example, abstract treatises on jurisprudence.[11]

The literary, documentary, and material evidence offered by each society under investigation varies significantly. The mass of literature across different genres and the abundant archaeological record from ancient Egypt, as Spalinger provides, contrasts with the rich legalistic and diplomatic corpus that survives from Hatti that Cox writes on. Both of these bodies of evidence contrast again strict sources relied upon by Solomon, when writing on Jewish laws of war. Those chapters looking at African practice of mitigating the effects of warfare relied upon documentary and qualitative interviews.

There is folly in limiting legal research to that which is written. It is of course far easier to do so; and it takes time, effort, money and health to be able to conduct field research. But the results are important. In Volume III, Emily Defina in her *Papua New Guinea Laws of War*, and the co-authors Marco, Ruben and Justin in *South Sudanese Laws of War* highlighted the importance of qualitative interviews, as does Ayan Abdirashid Ali in this Volume. Ayan's chapter is of course the most substantive of all chapters in the Volume (and indeed, so far throughout the series). This reflects the breadth of her interviews and the depth of the oral history of Somalia.

Collectively and individually, their ground-breaking work has had practical implications. On the 75th Anniversary of the Geneva Conventions, past and present contributors to this *Laws of Yesterday's Wars* series were invited to the Headquarters of the International Committee of the Red Cross to reflect on the wider history of IHL. One key consequence of that meeting was a recommitment to cultural understandings of IHL when conducting dialogues – the effectiveness of which has been highlighted through the success of Tamalin Bolus & Sarah Jean Mabeza's *Toolkits on African Laws of War*. Their work is expanded and reflected in this Volume, but was a rightful cornerstone of the 75th anniversary celebrations.

Collectively, the work in these Volumes highlights the risk in unthinkingly subscribing to the 'straight line history of eternal progression' of international law.[12] This is a model where a Great White Man (Grotius, Vitoria, Augustine) discovered international law and it was developed progressively into the modern

11 Rory Cox, *Origins of the Just War* (Princeton University Press, 2023) p. XXX.

12 Alonso Dunkelberg, 'It's a Trap! Re-Thinking Samuel Moyn's *Humane* Beyond the North Atlantic' (2021) 12 *Journal of International Humanitarian Legal Studies* pp. 345, 350.

era. For many parts of European law, this is without a doubt correct – one need only read the history of the laws of war in Roman,[13] Medieval Europe,[14] and the Renaissance[15] as well as how they shaped the framework of the American Civil War.[16] It is not the universal experience. There is clearly a deep history of the development and growth of international law (including IHL) outside of Europe. By remaining focused upon the Great White Man, we ignore the wider patterns and lessons of international law – such as the fact that models of conflict management exist that are not focused on 'victory at a proportionate cost'.

The risk of focusing solely upon Europe in addressing the history of the laws was championed in 1795 by Robert War, when he wrote:

> We expected too much when we contended for the *universality* of the duties laid down by the Codes of the Laws of Nations … however desirable such universality might be … what is commonly called the Law of Nations … is not the Law of *all* Nations but only of particular classes of them; and thus there may be a *different* Law of Nations for *different* parts of the globe.[17]

The answers can be across *The Laws of Yesterday's Wars: From Indigenous Australians to the American Civil War*,[18] *Volume II: Ancient India to East Africa*[19] and *Volume III: From the Highlands of Papua New Guinea to the Island of Malta*. The question remains the same with this Volume, and successive works to follow (such as Volumes V–IX which are currently in production). Whilst in many ways the primary question remains the same – how international is international humanitarian law – it is clear that the results can start to address contemporary challenges in the laws of war.

Finally, lest it be unsaid, there are of course errors that can be drawn from a wide-ranging description of a cultural understanding of warfare. From whose

13 Samuel White, 'Roman Laws of War' in Samuel White (ed.) *Laws of Yesterday's Wars: Volume II*, Brill Nijhoff, the Netherlands, 2023 pp. 110–126.

14 Samuel White 'The Late Middle Ages' in Samuel White (ed.) *Laws of Yesterday's Wars* Brill Nijhoff, the Netherlands, 2022 pp. 101–127.

15 Kyle Walker, 'The Renaissance' in Samuel White (ed.) *Laws of Yesterday's Wars* Brill Nijhoff, the Netherlands, 2022 pp. 127–150.

16 Christopher Bailey, 'Code of Necessity – Lawfare During the United States Civil War' in Samuel White (ed.) *The Laws of Yesterday's Wars* Brill Nijhoff, the Netherlands, 2022 p. 187.

17 *Enquiry into the Foundation and History of the Law of Nations in Europe* (London, 1795) 1, xiii–xiv and 169.

18 (Brill Nijhoff, 2021).

19 (Brill Nijhoff, 2022).

perspective is it to be drawn? Can culture ever be captured on page, as it constantly changes? To that I would say that the difference between writing on legal history, rather than a legal brief, is that one actually looks forward to having errors pointed out.

Samuel White

CHAPTER 1

Ancient Egyptian Directives of Warfare

Anthony Spalinger

1 Introduction

This Chapter looks to explore the laws (or more specifically, directives) of Ancient Egyptian warfare. The relevant time period this Chapter explores is the Egyptian New Kingdom of Dynasties XVIII–XX (ca. 1540 BC–1075 BC) and one event from the Kushite Era dated to ca. 730 BC. In their hieroglyphic records the ancient Egyptians officially prescribed no lists, sets, or promulgations with respect to how they engaged in war much less than establishing an official code of military behavior. We are equally unfortunate that no handbook for warfare is extant although it may be argued that the entire military institution, even at its most elemental stage, would have had declared objectives of practice, goals to be pursued and the like.[1] After all, the military is a corporate body instituted for warfare, violence, and as such it logically reveals typical bureaucratic norms of conduct.[2] With the exception of one striking example, we do not possess any catalogue or register of how the soldiers were to fight. By and large, when we turn to the sources in the New Kingdom indirect evidence must be employed in order to determine the acceptable standards of combat. To be sure, the connecting of hunting, violence, and warfare has not been overlooked.[3] Those expectations of typical conduct can by and large be

1 Part of the background to this issue will be presented in the forthcoming volume, Anthony Spalinger (ed.). *Brill's Companion to Warfare in Ancient Egypt*. Warfare in the Ancient Mediterranean World Series (Leiden: Brill, forthcoming). For the related issue of violence, see Uroš Matić, *Violence and Gender in Ancient Egypt* (London and New York: Routledge, 2021) with his earlier *Body and Frames of War in New Kingdom Egypt: Violent Treatment of Enemies and Prisoners* (Wiesbaden: Harrassowitz, 2019). Add the useful detailed study of Andrea Gnirs, "Coping with the Army. The Military and the State in the New Kingdom." In Juan Carlos Moreno García (ed.). *Ancient Egyptian Administration*, (Leiden: Brill, 2013), pp. 639–717. See now Rory Cox, *Origins of the Just War. Military Ethics and Culture in the Ancient Near East* (Princeton: Princeton University Press, 2023), Part 1.

2 I have discussed this aspect in *Leadership under Fire: The Pressures of Warfare in Ancient Egypt* (Paris: Soleb, 2019), Chapter 1 ("Generalship and Leadership: An Introduction").

3 John Darnell, "Hunting and Warfare: The Ritualisation of Military Violence in Ancient Egypt." In Garrett Fagan, Linda Fibiger, Mark Hudson *et al.* (eds.). *The Cambridge World History of*

 | DOI:10.1163/9789004703094_003

seen in the numerous military war records of pictorial nature that decorated the walls of the various temples.[4] In addition, we are able to combine those visual exploits with the conduct, exemplary or not, that is recorded in the various war records of the same time period.[5] Inter-diplomatic political relations, ones that involved embassies, treatment of foreigners, political juxtapositions of hostility, neutrality, and friendship need not be covered in this discussion. In essence, they lie in a different arena, one connected to warfare but standing outside of overt hostile manoeuvring.[6] The foreigner, alien, was always strange and thus to be despised, vilified, and not infrequently attacked. But speaking regularly, the Egyptians were never in an ever-present or 'constant' state of war. When, however, war became persistent with the kingdom of the Hittites or even earlier with Mitanni in Syria, then the warfare was over territory then in contest between various empires.

The related issue of violence in Egyptian warfare, especially related to captives, prisoners, children/women is a subject that will be only briefly discussed here as it has been the subject of many separate analyses by Uroš Matić.[7]

Violence Volume 1, The Prehistoric and Ancient Worlds (Cambridge: Cambridge University Press, 2020), pp. 181–197. Cox, *Origins of the Just War. Military Ethics and Culture in the Ancient Near East*, 134–142, provides a survey of the material.

4 Spalinger, *Icons of Power: A Strategy of Reinterpretation*, (Prague: Charles University of Prague, Faculty of Arts, 2011); and Nicholas E. Wernick, "The Images of Fortifications in the Sety I Battle Reliefs; Comparing Art and Archaeology." In Judith Corbelli, Daniel Boatright, and Claire Malleson (eds.). *Current Research in Egyptology 2009: Proceedings of the Tenth Annual Symposium* (Oxbow: Oxford, 2011), pp. 157–170.

5 Labib Habachi, *The Second Stela of Kamose, and His Struggle against the Hyksos and his Capital* (Glückstadt: J.J. Augustin, 1972). Harry Smith and Alexandra Smith, "A Reconsideration of the Kamose Texts," *Zeitschrift für ägyptische Sprache*, Vol. 103, 1976, pp. 48–76. Add Cox's discussion in Cox, *Origins of the Just War. Military Ethics and Culture in the Ancient Near East*, Chapter 3.

6 I thus avoid discussing the Teaching of Merikare which covers in a few lines issues related to military and diplomatic relations of Heracleopolis to the southern kingdom. For the vexed problem of dating see Joachim Quack, *Studien zur Lehre für Merikare* (Wiesbaden: Harrassowitz, 1992), pp. 120–136; and Andréas Stauder, *Linguistic Dating of Middle Egyptian Literary Texts* (Hamburg: Widmaier Verlag, 2013), pp. 175–199, where the linguistic typology places it to the timeframe of Dynasty XII–XVIII but not early Dynasty XII. Quack followed up his first dating attempt with a very useful critique in "Irrungen, Wirrungen? Forscherische Ansätze zur Datierung der alteren ägyptischen Literatur." In Gerald Moers *et al.* (eds.). *Dating Egyptian Literary Texts* (Hamburg: Widmaier Verlag, 2013), pp. 409–469. He is particularly emphatic against the later arguments for a New Kingdom dating proposed by Andrea Gnirs and Susanne Bickel.

7 See his two key volumes referred to in note 1 above. But see the study of Christian Langer referred to in note 39 below.

2 Means and Methods of Warfare

It is best to commence with the war narrative, even if incomplete, on Kamose's (ca. 1555–1550 BC) second stelae. He commanded that an entire records of his warfare against the northern enemy, the Hyksos, be recorded on two limestone monuments set up in Karnak, the temple of Amun in Thebes, his capital.[8] Although we are in the middle of things, the first person account explicitly shows the listener or reader the focus of the Theban king's orientation in war.[9] It is one-sided to be sure, and presents the obvious case of self-importance. The enemy are nothing, bombastic declarations, and successes in combat. But we can garner a few useful significant facets in this historical narrative orientation as well as perceiving the assumed way of fighting at this time, very late in Dynasty XVII Egypt (ca. 1545 BC).

At Niy in Syria, for example, the Memphis Stela of the king Amunhotep II (ca. 1427–1401 BC) states "Its prince, its people – its men and women were in peace (*ḥtp*) to his majesty, and their faces staring (?)." (One assumes with wonderment.) During his second campaign the local prince is said to have come out of his city in peace. He had automatically recognized the might of the Egyptian ruler. This type of expected immediate obedience appears to have been the expected norm for Amunhotep and, in fact, was an official sign, a pre-arranged symbolic performance on the part of the locals who showed their loyalty through a public act of deference and obedience. Thus the situation was straightforward and overt: gates open, local ruler (plus others) comes out in docility to greet pharaoh. Gates shut equals hostility. Hence, an agreed-upon public conduct was assumed by both parties. One might argue that such is akin to offering bread (hunger) and salt (life) to an arriving enemy army, a custom particularly prominent in Slavic cultures but known elsewhere in Europe and the Middle East, transforming a home-based ritual connected to guests to the troops of a foreign land.

8 Two later, and somewhat improved translations, will be found in Donald B. Redford, "Textual Sources for the Hyksos Period." In Eliezer Oren (ed.). *The Hyksos: New Historical and Archaeological Perspectives* (Philadelphia: The University Museum, 1997), pp. 13–15 and pp. 30–31; and Robert Ritner, "The Kamose Texts." In William Simpson (ed.). *The Literature of Ancient Egypt*, 3rd ed. (New Haven/London: Yale University Press, 2003), pp. 345–350. See as well, Roland Enmarsch, "Some Literary Aspects of the Kamose Inscriptions," *Journal of Egyptian Archaeology*, Vol. 99, 2013, pp. 253–263, Roxana Flammini, La Segunda Estela de Kamose (Atlanta: SBL; 2025).

9 Spalinger, *The Books behind the Masks. Sources of Warfare Leadership in Ancient Egypt*, Leiden/Boston: Brill, 2021, Chapter 1 ("Kamose's War Records").

The overarching issue is that Kamose's expectations for combat, his expected vituperative orientation, are contained within a lengthy promulgated record where only the protagonist, the hero, speaks. We must follow him to determine the conduct of war. His opening address to his high officials sets the tone for the ensuing narrative:[10]

> His Majesty spoke in his palace to the council of officials which was in his following: To what effect do I perceive it, my might, while a ruler is in Avaris and another in Kush, I sitting joined with an Asiatic and a Nubian, each man having his (own) portion of this Egypt, sharing the land with me. There is no passing him as far as Memphis, the water of Egypt. He has possession of Hermopolis, and no man can rest, being deprived by the levies of the Setiu. I shall engage in battle with him and I shall slit his body, for my intention is to save Egypt, striking the Asiatics.

When we encounter the first line of his second stela Kamose has already repelled his Hyksos opponent, Apophis, who has in fact retreated to his capital-fortress of Avaris in the northeast Delta and it is quite possible that a small encounter occurred at the landing place where the Theban monarch docked. (Note the ever-present river, a water-orientation, of the military encounter.) There is a speech of Kamose,[11] presumably directly to the Hyksos ruler as well as his compatriots, all of whom remain in their city while Kamose controls the important waterways surrounding the enemy's capital. But he never takes the city.

2.1 *Fighting on the Field*

True, the region is devastated, or so says Kamose the Theban king, but he and his army cannot effect a siege and eventually overcome his opponent.[12] This is strikingly in contrast to the small military encounter that Kamose faced earlier

10 Ritner, "The Kamose Texts," 344. Avaris is the capital of the Hyksos opponent in the northeast Delta, Kush with its Nubian king lay immediately south of Egypt; Hermopolis was a key metropolis on the Nile in Middle Egypt, and the Setiu refers to the Asiatics. Note the non-Egyptian aspects emphasized by Kamose.

11 The entire account is in the first person, the king's: Stauder, *Linguistic Dating of Middle Egyptian Literary Texts*, pp. 43–50.

12 On sieges and fortresses from an Egyptian point of view: Franck Monnier, "Une iconographie égyptienne de l'architecture defensive," *Enim*, Vol. 7, 2014, pp. 173–219, and "Des grandes voiles dans les descriptions de villes assiégées à l'époque pharaonique," *Égypte. Afrique et Orient*, No. 196, 2022, pp. 17–26.

on the River Nile at Nefrusy. At this earlier juncture, the foes are defeated in the field. The order of military operations at that time was as follows:

1. Combat
2. Success, and the enemy forces are driven back to their city.
3. Kamose gets hold of the city. The report remarks on the walls of the opposing city being destroyed.

This order, so to speak, follows a pre-arranged pattern, one that can be subsumed under the often expressed term *homo ludens* in which two protagonists fight close to a citadel or fortress-city.[13] The aggressive, and ultimately successful warrior hero fights his opponents outside of his protective battlements in order to determine who shall be victor. Staying inside must have been equated with cowardice. The two sides, in fact, proceed in combat along an established vector of movement and military strategy. At Nefrusy, the case just briefly described, Kamose later has the wife of the opponent go down to the shore of the Nile River, just as Herodotos reported the same submissive performance when the Persians conquered Egypt (III 14): "I had his wife go down to the shore."[14] In this very interesting case a slight reversal is enacted: the *defeated* enemy follows an apparently standard Egyptian practice. In this case the victor Kamose demands the overt humiliation, and the chief of Nefrusy is, after all, Egyptian.

Then too, if things went ill for the enemy they could always retire into a well-designed secure place. This is, after all, what Apophis (Kamose's great enemy) did at Avaris. Again, it is earlier that we encounter Kamose's army finding it easy to capture an enclosure and he further observes that the enemy chariots fled inside a second city (Per-Shaq). The situation is, in fact, always the case for the Egyptians of the Late Bronze Age. The pictorial evidence from the temple walls of Egypt reveals this to be the standard. Namely, it was the norm for both foes to fight close to a city, and that location would been in Palestine or

13 Spalinger, "Ramesses Ludens et Alii," *Studies on the Ancient Egyptian Culture & Foreign Relations*, Vol. 1, 2007, pp. 71–86, referring back to Mario Liverani *Prestige and Interest. International Relations in the Near East ca. 1600–1100 B.C.* (Padova: Sargon, 1990); and especially Erik Hornung, "Pharao Ludens," *Eranos Jahrbuch*, Vol. 51, 1982, pp. 479–516.

14 Passage in Ritner, "The Kamose Texts," 348. See especially Jean-Marie Kruchten, "From Middle Egyptian to Late Egyptian," *Lingua Aegyptia*, Vol. 6, 1999, p. 12 (note 51): "So, in practice, between dawn ("*as soon as earth lit up*") and breakfast time (*nw n sty-rꜣ*), Kamose crushed (*sꜣsꜣ*) his enemy on the field, then he destroyed (*ẖb*) the wall of his town, slaughtered (*smꜣ*) its inhabitants and lastly obliged his wife to draw water from the river (*dy hꜣ ḥmt=f r mryt*) like a maidservant, the utmost mortification of the vanquished, as we know thanks to the story of the daughter of Psamtik III and Cambyses as told by Herodotus (*L'enquête*, III, 14)."

Syria during the later Empire period. Any appreciation of the Egyptian battle reliefs will show one that there are essentially no alternatives to this scenario. The fortress-city had become an effective and dominant visual sign, a real icon, of warfare.[15]

At Avaris, Kamose taunts his Hyksos opponent.[16] Naturally, this is the grandiloquent ideological native feeling of the pharaoh who expressly required his treasurer to prepare the written stone document. The words place on record the boasts of the Theban in contrast to the absence of Apophis. The latter comes not out to fight, most probably knowing that the Theban could not remain long in his vicinity owing to the topographic nature of the area as well as the difficulty in provisioning. They could not "live off the land" for a long time. In truth, Apophis had finessed the rules of war. He avoided direct confrontation and Kamose had to return upstream. Assuredly, the combat would have been arranged outside of his city on the somewhat moisture-laden fields close to the port, a not very effective region for the use of chariots and horses. Apophis and Kamose were aware of the expected scenario, to occur after sunrise to be sure, once the Theban king reached the embattlements of his enemy's metropolis.

2.2 *Targeting the Environs*

Furthermore, when we turn to more abbreviated accounts of Egyptian New Kingdom warfare we find no exception. Amunhotep II, for example, shows again and again the scenario of the pharaoh reaching an enemy city.[17] Combat there then takes place, and a stress is placed upon the royal chariot of Amunhotep.[18] Amunhotep II remains always severe, if not barbarous (as

15 The classic study on this issue of Eliezer Oren and Joseph Shereshevski, "Military Architecture along the Ways of Horus," *Eretz Israel*, Vol. 20, 1989, pp. 8–22.

16 For the probable contemporary representation (too schematic but absolutely iconographic), see Steven Harvey, "The Cults of King Ahmose at Abydos" (PhD. Dissertation, University of Pennsylvania, 1998), pp. 303–312 and figs. 88–97, pp. 541–550; and Spalinger, *Icons of Power. A Strategy of Reinterpretation*, pp. 120–121 with Plate IX, fig. 22.

17 The standard work on the reign of Amunhotep II and his northern wars is Peter der Manuelian, *Studies in the Reign of Amenophis II* (Hildesheim, Gerstenberger Verlag, 1987), with Chapter 1 in particular. The most recent approach, and important revision, is now that of Camille Pierre, "La stèle d'Aménophis II au VIIIe pylône de Karnak," *Bulletin de l'Academie Belge pour l'Étude des Langues Ancienne et Orientales*, Vol. 12, 2023, pp. 11–28. There is also her Thesis as well, "Les campagnes militaires d'Amenhotep II en Asie" (PhD Thesis, Louvain-la-Neuve, UC Louvain, 2018).

18 Pictorially, see the return home: Abdel Zayed, "Une représentation inédite des campagnes d'Aménophis II." In Paule Posener-Kriéger (ed.). *Mélanges Gamal Eddin Mokhtar* (Cairo, Institut Français d'Archéologie Orientale), 1985, pp. 5–17.

previously felt).[19] Plundering of the environs was commonplace and slight data is presented indicating the king's tent as in the later Piankhy Stela which we shall discuss below. In the king's account on his Memphis Stela there is no mention of any siege, short lasting or otherwise. Combat took place very early in the morning, which is to be expected, and, as with Kamose (and later also Thutmose III) the foe could flee back for safety to their city. Other occasions involved the immediate recognition on the part of the local potentate of the Egyptian monarch's power.

2.3 *Plundering*

The Megiddo account of Thutmose III serves as a "developed form" of this type of combat guideline. The clash occurred in the morning – how and when else? – and the Egyptians won. Yet many of the high ranking opponents got back to their refuge without harm, mainly owing to the failure of Thutmose's soldiers to move against them immediately. As is well known his troops plundered the camp of the enemy. The reason for this is not hard to imagine. In this specific case Thutmose's chief opponents included key figures from Syria and Palestine, and especially the prince of the city of Kadesh on the River Orontes. Hence his camp (plus horses and chariots) was considerably more resplendent, and reveal his importance and wealth. One can add, to be sure, the war materiel and accoutrements of the prince of Megiddo as well. In a nutshell, unlike the "expected" military encounters in Palestine and Syria of Amunhotep II, here there was a decided difference.

How could the original expectation have taken place? The so-called "Annals" of Thutmose III never reveal that significant fact.[20] Was it assumed that, with chariots, the Egyptians could reach the enemy city's wall faster than the fleeing demoralized and defeated opponent? I believe so. For why else does the narrative emphasize that the failure to take Megiddo immediately after the victory lay with the avaricious royal troops of Thutmose. Clearly, Thutmose expected the city to surrender after a short period of time. That was *la règle du jeu*. It did not, however.

On an earlier occasion I discussed the quite different case of Ramesses II outside the walls of Kadesh.[21] There, I pointed out the concept of Johann Huizinga's

19 Lutz Popko, "Zum Einfluss des Historikers auf die Historie am Fallbeispiel Amenhoteps II." In Alexandra Verbovsek, Burkhard Backes, and Catherine Jones (eds.). *Method und Didaktik in der Ägyptologie* (Munich: Wilhelm Fink, 2011), pp. 649–665.

20 We can now rely upon the study of Redford, *The Wars in Syria and Palestine of Thutmose III* (Boston/Leiden: Brill), 2003.

21 See note 11 above. Subsequently, I applied that approach to pharaoh Piankhy of Kush in "Piankhy/Piye. Between Two Worlds." In Christina Karlshausen and Claude Obsomer

homo ludens, partly following Eric Hornung as well as Mario Liverani, in an effort to explains some of the presumed chronological peculiarities of the Thutmose at Megiddo as well as Ramesses at Kadesh. Here, it is not difficult at this juncture to emphasized that such combat was recognized not only by the Egyptians themselves but also by their West Asiatic enemies. To be sure we are speaking of urban cultures only, not Bedouin, semi-nomads, marauders and the like. That is why Kamose's declaration on the shore at Avaris has a resounding significance. It is not merely that he is victorious up to the very gates of Avaris, but that Apophis, his enemy, refuses combat.

At this time in the Late Bronze Age the military rule of warfare had been to engage your opponent in the field and outside of your citadel of security. If defeated, the norm was to accept that result, and thereafter to surrender. The killed were *essentially* only soldiers, but captives, including the local princes elite entourage might be "deported" to Egypt.[22] (The same qualification can be applied to women and children.) Sieges were not in the cards. Indeed, ultimately the Egyptians would have been successful at any rate, such as the seven month investiture of Megiddo demonstrates.

At Kadesh Ramesses II managed first to deflect and then to defeat chariot attacks by the Hittites but he was never able to cross the Orontes River and attempt to invest Kadesh.[23] The enemy was still too strong and, in fact had lost little infantry, if any. Thus Ramesses, and his Hittite opponent Muwatallis, were forced, so to speak, to fight on the following day, but whether the foe did in person remains *sub judice*. (Note that on the first day of combat the Hittite ruler stayed totally out of contact.) Then too, the first day's warfare was purely that of chariotry on the part of the Hittites, an arrangement different from the expected normal of warfare in the field.

Observe as well that such typical military encounters were at least for the Egyptians, commonplace at a time preceding their foray into Palestine.

(eds.). *De la Nubie à Qadech/From Nubia to Kadesh. La guerre dans l'Égypte ancienne/War in Ancient Egypt.* (Brussels: Safran, 2016), pp. 235–241. But there the historiographic background was filled out in detail.

22 See Matić's two studies referred in note 1 above, but add his more specific chapter, "Children on the Move: *ms.w wr.w* in New Kingdom Procession Scenes." In Jana Mynářová, Pavel Onderaka, and Peter Pavúk (eds.), *There and Back Again – the Crossroads II* (Prague: Charles University of Prague, Faculty of Arts, 2015), pp. 373–389. Captives including women and children were brought to Egypt, especially when the enemy were Libyans intent upon settling in the Delta.

23 Peter Brand, *Ramesses II. Egypt's Ultimate Pharaoh* (Columbus: Lockwood Press, 2023), Chapter 5 ("The Battle of Kadesh"); Spalinger, *Leadership under Fire: The Pressures of Warfare in Ancient Egypt*, Chapter 3 ("Ramesses II: Pharoah as Warrior").

Kamose's war records is proof of that. Hence, this rule of warfare has far less to do with the unique occurrence in Egypt it major waterway. The Nile easily served as the means of rapid transportation for troops etc. centuries before horses and chariots warfare had become standard for the Egyptians.[24] In a similar fashion observe that Ramesses II and his Hittite protagonist, had to fulfil the martial requirements of the day. To compare what occurred at Kadesh in the fifth regnal year of Ramesses with the events that were enacted at Megiddo under Thutmose III (ca. 1479–1425 BC) will be worthwhile as both cases were unprecedented and do not belong, properly speaking, in the realm of "proper conduct." Yet both starkly indicate the *homo ludens* character of the day.

In the earlier case Thutmose marched out from Egypt in order to re-establish full Egyptian control over Palestine owing to a revolt which was centered in the Esdraelon Valley at Megiddo. The latter was led by its local potentate but had full support from the prince of Kadesh whose city lay far north in southern Syria. Ramesses, as is well-known, was intent many years later upon re-seizing Kadesh. Unbeknownst to him his opponent, the Hittite king, was situated there, hiding behind the city.

Thutmose III[25] at Megiddo	Ramesses II[26] at Kadesh
Arrival at city on day 19 of the first month of summer.	Arrival opposite Kadesh on the third month of summer, day 9. Surprise Hittite chariot attack

24 An excellent early case involving warfare may be seen in the tomb of Anchtify at Moalla where he states that the front of his fleet was at point X and the rear at Point Y: Wolfgang Schenkel, *Memphis. Herakleopolis.Theben. Die epigraphischen Zeugnisse der 7.–11. Dynastie Ägyptens* (Wiesbaden: Harrassowitz, 1965), p. 50. For this far earlier epoch (First Intermediate Period), see Spalinger, "The Organisation of the Pharaonic Army," in Juan Carlos Morena García (ed.), *Ancient Egyptian Administration* (Leiden/Boston: Brill, 2013), pp. 437–460.

25 Redford, *The Wars in Syria and Palestine of Thutmose III*, 25–42; and Spalinger, "Some Notes on the Battle of Megiddo and Reflections on Egyptian Military Writing," *Mitteilungen des Deutschen Archäologischen Instituts, Abteilung Kairo*, Vol. 30, 1975, pp. 221–229.

26 Christopher Eyre, "The Accessibility of Ramesside Narrative." In Sabine Kubisch and Ute Rummel (eds.). *The Ramesside Period in Egypt. Studies into Cultural and Historical Processes of the 19th and 20th Dynasties. Proceedings of the International Symposium Held in Heidelberg, 5th to 7th June 2015* (Berlin/Boston: De Gruyter, 2018), pp. 89–102.

Day 20: no warfare; preparation for combat on the following day.	
Combat soon after sunrise on day 21.	Second day of fighting took place immediately thereafter, at dawn

Additional related influences:

Day 21 was the first lunar day, and thus an auspicious one. I am sure that this was taken into consideration by the pharaoh.	Took place at dawn; surely prearranged in some way; assuredly the new combat was expected; Hittite troops had to cross the Orontes westward, and that was in the full sight of all.

I do not want to extend the argument too much by assuming, as Alexandra Mironova does, that certain significant Egyptian festivals – she refers explicitly to the *heb sed* – are automatically linked with these kings' campaigns.[27] Yet when certain key secular anniversaries occur we should not overlook them as they seem to influence strongly the events of combat. One can think of Amunhotep II in his year nine campaign as recorded on his Memphis Stela and there we also witness a propitious event, the king's dream as well as soon thereafter the anniversary of his accession.[28] But even so, his two war records simply reinforce the basic parameters of expected combat, at least in Asia. By viewing their visual counterparts, the pictorial representations of battle, a similar pattern automatically. The key snapshot is that of the king in his chariot with his own troops around him as a rule, attacking an enemy citadel. Thereafter, the visual record can often join that dramatic occurrence with that of the battlefield trophies, a later episode that is regularly present with Amunhotep II as well as in the New Kingdom pictorial accounts. True, the concept of a post bellum "deserted" enemy city occurs but once in the pictorial repertoire and one can even see birds flying up and away from the ramparts.[29]

27 Alexandra Mironova, *Calendars and Festivals of Ancient Egypt* (Moscow: Moscow Publishing House, 2022), pp. 269–275.

28 Spalinger, "A Lost Dream Episode?" In Kasia Szpakowska (ed.). *Through a Glass Darkly. Magic, Dreams, and Prophecy in Ancient Egypt* (Swansea: Classical Press of Wales, 2006), pp. 227–242.

29 Spalinger, *Icons of Power. A Strategy of Reinterpretation*, pp. 64–67.

Moreover, there are cases of the fortress being attacked at its main gate. By and large, however, the battle taking place immediately in its environs is the crucial depiction. Thutmose III himself has been compared with Sargon of Agade in an intriguing study that reinforces my feelings concerning a communality of thought patterns, societal norms that included warfare, during this epoch, that of the Late Bronze Age.[30]

3 Prohibited Conduct

With Pianchy of Kush we move into the center of Kushite-Egyptian warfare for a detailed narrative for first time, and at a date ca. 730 BC or so. At this time his father had already moved Kushite control north into Egypt and was recognized at the southern religious capital of Thebes. Pianchy's control had extended downstream to Middle Egypt and various regional potentates recognized him as pharaoh. By and large this control appears to have been easily accomplished, mainly due to the patchwork quilt political arrangement, then omnipresent in Egypt at this time. But the rival city of Sais in the northwest Delta, led by its ruler Tefnacht, had come to challenge this indirect domination and found in the local king Namlot of Hermopolis, a new ally.

In Pianchy's Great Stela there are two separate factors to evaluate.[31] The first is the theoretical, so to speak, and the second the actual events as they unfolded. Because the former has been discussed frequently in the scholarly literature let me outline it here. Piancy enjoins at his capital Napata (Gebel Barkal) upon his troops before they leave his homeland, Here are first the requirements for warfare, granted that they are not actual rulers of behavior as much as accurate tactical instructions:[32]

30 Hans-Werner Fisc her-Elfert, "Thutmose III. and Sargon of Akkad – Reflections of Akkadian Literature in the New Kingdom," *Universum Humanitarium*, Vol. 1 [2], 2016, pp. 212–233.

31 For an evaluation of the stela, Spalinger, *The Books behind the Masks. Sources of Warfare Leadership in Ancient Egypt*, Chapter 6 ("Pharaoh Pianchy and his Great Stela").

32 Alan H. Gardiner, "Pianchy's Instructions to His Army," *Journal of Egyptian Archaeology* Vol. 21, 1935, pp. 219–223; Dan'el Kahn, "Piankhy's Instructions to his Army in Kush and their Execution." In Mordecai Cogan and Dan'el Kahn (eds.). *Treasures on Camels' Humps: Historical and Literary Studies from the Ancient Near East Presented to Israel Eph'al*, (Jerusalem: Magnes Press, 2008), pp. 184–194; and Spalinger, *Leadership under Fire: The Pressures of Warfare in Ancient Egypt*, pp. 206–209.

> Advance in a battle line!
> Fight it! Surround it!
> Hem them in!
> Seize its people, its cattle, and its ships on the river!
> Do not allow its cultivators go to the field(s)!
> Do not let the plowers plow!
> Ham in the Hermopolite Nome's foreland!
> Attack it every day!

Here we see the keen appreciation of actual combat by Pianchy. But it is in the words of his regulations – they are just that – which he gave to his army about to leave northwards for Egypt that most attention has been given. Pianchy indicates how his troops are to fight right from the start of actual hostilities. They are essential precepts, rules, and regulations for the conduct of warfare when two armies are about to encounter each other. Importantly, the five outlined below cover the conduct in war.

3.1 *Fight When It Is Visible and Assuredly Not at Night*

This admonition is an obvious one considering the epoch, yet I find it significant that Pianchy commences his injunctions with the case of daylight versus darkness as if such could have occurred.

How factual these military encounters were can be laid to the side but for additional remarks which both Kamose and the Annals of Thutmose III supply. Between dawn and breakfast time the Theban pharaoh crushed the enemy on the field and presumably – though surely the account is temporal very fluid at this point – destroyed the walls of the town, and at some later date perhaps slaughtered its inhabitants. For all practical purposes I feel that it is sufficient to maintain that, as was to be expected, a fully laid out morning battle was designed. Kamose did not surprise his enemy. The same most assuredly can be said for Thutmose III waiting for down outside the city of Megiddo. He too engaged the enemy in the early morning. Leaving off Pianchy till the second half of this discussion, remember that the same thing occurred on day two of the Battle of Kadesh.

Assuredly, there is nothing abnormal or unexpected about these temporal citations. Armies rise early and depart on a prescribed or pre-planned rout to move elsewhere. Classically, I can refer back to Thutmose III and remark that he moved out of the royal tent at Aruna Pass close to sunrise, setting forward rapidly to his goal, Megiddo. This was definitely after daybreak. Amunhotep II similarly provides two additional references indicating the same situation.[33] The first was after his fateful dream and the second after the well-known holocaust which he performed. Naturally, considering the logistic constraints at this bygone time as well as the need to decamp and march rapidly to a destination, morning is the obvious time and there is nothing unusual here. But so to it would have been for the enemy, and the cases of the Megiddo coalition during the reign of Thutmose III as well as the Hittite king's set piece, as one might call it, on day two outside of Kadesh are clear-cut cases of such standard rules of warfare. In particular, note that Muwatallis would have had to send his troops once more westward, across the Orontes River, in order to meet Ramesses's refreshed contingents. Indeed, now here in the lengthy account of the Kadesh Poem do we read the pharaoh ever crossing the river to the east, to the location where Muwatallis lay. Then too, on this second occasion once more the Hittite king did not engage his Egyptian foe in person.

One of the singular characteristics of this great military encounter it may be worthwhile to speculate upon the absence of Muwatallis. Ramesses insured that he be depicted as a coward, surrounded and protected by his bodyguard on the opposite side of the river. Furthermore, the ensuing combat remained, at least for the first day, to be that of chariots against the Egyptian infantry and chariots. Those fast moving war vehicles are naturally emphasized in the lengthy Egyptian narrative. It would appear that the same occurred on day two. Hence, one might argue that both clashes hinged solely upon the Hittite chariots versus the depleted Egyptian force. Did Muwatallis purposely avoid personally involving himself owing to the lack of his own infantry support? That is possible and should not be automatically dismissed, even if it is a highly speculative analysis. In any case the outcome of the military encounters on the first day had to depend upon the rapid success of the Hittite chariots surrounding Ramesses at his camp. This failed. So why then, does it appear that Muwatallis sent a message to his Egyptian opponent on day two if likewise he stayed somewhat remote from the clash. It would then appear that this set battle at that time was staged to some degree, an interpretation that I previously offered under the rubric of the title "Ramesses Ludens."

3.2 *A Challenge Is Then Given "From Afar"*

Here, the injunction is strict even as it reflects the ludic nature of warfare. Before commencing any hostile movement or action it is necessary to announce the desire for combat. All is straightforward and transparent. "Fight when he [= the

---

33 See note 28 above.

enemy] proposes" is added on to this requirement. In addition, if the foe is awaiting further support, then his troops are to await their arrival, a remarkable statement but one that fits neatly into Pianchy's concept of warfare in which the *homo ludens* structure permeates these injunctions.

3.3 *All the above Recognizes That We Must Marshal the Troops Efficiently*

Pianchy specifically knows the necessity of having full contingents of infantry and chariot support. He explicitly notes that *we must* "harness the best steeds" and then form the battle line.

3.4 *Allies Are Recognized*

This requirement is noted in 2 above, but see as well that the more elite cohorts of the enemy, in fact his allies, are to be challenged to battle (NB) "in advance" of the fighting.

3.5 *Fight When the Enemy Proposes To*

This is added on to requirement 2. Keep in mind that Piancy's side proposes and the other side, the enemy, disposes.

4 Analysis

So far these strictures, though uniquely present in the entire hieroglyphic record of ancient Egypt, are not unusual. They, in fact reflect Pianchy's attitude forward the enemy insofar as the latter are considered to be human, enemies to be sure but men worthy of recognition as true compatriots in war. Pianchy additionally states that the high ranking civil-military leaders (*ḥ3tjw-ʿ*) as well as effective "Libyan troops" (*Ṯḥnw mḥ-jb*) which can only be an elite cohort allowed to be challenged. Thus the ludic nature of warfare is once more revealed in the ancient text. The ensuing combat appears to be one in which horses (i.e., chariots) solely participated. Therefore, I believe that the final emphasis given by the Kushite monarch is to the elite sectors of his opponent's army and his own, to be sure.

This short passage of instruction assumes a standard means of combat and martial antagonism, one that was accepted on both sides and thereby it reflects the ethos of the age, one during which Egypt was divided and ruled by various potentates. But it equally discloses the other side. That is to say, Pianchy recognizes the inherent worth of his opponent. I contest that the underlying assumptions are clear on at least one side. Independent of any tactical considerations, advantages or otherwise, Pianchy assumes a few basic parameters of fighting in which challenges take place. They must be verbal, of course. Allowing your opponent to wait for allied support is another, and perhaps a surprising attitude on the part of the Kushite monarch. In addition, it is the opponent who actually inaugurates the combat, of his own troops. All in all these rubrics of behavior are extremely revealing as they indicate some type of communality, to military encounters, ones associated with Kushites in the distant south upstream, the Libyan potentates within Egypt proper, and other Egyptian armies.

In actual combat Pianchy's attacks against Hermopolis in Middle Egypt as later at Memphis deserve amplification, if only as we witness the actual unravelling of warfare and not a series of royal prescriptions.[34] During the first a siege took place and eventually Hermopolis pleaded for surrender. Pianchy would not accept that even when the Libyan potentate gave visual evidence of surrendering his crown. What actually eventuated is interesting, Namlot, his opponent, sent his wife to the royal wives of Pianchy and other significant women of the king's entourage to implore for peace.[35] Although the timeframe is not specified precisely in the account Namlot is then introduced imploring for peace literally at the feet of Pianchy. This took place outside of the city of Hermopolis itself and in the local "portable" palace.

In summary, although the siege of Hermopolis is never presented the events follow are more revealing, and this is why I believe the editor-authors of the composition ignored the local sallies and methods of offence-defence and turned instead to the evens of Namlot's wife. Additional reasons for this narrative switch have been discussed elsewhere but we may conclude by remarking on the necessity of a siege and the emphasis upon ships in the context of the warfare.

But it was earlier at Heracleopolis that we first see evidence that Pianchy's "system," one that I maintain was commonplace in the Nile Valley at this time, occurred. At Heracelopolis Pianchy's troops had earlier challenged the enemy to battle (in Egyptian *sr ꜥḥꜣ*).[36] And here the narrator provides full details of the enemy coalition plus a total of the enemy dead. That is to say, an official terse but specific report of the battle was given to Pianchy by written message and thus preserved for future use, as here on this stela. At this point, one in which

34 A summary may be found in my *Leadership under Fire. The Pressures of Warfare in Ancient Egypt*, pp. 212–227.

35 *Ibid.*, 218–219.

36 *Ibid.*, pp. 213–214.

the Kushite pharaoh was not present, the war report had to include the following data. This aspect must be included in the "rulers of war," but in essence it covers the war reports:

1. Leaders of the enemy: name and titles/ranks indicated; two-pharaohs present
2. Libyan chiefs, soldiers of lesser chiefs/generals
3. List of enemy dead; chariots probably included as well.

The third group is commonplace in earlier military accounts and, in fact, belongs always at the end of any successful combat of the Egyptian rulers with. In contrast, the enemy coalition, represented by Namlot, acted, so says the Great Stela, under the aegis of the west Delta city of Sais, led by its pharaoh, Tefnacht, and there is a very indirect reference given regarding Namlot's allegiance to him.

Up to the apex of the Delta at Memphis, but included key northern Upper Egyptian cities, the events roll out quickly. At this point Pianchy employs the all too common technique of addressing the inhabitants once more. For example, the narrative devotes a small portion of its account to the interchange between Pianchy and the inhabitants of Per-Sekhemkheperre. It possesses a dramatic, thespian flair even if the exposition is short. First the city is shut (always mentioned) and hence opposed to the king. Pianchy sends his messenger into the city, and they reply likewise, acknowledging his domination. A son of a Libyan chief leaves the metropolis as the chief of the delegation. No violence is set into motion: the act of contrition is completed. Two more abbreviated scenarios may be found when Pianchy reaches Mer-Amun, and Itj-tawy, both south of Memphis. All of these events reveal the expectation of military success being played out by erstwhile former enemies now clamoring for peace. But they nonetheless first meet Pianchy with a firmly closed, and one presumes ably defended municipality. In essence, the locals must perform their role of antagonist, awaiting the words of Pianchy. Then they reply to his demands – I presume all of this was done orally and not by written message. One feels that all is stage directed here. In fact, the entire storyline parallels almost perfectly the written and pictorial accounts of Egypt in Asia during the New Kingdom.

Piancy then reached Memphis and acted the same. An official message was sent into the city. Clemency is promised. In this case, however, troops were dispatched from Memphis. But first "they closed they fort" (line 86). Hence, the reaction – visually emphatic – is totally opposite to the preceding three cases. Memphis, though also promised mercifulness, does not acquiesce. The soldiers dispatched earlier to meet Pianchy must have been a token force, performing their ritual of physical opposition but in no way did they intend to defeat the

Kushite ruler. How could they do so?[37] In fact, those troops were dispatched against the engineering cohorts which Pianchy had sent to Memphis to secure his entrance at the harbor. In fact, that is where he would subsequently enter the opposing city. In truth, the sally by the opposition was not a major one as it was aimed solely at the preparations which Pianchy was doing in order to get into the effectively bottled up and secured city: his main army was not faced, and not he in particular. This action might equally be understood as following some type of set precepts for military behavior even though the intent was aimed at retarding the Kushite foe's encircling and battlement tactics. Indeed, Pianchy himself had not yet reached Memphis so any ludic interpretation seems improbable. And it must not be forgotten that Tefnacht had already reached Memphis and encouraged it to resist. In other words, Pianchy's opponent may have altered the original plans of that city to surrender although this interpretation is somewhat speculative.

The important event occurred on the following day, again at dawn, when Pianchy reached the capital. At that time he reveals his logistic and intellectual engineering aspect by determining how, specifically, to take the city. It was taken successfully, and I suspect easily as the narrative dwell over this discuss in any form. In this case it is important to refer to a few key tactical aspects. Pianchy attacks the harbor region, not the north of Memphis where he had moored. He avoided surmounting the city's walls or blocking the locality. In addition, he arranged as many shops that he found and brought with him to form a sort of massive ferry in order to move against the enemy.

But here the method of attack as well as the actual combat was far different than the expected, indeed battle-oriented system that hitherto one would have expected. The reason for that was owing to the topography of Memphis itself and its lack of isolation from the River. Thus it is fair to state that the expected norms of combat were in place so that any battle encounter would follow a prearranged set pattern in which it appears that respect because one's opponent always held but only when a battle was to take place in the open, so to speak. Sieges were otherwise, and the resistance of Memphis followed that undesirable resistance.

37 The account in line 87 stresses that the enemy moved against the "craftsmen, builders, and sailors."

5 Conclusion

The key issues presented in this discussion reflect different time frames, and also with the case of Pianchy different cultures. As can be ascertained from Kamose, he expected to engage Apophis in a personal battle, a duel situation one that fits automatically in the concept of the ludic nature of warfare. That did not take place with Apophis although it is had, in fact, occurred earlier on the Nile River but only again the enemy's generals and officials. Except for the importance of the city's port, and here every major Egyptian city was flanking the Nile or one of its arms in the Delta, has to be taken into consideration, but this aspect is most definitely one that influenced strategy more importantly tactics. In Asia, as can be seen from the pictorial representations of battles the fortress-citadel of the enemy served as the icon par excellence of the enemy. In front of the metropolis, wherever specifically does not matter, a battle was expected by both sides. Hopefully, no siege would follow, but the abnormal situation which occurred outside of Megiddo led directly to that unexpected case.

Unfortunately it was for all as eventually the metropolis would have to surrender. When we descend in time to the reign of Pianchy his movement were, as with all combat along the Nile, determined by the royal flotilla and the possibility of another investment. What is singular in the length account on his stela is that he provides us with a backdrop in which basic rules of warfare were enunciated. Yet once more we view the encirclement of key cities just as the Egyptians of earlier New Kingdom did in Palestine and Syria. Note that the civilian populace never enters the equation, but this was to be expected, at least in the narrative presentation of the authors of the Egyptian accounts.

The issue of captives and the treatment of the dead has recently been covered in the scholarly literature.[38] Deportations, especially during the New Kingdom, were frequent and here a very recent exemplary study of Christian Langer is recommended for consultation.[39] Exact policies for these issues remain unclear as there is no specific indication of an official pharaonic rule concerning the defeated. Amunhotep II of Dynasty XVIII is often brought up as

38 The two key studies are those of Matić, cited in note 1. Add the references in Spalinger, *Leadership under Fire: The Pressures of Warfare in Ancient Egypt*, pp. 76–77 (note 115) with Matić's "Traditionally Unharmed? Women and Children in New Kingdom Battle Scenes." In Andrea Kahlbacher and Elisa Priglinger (eds.). *Tradition and Transformation in Ancient Egypt: Proceedings of the 5th International Congress for Young Egyptologists, Vienna, 15–19 September 2015* (Vienna: Akademie der Wissenschaften, 2019), pp. 245–260.

39 Christian Langer, *Egyptian Deportations of the Late Bronze Age. A Study in Political Economy* (Berlin/Boston: De Gruyter, 2021).

a man personally vituperative, effectively ferocious, and highly frightening.[40] In contrast, see the more "diplomatic," careful, and painstaking approach of Pianchy.

In another context, but one somewhat parallel to the issue of deportations, I have commenced a study of the number of captives listed as well as the grand totals of enemy dead with Hans Delbrück's summary his previous research concerned with this administrative-bureaucratic practice in antiquity.[41] A recent study of the Neo Assyrian data shows how complicated it is to determine the reasons for these final reckonings. At the minimum, simple boasting comes to mind, pure lying.[42] Errors, copying changes, incorrect use of the war records provide explanations for the figures of slain or captured, but there remains the key psychological one of overt falsehood. The now famous "severed hands" at Tell ed Daba/Avaris is argued to be a clear case of mutilation after the fact (death), and perhaps an original non-Egyptian practice.[43] But none of that extensive data is even indirectly associated with any operative procedure followed. My comment that "Would that we had even a fragmentary portion of an Egyptian military handbook," still holds.[44] But we can see, nonetheless, certain practices by the New Kingdom and later that enable us to formulate a common system of behavior in combat. They even apply when Pianchy marched northwards into Egypt, notwithstanding his Kushite – hence non-Egyptian – background. Moreover, New Kingdom pictorial data even

40 Spalinger, *Leadership under Fire: The Pressures of Warfare in Ancient Egypt*, p. 50.

41 Hans Delbrück, *Numbers in History* (London: University of London Press, 1913). Jordi Vidal, is equally worthwhile to consult in this matter: "Calculating Percentages of Battle Casualties: On the Reliability of Assyrian Annals and Reliefs from the 9th Century B.C.," *Altorientalische Forschungen*, Vol. 40, 2013, pp. 183–192. My study is titled "Trophies: Numbers and Locations."

42 Kai Ruffing, Kerstin Dross-Krüpe, Sebastian Fink, Robert Rollinger (eds.). *Societies at War. Proceedings of the 10th Symposium of the Melammu Project held in Kassel September 26–28 2016 and Proceedings of the 8th Symposium of the Melammu Project held in Kiel November 11–15 2014* (Vienna: Akademie der Wissenschaften, 2020), pp. 15–98. To this compendium we can add Marco de Odorico, *The Use of Numbers and Quantifications in the Assyrian Royal Inscriptions* (Helsinki: University of Helsinki, Neo-Assyrian Text Corpus Project 2001).

43 Julia Gresky, Manfred Bietak, Emmaneuele Petiti *et al.*, "First osteological evidence of severed hands in Ancient Egypt," *Science Reports* 13, 5239 (2023) – https://doi.org/10.1038/s41598-023-32165-8. Earlier, see Danielle Candelora, "Grisly Trophies: Severed Hands and the Egyptian Military Reward System," *Near Eastern Archaeology*, Vol. 84, 2021, pp. 192–199.

44 Spalinger, *Leadership under Fire: The Pressures of Warfare in Ancient Egypt*, p. 16 (note 1); see Brian Campbell, "Teach Yourself How to Be a General," *Journal of Roman Studies*, Vol. 77, 1987, pp. 13–29.

reveal a common West Semitic practice of *Xitpu* in which the corpse of a male child is dropped from the besieged city for the enemy to see.[45]

The aforementioned convention was geared in all of the cases of a chariot attack combined with infantry. There was no difference within the Nile Valley in Pianchy's time. Ramesses II was caught by the chariots at his camp but that was a singular result due to the advance knowledge of his plans by Muwatallis, Ramesses's sharp minded foe. Still, the murky combat on day two exemplifies to a tee the premisses of military "rules of combat." The reliance on an initial "duel-like" situation brings forward the vexed problem of how did the chariots fight? After initially arguing for their great importance, Alan Schulman later presented five major limitations, or at least inconveniences, associated with these moving vehicles:[46]

1. It was not suitable, indeed not at all useful for attacking cities or any fortified location.
2. As a means of transport the carrying capacity was small and all depended ultimately on the size of the chariot cohort.
3. The obvious problem of terrain enters. Flat ground is best; to high vegetation, gorse, is clearly disadvantageous.
4. They cannot hold open ground.
5. Unbroken enemy formations were too resilient to direct chariot attack.

But we must be equally careful not to take any of these restrictions too strongly. The Egyptian pictorial representations of battle do not show chariots versus chariots to be sure, and the Kadesh encounter is an obvious case of a surprising switch in tactics owing to the strategic weakness of Ramesses. But the Egyptian

45 Spalinger, "A Canaanite Ritual Found in Egyptian Military Reliefs," *Journal of the Society for the Study of Egyptian Antiquities* Vo. 8, 1978, 47–60. Jack Sasson, "Human Sacrifice and Circumcision," *Biblical Archaeology Review*, Vol. 13.2, March 1987, pp. 12, 14–15, 60, followed up the discussion, and he was aided by in the same volume by James Hoffmeier, "Further Evidence for Infant Sacrifice in the Ancient Near East," pp. 60–61 (reproducing Spalinger's study). Later, see William W. Hallo, "A Ugarit Cognate for Akkadian *Ḥitpu*." In Baruch Levine and Robert Chazan (eds.). *Ki Baruch Hu. Ancient Near Eastern, Biblical, and Judaic Studies in Honor of Baruch A. Levine* (Winona Lake: Eisenbrauns, 1999), pp. 43–50. Aaron Burke, More light on Old Reliefs: New Kingdom Siege Tactics and Asiatic Resistance." In J. David Schloe (ed.). *Exploring the longue Durée: Essays in Honor of Lawrence E. Stager* (Winona Lake: Eisenbrauns, 2009), pp. 57–68, ignored these commentaries.

46 Brett Heagren, "The Art of War in Pharaonic Egypt" (PhD Thesis, University of Auckland, 2010), pp. 80–87; Alan R. Schulman, "The Egyptian Chariotry: a Reexamination," *Journal of the American Research Center in Egypt*, Vol. 2, 1963, pp. 75–98, with "Chariots, Chariotry, and the Hyksos," *Journal of the Society for the Study of Egyptian Antiquities*, Vol. 10, 1980, pp. 105–153; and Werner Mayer and Ruth Mayer-Opificius, "Die Schlacht bei Qadeš," *Ugarit Forschungen*, Vol. 26, 1994, pp. 321–368.

artists liked above all to represent their chariot divisions pursing fleeing enemies as it was only after the infantry were broken that the chariots were able effectively to close upon the enemy. And then the archer could exchange his bow for a spear or javelin, and the importance of the individual warrior, the solitary hero, then arose more importantly in the melee. Essentially, however, the vehicles were employed a mobile platforms for archers, who shot their arrows against infantry or other chariot soldiers. It is only that the method of attack is still disputed: parallel movements or flanking ones are the two possibilities discussed and disputed.

Predating the New Kingdom then, as the narrative of Kamose's stelae shows, a system of warfare had already been developed in which an initial clash was expected outside of and very close to a fortress, citadel, or city. The use of chariots merely expanded the role of mobility within this expected "rule of combat." Thanks to Pianchy's strictures that he imposed upon his army we can understand more of the background expectations to military conduct in the field and at the same time witness the fair interchange of the elite warrior ethos. If the foe chose not to engage, then he would be subject to vile taunting deprecations, as in fact Kamose shouted near to the palace of Apophis in Avaris. The expectations to battle are easily subsumed under the theoretical umbrella of *homo ludens*, but they also were commonly accepted rules and regulations of war.

CHAPTER 2

Hittite Laws of War

Rory Cox

Introduction[1]

The kingdom of Hatti rose to prominence around 1650 BCE, eventually coming to dominate most of Anatolia and northern Syria-Palestine. Its empire stretched from the shores of the Aegean to the banks of the River Tigris. At its height, between 1400 and 1250 BCE, it was the leading military superpower of the Near East.[2] Calling themselves 'men of the Hatti land', the Hittites took their name from their capital of Hattuša (about 150 km east of modern Ankara), where excavations have revealed extensive fortifications, temple precincts, huge grain silos, palaces, and a vast royal archive of tens of thousands of clay tablets.[3] Then, around 1180 BCE, the Hittite kingdom crumbled completely. It was thus the most significant victim of what historians have dubbed the 'Late

1 This chapter, intended as an introduction to Hittite military ethics and law, has been adapted from a lengthier and more detailed analysis published in Rory Cox, *Origins of the Just War: Military Ethics and Culture in the Ancient Near East* (Princeton: Princeton University Press, 2023), Part II, 163–266.

2 For a concise overview of Hittite history, see J.G. Macqueen, 'The History of Anatolia and of the Hittite Empire: An Overview', in *Civilizations of the Ancient Near East*, edited by Jack M. Sasson, John Baines, Gary Beckman, and Karen S. Rubinson, 4 vols. (Peabody, MA: Hendrickson, 2000) [henceforth *CANE*], 2:1085–1105. For more in-depth general treatments, see Billie Jean Collins, *The Hittites and their World* (Atlanta, GA: Society of Biblical Literature, 2007); Trevor Bryce, *The Kingdom of the Hittites* (Oxford: Oxford University Press, 2005); Horst Klengel, *Geschichte des Hethitischen Reiches* (Leiden: Brill, 1999). For a survey of Hittite historical writing: Hans G. Güterbock, 'Hittite Historiography: A Survey', in *History, Historiography and Interpretation: Studies in Biblical and Cuneiform Literatures*, ed. H. Tadmor and M. Weinfeld (Jerusalem: The Magnes Press, 1983), 21–35.

3 Theo van den Hout, 'Institutions, Vernaculars, Publics: The Case of Second-Millennium Anatolia', in *Margins of Writing, Origins of Cultures*, edited by S. Sanders (Chicago: Chicago University Press, 2006), 221–60, at 223, 225; Bryce, *Kingdom of the Hittites*, p. xvii, 2; Trevor Bryce (ed.), *Letters of the Great Kings of the Ancient Near East: The Royal Correspondence of the Late Bronze Age* (Abingdon and New York: Routledge, 2003), 161–2; Collins, *Hittites and their World*, 6, 141–2.

 DOI:10.1163/9789004703094_004

Bronze Age Collapse', brought about by a combination of factors, including climate change and the mass migration of people from West to East.[4]

Hittite history can be roughly divided into two periods: the Old Kingdom (*c*.1700–*c*.1400 BCE) and the New Kingdom (*c*.1400–*c*.1180 BCE).[5] The Old Kingdom represents a period of formation and consolidation in Anatolia, with intermittent territorial contractions and expansions as the Hittites experienced military defeat or victory. The New Kingdom marks a period of true empire, when Hatti achieved its greatest territorial extent and political influence.

A remarkable variety of textual and material evidence survives that helps to shed light on ancient Hittite culture, society, and politics. Indeed, the Hittite New Kingdom, especially the century between *c*.1300 BCE to *c*.1200 BCE, is one of the most richly documented periods in ancient Near Eastern history.[6] Sources include royal annals, proclamations, prayers, and, importantly, more than twenty diplomatic treaties between Hatti and its vassal states or peer competitors.[7] Hittite religious records include temple regulations, inventories of cultic sites, ritual instructions, oracular enquiries, and hymns and prayers used in both religious liturgy and for the training of young scribes.[8] Taken together, these sources can help scholars to reconstruct Hittite approaches to war: ethical, legal, and operational.

1 Hittite Warfare

Achieving military dominance in the ancient Near East was extremely difficult. The kingdoms of Egypt, Babylon, Mitanni, and Assyria all had similarly grand ambitions at various points in time, seeking to exploit the cities and rich

---

4 William A. Ward and Martha S. Joukowsky (eds), *The Crisis Years: The 12th Century B.C.: From Beyond the Danube to the Tigris* (Dubuque, IA: Kendall Hunt, 1992).

5 Bryce, *Kingdom of the Hittites*, 6.

6 Itamar Singer, *The Calm Before the Storm: Selected Writings of Itamar Singer on the Late Bronze Age in Anatolia and the Levant* (Atlanta, GA: Society of Biblical Literature, 2011), 3; H.G. Güterbock, 'The Deeds of Šuppiluliuma as Told by his Son, Muršili II', in *Journal of Cuneiform Studies* 10 (1956): 41–68, 75–98, 107–119; The 'Ten Year Annals' and the more detailed 'Comprehensive Annals', the latter of which cover Muršili II's entire reign. See Albrecht Götze, *Die Annalen des Müršiliš. Mitteilungen der Vorderasiatisch-Aegyptischen Gesellschaft 38* (Leipzig: J.C. Hinrichs, 1933).

7 For a useful list of sources pertaining to Hittite warfare, see Victor Korošec, 'The Warfare of the Hittites: From the Legal Point of View', *British Institute for the Study of Iraq* 25(2) (1963): 159–166, at 159–60.

8 Gary Beckman, 'The Religion of the Hittites', *Biblical Archaeologist* 52 (2/3) (1989): 98–108, at 98–99.

trade routes of Syria and the Levant. The constant threat of incursions from the coastal and island states of the Aegean, and from the semi-nomadic Kaškaean (*also* Gašgaean) peoples of north-eastern Anatolia, brought further challenges and disruption.[9]

The character of Hittite warfare was similar to other Bronze Age societies of the Near East. The Hittite army consisted of a standing force of warriors made up of both infantry and elite chariotry. This standing army performed garrison duties and even seems to have acted as a proto-police force when not on active campaign.[10] The king possessed a personal guard and retinue that provided the core of his army, though he remained reliant on his leading retainers to provide the bulk of his military forces. This has led one scholar to insist that, although sustaining a principle of hereditary monarchy, the Hittite king was 'merely *primus inter pares*.'[11]

In addition to the main army, all Hittite subjects were eligible to serve as levies during specific campaigns or to fulfil garrison duties.[12] Hittite kings also relied heavily on auxiliary troops provided by vassal states. Virtually every Hittite vassal treaty stipulated very specific military obligations, and these were treated with the utmost seriousness by the royal capital.[13] Occasionally,

9 See Claudia Glatz and Roger Matthews, 'Anthropology of a Frontier Zone: Hittite-Kaska Relations in Late Bronze Age North-Central Anatolia', *Bulletin of the American Schools of Oriental Research* 339 (2005): 47–65, at 49.

10 See Richard H. Beal, *The Organisation of the Hittite Military* (Heidelberg: C. Winter, 1992), 37–55; Richard H. Beal, 'The Organization of the Hittite Military', PhD Dissertation, University of Chicago (1986), 563–685. For a more concise summary, see also Richard H. Beal, 'Hittite Military Organization', in *CANE*, 1:545–54. For overviews of contemporary weaponry and tactics, see Yigael Yadin, *The Art of Warfare in Biblical Lands in the Light of Archaeological Discovery* (London: Weidenfeld and Nicolson, 1963), 76–247; William J. Hamblin, *Warfare in the Ancient Near East to 1600 BC: Holy Warriors at the Dawn of History* (Abingdon and New York: Routledge, 2006), 290–303; Albrecht Goetze, 'Warfare in Asia Minor', *Iraq* 25 (2) (1963): 124–30.

11 Ekrem Akurgal, *The Art of the Hittites*, translated by Constance McNab (New York: Harry N. Abrams, 1962), 86.

12 Beal, *Organization of the Hittite Military*, 56–117; Beal, 'Organization of Hittite Military', 133–9; 'Hittite Laws', translated by Harry A. Hoffner, Jr., in *Law Collections from Mesopotamia and Asia Minor*, edited by Martha T. Roth, with a contribution from Harry A. Hoffner, Jr. (Atlanta, GA: Scholars Press, 1995), 245.

13 Beal, *Organization of the Hittite Military*, 71–92; Beal, 'Organization of Hittite Military', 220–39, 258. For examples of military obligations within vassal treaties, see Gary Beckman, *Hittite Diplomatic Texts*, edited by Harry A. Hoffner, Jr., 2nd edn. (Atlanta, GA: Scholars Press, 1999), 16, 23–4, 29, 37–8, 61, 106, 164–5, 166; *The Ancient Near East: An Anthology of Texts and Pictures*, edited by James B. Pritchard, 2 vols. (Princeton: Princeton University Press, 1958–1975), 2:42–5.

monetary payment could be offered in lieu of troops, and this would have been used to hire foreign mercenaries.[14]

The sizes of Hittite armies are difficult to reconstruct with any accuracy. An early inscription mentions an army of 1,400 infantry and 40 teams of horses (i.e. chariots),[15] while Hattušili I (reigned *c.*1650– *c.*1620) was able to garrison 3,000 troops in two different locations in response to an invasion from neighbouring Mitanni. From the beginning of the Old Kingdom there existed two military officers who each bore the title 'Overseers-of-One-Thousand-Chariot-Fighters', although whether 'One-Thousand' refers to the number of chariots or to the number of crew is unclear (Old Kingdom chariots operated with two-man crews rather than the later three-man crews of the New Kingdom).[16] Given that the early-second-millennium BCE kingdoms of Babylon and Assyria could field armies in excess in 10,000 men, it is probably safe to assume that Hatti was capable of mustering comparable forces from *c.*1600 BCE onwards. What is more certain is that army sizes swelled during the Hittite New Kingdom. From *c.*1400 BCE onwards, major campaign armies were probably exceeding 30,000 troops.[17] The Egyptian pharaoh Ramses II claims that the combined Hittite forces at Qadesh in 1274 BCE numbered an impressive 47,500 troops.[18]

Within such armies, the chariot corps was the undisputed elite. The Hittite chariot was employed as a highly mobile platform to transport elite troops around the battlefield, with charioteers carrying bows, spears, and shields. Archers would have been able to shoot from moving chariots, and there was absolutely no stigma attached to the bow as a weapon of war, or to archers as warriors.[19] Archery was held in great esteem throughout the ancient Near East, practised by common soldiers and kings alike. Nonetheless, it is likely that warriors dismounted for hand-to-hand fighting, much like we read in Homeric descriptions of battles on the plains of Troy. Indeed, there is compelling evidence that Hittite and Anatolian culture helped to shape the form of Homeric

14 See 'No 37: Edict of Tudhaliya IV releasing Ammistamru II of Ugarit from participation in war against Assyria', in Beckman, *Hittite Diplomatic Texts*, 183.

15 'The Anitta Inscription', ll. 68–72, in Trevor R. Bryce, *The Major Historical Texts of Early Hittite History* (Brisbane: University of Queensland Press, 1983), 27.

16 Beale, *Organization of the Hittite Military*, 277–9, 282; Beale, 'Organization of Hittite Military', 341–62.

17 Macqueen, *Hittites*, 56.

18 On the veracity of this claim, see Beal, *Organization of the Hittite Military*, 291–4.

19 Goetze, 'Warfare in Asia Minor', 125–6; Beal, *Organization of the Hittite Military*, 142–90.

epic.[20] Cavalry also played a role in Hittite armies, probably acting as scouts or messengers, with some cavalrymen possibly fighting from horseback.[21]

The bulk of Hittite forces, however, were made up of infantrymen. Hittite sources give little attention to the armaments of Hittite infantry on campaign, but it is almost certain that the spear and shield were the main weapons of such troops. Spears are frequently mentioned in Hittite texts, the foot-soldiers of the Hittite royal guard were armed with spears, and contemporary Egyptian reliefs depict Hittite infantry armed with spears and shields.[22] These troops would also have carried a variety of other bronze and stone melee weapons such as axes, maces, and daggers. Wealthier troops would also have carried expensive weapons such as bronze swords and worn leather and/or bronze body armour.

As far as Hittite fortifications are concerned, the archaeological remains of Hattuša's massive walls provide ample proof that the Hittites were expert in defensive architecture and construction. One historian has even claimed that the Hittites were 'the most skilful fortress builders of the Ancient Middle East'.[23] However, like other Late Bronze Age militaries, Hittite siege technology was rudimental. There are references to what sound like siege towers, ramps, and battering rams, but in general the besieged undoubtedly held the advantage over their besiegers.[24] Rather than direct assault, blockade and treachery were probably the most effective techniques for capturing fortified cities.[25]

---

20 See Mary R. Bachvarova, *From Hittite to Homer: The Anatolian Background of Ancient Greek Epic* (Cambridge: Cambridge University Press, 2016).

21 Beal, *Organization of the Hittite Military*, 190–8; Beal, 'Organization of Hittite Military', 103–5, 580. For references to Hittite commanders scouting the enemy and setting the army on alert, see Harry A. Hoffner, Jr., *Letters from the Hittite Kingdom*, by edited by Gary M. Beckman (Atlanta, GA: Society of Biblical Literature, 2009), Letters 7, 12, 13 at 97, 105–107.

22 Beal, *Organization of the Hittite Military*, 198–201, 212–31; Beale, 'Organization of Hittite Military', 605–19; Macqueen, *Hittites*, 59–64. See also the Hittite Laws: '§126… If anyone steals a bronze spear in the gate of the palace, he shall be put to death.' *The Laws of the Hittites: A Critical Edition*, edited by Harry A. Hoffner, Jr. (Leiden: Brill, 1997), 114–116, at 116.

23 Akurgal, *Art of the Hittites*, 107–108. On fortifications, see also Goetze, 'Warfare in Asia Minor', 127; Macqueen, *Hittites*, 64–73.

24 'Letter 111: To the King from Kaššu', in Hoffner, *Letters from Hittite Kingdom*, 340–4, esp. 341. See also Gary Beckman, 'The Siege of Uršu Text (CTH 7) and Old Hittite Historiography', *Journal of Cuneiform Studies* 47 (1995): 23–34, at 26.

25 For example: 'Since it was impossible to proceed by horse, I, the Sun, went by foot at the end of my troops, and I ascended by foot on mount Arinnanda. I besieged the prisoners through hunger and thirst. And when they were starving and thirsty, and the situation became difficult for them, the prisoners came out and fell down at my feet: "Our

Such impressive military capabilities obviously required a sophisticated machinery of command and organization. The Great King was the commander-in-chief of the Hittite military, but below him was a complex web of high-ranking officers and regional commanders, apparently lacking a rigid chain of command. For example, if the king himself did not lead a campaign, there was no automatic second-in-command. While this duty frequently fell to the crown prince, other leading officers (often princes of the blood) could vie for command. As a result, Hittite armies were perhaps occasionally hampered by a lack of command unity;[26] yet the system must have been effective enough because, for several centuries, the Hittites were the dominant military power of the region.

Alongside their martial prowess, the Hittites were extremely capable political operators, developing a sophisticated system of diplomatic relationships based on formal treaties. Conquered territories were legally integrated into the kingdom and empire through vassalage treaties but, in a development novel to Hatti, treaties were also adapted to serve peaceful diplomacy. The Hittites created peace treaties with co-equal states (such as Egypt), with vassals over whom it ruled directly, and also with a third category of state (*kuirwana*), sitting somewhere between the first two in status: 'a sort of privileged protectorate', in the words of David Bederman.[27]

2 Hittite Legal Culture

Hittite culture was remarkably legalistic. A law collection, containing roughly 200 'cases', reveals Hittite normative thought about right and wrong action and suitable punishment.[28] Remarkably, these laws display a commitment (in theory at least) to applying justice equally across the social spectrum, from

lord, do not destroy us! Our lord, take us at your service and bring us to Hattusha!"', 54–7, translated in Mario Liverani, *International Relations in the Ancient Near East, 1600–1100 BC* (Basingstoke: Palgrave Macmillan, 2001), 89; cf. Bryce, *Kingdom of the Hittites*, 194–5.

26 Beal, *The Organisation of the Hittite Military*, 318–19. For an extended analysis of Hittite military offices, see ibid., 297–520.

27 David J. Bederman, *International Law in Antiquity* (Cambridge: Cambridge University Press, 2001), 27.

28 See *The Laws of the Hittites*, ed. Hoffner; Hoffner, 'Hittite Laws', in *Law Collections from Mesopotamia and Asia Minor*, ed. Roth, 213–48; Albrecht Goetze, 'The Hittite Laws', in *Ancient Near Eastern Texts Relating to the Old Testament*, edited by James B. Pritchard, 3rd edn. (Princeton: Princeton University Press, 1969), 188–97.

slaves to great lords.[29] Just as importantly, Hittite domestic law and diplomatic contracts had a deep and lasting influence on the laws and covenants of the Hebrew Bible, as well as Greco-Roman law.[30]

Hittite kings understood that Hatti was but one of several great powers and they were willing to recognize other great kings as 'brothers'.[31] Nonetheless, the Hittites – like other Near Eastern societies of the period – made a binary distinction between a core 'inner' territory (us/ours) and 'outer' peripheral lands that were presumed to be potentially hostile.[32] The Hittites could certainly find the manners of 'outer' peoples distasteful and even barbaric, although their xenophobia was markedly restrained compared to, say, Egyptian or Assyrian attitudes.[33] With a relatively pluralistic view of the world, Hittite kings never claimed a universal authority over other states, although they did assert rights of sovereignty through conquest.

Theoretically, the Hittite king's authority within his kingdom was absolute. Hittite kings did not claim personal divinity – although they did claim to become gods after death[34] – but they did insist that they ruled by divine appointment:

> The land belongs to the storm-god alone. Heaven, earth, and the people belong to the storm-god alone. He has made the Labarna, the king, his

29 Victor Korošec, *Hethitische Staatsverträge: ein Beitrag zu ihrer juristischen Wertung. Leipziger Rechtswissenschaftliche 60* (Leipzig: Weicher, 1931), 39, 42; O.R. Gurney, *The Hittites*, revised 2nd edn. (Baltimore: Penguin, 1962), 88–103.

30 George E. Mendenhall, 'Ancient Oriental and Biblical Law', *The Biblical Archaeologist* 17 (2) (1954): 25–46; idem., 'Covenant Forms in Israelite Tradition', *The Biblical Archaeologist* 17 (3) (1954): 49–76; idem., *Law and Covenant in Israel and the Ancient Near East* (Pittsburgh: Biblical Colloquium, 1955); Bryce, *Kingdom of the Hittites*, 373; Collins, *Hittites and their World*, 118–20; Bruce Wells, 'Law and Practice', in *A Companion to the Ancient Near East*, edited by Daniel C. Snell (Malden, MA: Blackwell, 2005), 183–95.

31 'No 13: Treaty between Muwattalli II and Alaksandu of Wilusa', Beckman, *Hittite Diplomatic Texts*, 90; Collins, *Hittites and their World*, 219; Richard H. Beal, 'Making, Preserving, and Breaking the Peace with the Hittite State', in *War and Peace in the Ancient World*, edited by Kurt A. Raaflaub (Malden, MA: Blackwell, 2007), 83; Bryce (ed.), *Letters of the Great Kings*, 2; Bederman, *International Law in Antiquity*, 26–7.

32 See the classic study by Liverani, *International Relations*.

33 Gary Beckman, 'Foreigners in the Ancient Near East', *Journal of the American Oriental Society* 133 (2) (2013): 203–216, at 204.

34 Beckman, 'Religion of the Hittites', 101. A possible exception is Tudhaliya IV, who may have claimed personal divinity during his life: Stefano de Martino, 'Symbols of Power in the Late Hittite Kingdom', in *Pax Hethitica: Studies on the Hittites and Their Neighbours in Honour of Itamar Singer*, edited by Yoram Cohen, Amir Gilan, and Jared L. Miller (Wiesbaden: Otto Harrassowitz Verlag, 2010), 87–98, at 95.

> administrator and given him the entire Land of Khatti. The Labarna shall continue to administer with his hand the entire land. May the storm-god destroy whoever should approach the person of the Labarna, the king, and the borders of Khatti![35]

This authority is reflected in the Hittite law collection, which clearly established the king as 'the supreme judge', to whom all Hittite subjects could appeal.[36] This authority was reinforced through sanction. Although surprisingly few offences merited the death penalty in the Hittite law code (the earliest copies of which date from the Old Kingdom period), challenging or disobeying the judgement of the king was one such capital offence.[37]

The king's authority as political leader was established not only through his selection by the gods to govern the Land of Hatti, but also through his cultic function as the kingdom's chief priest, essential for mediating human and other worldly interactions with the divine, as seen in this royal prayer:

> Divine lords – Sun-goddess of Arinna, my lady, and all the gods of the Land of Hatti, my lords – whose priest I am, who have conferred upon me, from among all others, the rulership over Hatti.[38]

The concept of the king as an agent of the gods, and thus also protected by the gods, was explicitly stated in Hittite royal documents, especially vassal treaties and royal edicts: 'The word of Tabarna, Great King, is not to be discarded or broken. Whoever disregards it shall be the legal adversary of the Powerful Storm-god, my lord, of the Sun-goddess of Arinna, my lady, and of all the gods.'[39] Here we see a royal ideology that not only sanctioned the king's authority by

35 Cited Gary Beckman, 'Royal Ideology and State Administration in Hittite Anatolia', in *The Civilizations of the Ancient Near East*, in CANE, 1:529–43, at 530.

36 *Laws of the Hittites*, ed. Hoffner, 4–5.

37 Note that in cases of resisting royal judgement the offender's family was also punished by the destruction or seizure of the offender's property after death: '¶173a If anyone rejects a judgment of the king, his house will become a heap of ruins. If anyone rejects a judgment of a magistrate, they shall cut off his head.' *Laws of the Hittites*, ed. Hoffner, 217–20, 234. See also Hoffner, 'Hittite Laws', in *Law Collections*, ed. Roth, 213–14, 234; Edwin M. Good, 'Capital Punishment and Its Alternatives in Ancient Near Eastern Law', *Stanford Law Review* 19 (5) (1967): 947–77, at 965. Cf. Deut. 17:8–13, which prescribes death for the failure to abide by a court decision.

38 'Prayer of Muwatalli I, Prayer No. 20 (CTH 381)', in Itamar Singer, *Hittite Prayers*, edited by Harry A. Hoffner, Jr. (Atlanta, GA: Society of Biblical Literature, 2002), 87.

39 'No 29, Edict of Muršili II of Hatti recognizing the Status of Piyassili of Carchemish', in Beckman, *Hittite Diplomatic Texts*, 169.

rooting it in the divine, but by extension presented any challenge or threat to that authority as a challenge to the gods themselves. If individual Hittite kings were *primus inter pares* in terms of material power, this ideology was intended to raise the royal dignity above the level of other elite competitors.

Endowing kingship with an ideology of divinely mandated rule came with a raft of concomitant expectations and duties. Foremost among these was the maintenance of justice. As Martha Roth comments: 'Whether or not the king was always himself an active participant in the administration of the legal system, he was always its guardian, for the application of justice was the highest trust given by the gods to a legitimate king.'[40] Whether as an active judge and legislator or as a paradigm of moral action, the king symbolized the precepts of justice as demanded by the gods.[41]

The Great King's duty to execute justice also extended to his vassal states. Muršili II intervened between Mukish and Ugarit over a matter of lands contested by the two states and, having 'investigated this case, he determined that these cities have belonged to the land of Ugarit since long ago.'[42] Similarly, in a number of political treaties created for the subject principalities of western Anatolia in the wake of Muršili II's defeat of Uhha-ziti of Arzawa (*c.*1317 BCE),[43] the Hittite monarch positioned himself as judge and arbiter between the vassal kingdoms, should disputes arise: 'If you have some legal dispute, you shall not act rashly, nor … be angry. If you yourselves have a resolvable dispute, then set out and come before My Majesty, so that I, My Majesty, can set you on the proper path by means of a judgment.'[44]

3 A Hittite *Ius ad Bellum* Tradition

3.1 *Authority*

Enemies of the state – those who challenged the authority of the Great King – became *legal* adversaries of the gods. This is why gods feature so centrally in Hittite diplomatic treaties as enforcers of the legal contract sealed between the two parties. War was the terrestrial prosecution of a legal trial in the court of the gods. The Hittites understood that divine favour was

---

40 Roth, *Law Collections*, 4–5.

41 Roth, *Law Collections*, 5.

42 'No 31a: Edict of Muršili II concerning Frontiers of Ugarit', §2 (A obv. 3–16), in Beckman, *Hittite Diplomatic Texts*, 174

43 See Treaties 10, 11, 12: Beckman, *Hittite Diplomatic Texts*, 69–86.

44 'No. 10: Treaty between Muršili II of Hatti and Targasnalli of Hapalla', §10, in Beckman, *Hittite Diplomatic Texts*, 72.

dependent on correct moral action; therefore the victor would be the state and ruler whom the gods judged to hold the moral as well as the legal 'right'. Divine favour also depended on the proper observation of religious ritual, for which the king, as chief priest, was primarily responsible.[45] This cultic role coexisted with the obligation of the king to rule justly, so that Hittite kingship embodied a moral, legal, and religious leadership upon which Hittite society was focused.

The final aspect of Hittite kingship was the monarch's role as a war leader. Formulaic references to the king as 'hero' underlined the importance of martial prestige as a defining feature of Hittite kingship. Royal seal impressions often include the formula: 'Seal of Tabarna [followed by name of the king], the Great King, the hero'.[46] Seals depict kings accompanied by two hieroglyphs depicting a dagger and a blossom: symbols of the king as a war leader and as a source of fecundity, respectively.[47] The king was almost always depicted carrying weapons, proof of the central role that war played in Hittite society and culture. Such images are repeated on a monumental scale at the massive rock reliefs at Yazilikaya, located just outside the royal capital of Hattuša. Here, King Tudhaliya IV (reigned *c.*1245–*c.*1215 BCE) is shown wearing a long sword with an ornate scabbard; elsewhere in the sanctuary, a procession of twelve gods are depicted in military garb and carrying swords.

The protective duties of the king extended to his political vassals. In a treaty between Tudhaliya II (reigned *c.*1425–*c.*1390 BCE) and Sunashshura of Kizzuwatna, the Hittite king swears to defend Sunashshura and his heirs in the same manner that he defends Hatti: 'As His Majesty protects his own person and land, he must likewise protect the land and person of Sunashshura. His Majesty must protect for kingship whichever son of Sunashshura he designates as his successor.'[48] In return, Hittite kings expected their vassals to defend Hittite interests and continue to take responsibility for defending their own territory: off-loading defence costs to Hattuša was not acceptable.[49]

In sum, the Hittite king exercised power through an authority rooted in the divine. As a steward of the land and people, appointed by the gods, the king claimed untrammelled authority within the state. But this was a reciprocal relationship. In return for obedience and service, the king was obliged to rule in a manner appropriate to his divine appointment. He must act morally, he must rule according to the law, he must show mercy to his subjects, he must

---

45 Beckman, 'Religion of the Hittites', 101.

46 See Akurgal, *Art of the Hittites*, 60–72; Beckman, 'Royal Ideology', in *CANE*, 1:532.

47 Akurgal, *Art of the Hittites*, 74; Stefano de Martino, 'Symbols of Power', 87–98.

48 'No. 2: Treaty between Tudhaliya II of Hatti and Sunashshura of Kizzuwatna', §11, in Beckman, *Hittite Diplomatic Texts*, 17–26, at 19.

49 'No. 10: Treaty between Muršili II of Hatti and Targasnalli of Hapalla', §12, in Beckman, *Hittite Diplomatic Texts*, 73.

fulfil his cultic obligations to the gods, and he must lead his people to victory in war.

As the chief priest, the king acted as a kind of divine conduit for his army, channelling the gods support and strength. 'Give them a man's valiant, battle-ready, divine weapon!' beseeches Muršili I, 'Put beneath their feet the enemy lands, and may they destroy them.'[50] Through his relationship with the divine, a just king could expect divine protection and military success.[51] Throughout the *Deeds of Šuppiluliuma*, we are told that 'the gods helped him', enabling the king to slay his enemies and reconquer Hittite lands that had suffered encroachment.[52] Indeed, divine support could enable the killing of masses of enemies.[53]

Moral righteousness on behalf of the king and the subjects he represented remained crucial in order to secure divine blessing in war. Unlike other contemporaneous royal ideologies, the possession of moral righteousness by the Hittite monarch was not automatically assumed. For example, during the New Kingdom reign of Tudhaliya IV, Hatti faced various threats and military reverses, especially from Assyria. In a prayer to the Sun-goddess of Arinna, Tudhaliya IV's sense of desperation is reflected by his soul-searching: he admits to a lack of proper piety by neglecting certain religious festivals (thus incurring the goddess's displeasure), seeks forgiveness for his sins, and promises to give the goddess her due. By confessing his sins and making the appropriate concessions – that is, by acting justly – Tudhaliya IV hoped that, in return, the goddess would bestow military success upon him:

> If you, O Sun-goddess of Arinna, my lady, became angry with me on account of some festivals, take care of me again, O Sun-goddess of Arinna, my lady! May I defeat the enemy! If you, O Sun-goddess of Arinna, my lady, will step down to me, and I shall defeat the enemy, I shall confess my sin before you and never again shall I omit the festivals ... and if I shall defeat the enemy, when I return from the battle-field, I shall go up to Mount Tagurka, and I shall give you thousands [of offerings], and I shall make reparation.[54]

50 'No. 9: Muršili's hymn and prayer to Telipinu', §11, in Singer, *Hittite Prayers*, 55. Cf. Prayer No. 8.

51 For example, 'No. 11: Treaty between Muršili II and Kupanta-Kurunta of Mira-Kuwaliya', §3, in Beckman, *Hittite Diplomatic Texts*, 74.

52 Güterbock, 'Deeds of Šuppiluliuma', 78.

53 Güterbock, 'Deeds of Šuppiluliuma', 75–6; cf. 90–1.

54 'No. 24: Tudhaliya IV's prayer to the Sun-goddess of Arinna for Military success', §§1–5, in Singer, *Hittite Prayers*, 108–9.

There is even evidence, in a royal edict no less, of Tudhaliya IV contemplating defeat in the ongoing war against Assyria. This edict was sent to the king of Ugarit, and considers the future outcomes of the war: 'When the war with Assyria has come to an end, *if I, My Majesty, prevail over the king of Assyria, then we will make peace with one another.*'[55] The phrase 'if I prevail' introduces *doubt* regarding Hittite victory, and indicates a strategic awareness that defeat was possible. When considered alongside other ancient Near Eastern empires, such sentiments are highly unusual, if not unique. An Egyptian or Assyrian royal document would never have countenanced the possibility of defeat, and it suggests that Hittite kings did not take victory for granted.

This is of the highest importance when considering Hittite ethical and legal attitudes to war. Only when a society seriously considers the possibility of defeat can it truly engage with military ethics. In Hatti, defeat was understood as a result of divine disfavour, which was itself a consequence of immorality on the part of the king, his forebears, or his subjects. A deficiency of justice or piety risked military defeat. Because the Hittites could conceive of their own injustice, they could also entertain the possibility that some of their military actions could be unjust. Here, then, we have the beginnings of a genuine engagement with international justice as something other than wholly chauvinistic.

3.2 *Just Cause*

The Hittites certainly recognised certain injuries for which war was a necessary response, and it was obviously viewed as a legitimate tool of foreign policy.[56] Five causes for war clearly emerge from the sources: (i) self-defence; (ii) restitution of property; (iii) vengeance (for human and/or divine injuries); (iv) defence of allies; (v) suppression of rebellion. I shall deal with each of these in turn.

The justness of self-defence was an intrinsic concept for Hittite rulers. From the very earliest evidence of Hittite warfare, we can witness Hittite kings waging war to defend their kingdom against what they considered direct injuries. Very often this included references to the perennial enemies of Hatti, the nomadic Kaška tribes of north-eastern Anatolia,[57] as in this prayer to the Sun-goddess of Arinna by King Arnuwanda I (*c.*1360 BCE) and his queen, Asmunikal:

55 'No 37: Edict of Tudhaliya IV releasing Ammistamru II of Ugarit from participation in war against Assyria', §1, in Beckman, *Hittite Diplomatic Texts*, 183. Italics added.

56 Jonathan Rosner Ziskind, 'Aspects of International Law in the Ancient Near East' (Unpublished PhD submitted to Columbia University, 1967), 125.

57 The Kaška are mentioned in over 200 Hittite texts: Claudia Glatz and Roger Matthews, 'Anthropology of a Frontier Zone: Hittite-Kaska Relations in Late Bronze Age

> We shall surely continue to tell you gods how the enemies attacked the land of Hatti, plundered the land, and took it away ... and we shall continually bring our case before you ... the temples which you, O gods, had in these lands, the Kaska-men have destroyed and they have smashed your images, O gods. They divided up the priests, the holy priests, the priestesses, the anointed ones, the musicians, the gardeners, and they made them their servants.[58]

The invasion of Hatti's borders, the plundering of property, the violation of religious sites and the seizing and enslavement of non-combatant personnel dedicated to the temples are obviously regarded as heinous crimes, necessitating a military response.

In a series of letters between the royal capital and a provincial governor named Kassu, dating to around 1300 BCE, we see the Hittite royal machinery at work in responding to military threats:

> [King to Kassu] Concerning the matters about which you wrote to me: how the enemy is damaging the crops, how in Kappušiya he has attacked the property of the Queen, how they have taken one team of oxen belonging to the House of the Queen, and how they have led away 30 oxen and 10 men of the serfs – all this I have heard. Because the enemy thus marches into the land at a moment's notice, you should locate him somewhere, you should attack him.[59]

Conflict between Hatti and territorially defined kingdoms and principalities was also couched in terms of self-defence. In recounting the deeds of his father, Šuppiluliuma I, Muršili II describes self-defensive military action: 'because Hatti was attacked by the enemy, and the enemy had taken borderlands of Hatti, my father kept attacking the enemy lands and kept defeating them. He took back the borderlands of Hatii, which the enemy had taken

North-Central Anatolia', *Bulletin of the American Schools of Oriental Research* 339 (2005): 47–65, at 53–4.

58 'No. 5: Prayer of Arnuwanda and Asmunikal to the Sun-goddess of Arinna', §§11–18, in Singer, *Hittite Prayers*, 41–2

59 'Letter 14: King to Kassu', in Hoffner, *Letters from Hittite Kingdom*, 109. Kassu held the office of 'Chief of the Army Inspectors' (ibid., 95) and also apparently 'Chief of the Military Heralds': 'No. 73: From Hulla, the Commander of Chariot Warriors to Kassu', in Hoffner, *Letters from Hittite Kingdom*, 227–8.

and resettled them.'[60] Thus Hittite kings saw a straightforward relationship between aggressive actions committed against the state and the legitimacy of military responses to defend Hittite interests. It was the duty of the king to defend both his borders and his subjects.

It was also the duty of the king to restore stolen property or seek compensation for property that had been destroyed. Some of our earliest evidence from Hatti testifies that armed violence was considered a legitimate tool to achieve this. This itself was based on a legal system that operated on a combination of vindictive and compensatory principles.[61] This echoed older practices enshrined within the Hittite legal code, in which a number of laws deal with the killing or abduction of Hittites and their property.[62]

A deep concern with the legal ownership and restoration of property was continued into the later period. An edict issued to vassal military commanders during a border war demanded that they 'will bring the stolen goods' taken by the enemy back to Hatti. There are several clauses on the seizing and returning of property, with the king insisting that his servants 'will give back everything which still exists and is visible to the eye. They will not hold back as much as a strand of wool, but will give it back. And they will seize everyone who has escaped'.[63] This last clause almost certainly refers to slaves, who were also considered a form of property.

The importance given to the restoration of stolen property could lead to serious international conflict. The Assyrian king, Tikulti-Ninurta (*c.*1243–*c.*1207 BCE), was wary of provoking war with Hatti when he wrote to Tudhaliya IV insisting that, 'No one sinned against your land, no one removed a blade of straw or a splinter of wood from the march of your land.'[64] Similarly, Hattušili III, frustrated at the raiding of Hittite territory by the city Turira but wishing to avoid all-out war with Assyria, wrote to Adad-nirari I seeking confirmation of Assyria's claim over the city:

> When Turira plunders that land [i.e. Hittite territory], they keep taking booty to Turira ... If Turira is yours, smash it! But you shall not claim the

60 'No. 12: Muršili II's "first" plague prayer to the assembly of Gods and Goddesses', §4, in Singer, *Hittite Prayers*, 62.

61 'Treaty between a King of Hatti (perhaps Hantili II) and Paddatissu of Kizzuwatna', §7, in Beckman, *Hittite Diplomatic Texts*, 13.

62 Hittite Laws (late version) ¶¶ 3–7, 19a, 180, 185: in *Laws of the Hittites*, ed. Hoffner, 18–21, 29–30, 143–4, 147. See also Ziskind, 'Aspects of International Law', 24–6.

63 'No 27a: Indictment of Mita of Pahhuwa and Treaty with the Elders of several Anatolian communities', §§5, 9, 11, in Beckman, *Hittite Diplomatic Texts*, 162, 163.

64 Cited Liverani, *International Relations*, 56.

> possessions of my subjects who are dwelling in the city. If Turira is not yours, write to me, so that I may smash it. The possessions of your troops who are dwelling in the city shall not be claimed.[65]

Hittite commanders even had an obligation to restore goods previously seized from Hittite territory. When the spoils of a campaign were brought back to Hattuša, any property identified as having been plundered from Hatti in previous conflicts was subsequently returned to its Hittite owners.[66] By definition, of course, this meant that Hittites were seizing plunder of their own during military campaigns.

Vengeance was often sought in response to enemy actions that inflicted injuries on Hittite territory, subjects, and property: thus it was intimately connected to aspects of self-defence and restitution of property. The breaking of oaths constituted one of the most important just causes for declaring war. In this sense, international treaties may have had only a limited capacity to restrain war, but they made a substantial contribution to how these wars were justified, providing useful "evidence" of enemy perfidy and guilt. Such violations were political, legal, and religious crimes, as they broke oaths made before the gods. Seeking vengeance against enemies was thus viewed as legitimate and even necessary to punish crimes against the Hittite pantheon and state, and to satisfy mundane and divine demands of justice and honour.

A typical Hittite vassal treaty from the fourteenth century BCE listed the various punishments the 'oath gods' would inflict for any breaches of the treaty: 'these oath gods shall seize him ... and destroy him, together with his household, his fields, his vineyards, his threshing floors, his oxen, and his sheep, and together with his renown, his progeny ...'[67] In the case of international relations, war was the instrument through which this punishment was executed.[68]

But vengeance was not necessarily unlimited and war leaders could choose restraint. When Uhha-ziti, king of Arzawa, broke a treaty and declared war against Hatti in the late fourteenth century BCE, King Manapa-Tarhunta of the Seha River Land was also persuaded to take up arms against his Hittite

65 'No. 24B: Letter from Hattušili III to Adad-Nirari I of Assyria', §1, in Beckman, *Hittite Diplomatic Texts*, 148. See also Liverani, *International Relations*, 64–5; Bryce, *Kingdom of the Hittites*, 274.

66 Korošec, 'Warfare of the Hittites', 162.

67 'No. 1A: Treaty between Arnuwanda I of Hatti and the Men of Ismerika', §§3–4, in Beckman, *Hittite Diplomatic Texts*, 14.

68 Ziskind, 'Aspects of International Law', 87, 126. For examples of curses and punishment of oath-breakers in Hittite treaties, see Beckman, *Hittite Diplomatic Texts*, 22, 24, 29, 35, 52, 53, 113.

overlords. The Great King Muršili II launched a successful counter-campaign and, 'because Uhha-ziti had transgressed the oath in regard to me, the oath gods seized him, and I destroyed him.' But Muršili II was moved to mercy when dealing with Manapa-Tarhunta:

> I would have destroyed you likewise. But you fell down at my feet, and you dispatched old men and old women to me. And your messengers fell down at my feet. You sent to me as follows: 'Spare me, my lord. May my lord not destroy me …' Then I, My Majesty, had compassion for you, and because of that I acceded to you and made peace with you.[69]

Clearly, there were times when mercy was considered appropriate; on this occasion, of course, there may also have been some underlying *Realpolitik* motivation for Muršili II to stay his hand.

As in any imperial state, rebellion was a constant source of anxiety for Hittite kings (as the treaty above evinces).[70] Military resources were rarely sufficient to deal with internal and external threats at the same time. This anxiety is reflected in the surviving vassal treaties, in which one of the formulaic components were oaths of loyalty to the royal family and promises to report any seditious language or rebellious acts to the imperial capital. Moreover, Hittite society – like other ancient societies – was composed of free, semi-free, and unfree persons. Hatti's agrarian economy was dependent on slave and corvée labour, much of which was made up of prisoners-of-war or their descendants. Revolt was an ever-present fear, so the punishment for insurrection was severe.[71]

The suppression of revolt was understood as an extension of the principle of legitimate vengeance, because, given the Hittite practice of creating legally binding international treaties, most rebellious vassals were probably in breach of pre-existing treaty oaths. Even if not, rebelling against the king constituted an injury to the king's (and therefore also the kingdom's and the gods') honour. Punishing rebellion could thus be justified on at least four grounds:

69 'No 12: Treaty between Muršili II and Manapa-Tarhunta of Land of the Seha River', in Beckman, *Hittite Diplomatic Texts*, 83.

70 'Annals of Hattušili I', §5, translated by Gary Beckman, in *The Ancient Near East: Historical Sources in Translation*, edited by Mark W. Chavalas (Malden, MA: Blackwell, 2006), 220. See also Philo H.J. Houwink ten Cate, 'The History of Warfare According to Hittite Sources: The Annals of Hattusilis I (Part I)', *Anatolica* 10 (1983): 91–109, and Philo H.J. Houwink ten Cate, 'The History of Warfare According to Hittite Sources: The Annals of Hattusilis I (Part II)'*Anatolica* 11 (1984): 47–83, for an alternative translation.

71 'Annals of Hattušili I', §6, in *Ancient Near East*, ed. Chavalas, 220; 'Annals of Hattušili I', Houwink ten Cate, 'Warfare according to Hittite Sources', 48.

self-defence, restitution of property, vengeance for oath violation, and defence of honour.

The majority of the surviving Hittite treaties are essentially defensive and offensive alliances. As such, they are evidence of a series of symbiotic political relationships, at the heart of which was the desire for survival through securing military advantages in a highly dynamic, competitive, and dangerous geopolitical system. Hittite kings sought to create buffer zones that would ultimately guarantee the security of Hattuša and the Lands of Hatti, and so the defence of allies was effectively a form of self-defence.

A treaty created between Tudhaliya II of Hatti and Sunashshura of Kizzuwatna listed the following obligations, reflecting standard treaty norms:

- If some other land begins war against Sunashshura, His Majesty must inform Sunashshura as soon as he hears of it.
- If any city in the land of His Majesty begins war – as it is His Majesty's enemy, it will likewise be Sunashshura's – they will fight side by side.
- And if some city in the land of Sunashshura begins war – as it is Sunashashura's enemy, it will likewise be His Majesty's – they will fight side by side.[72]

It is evident that these obligations (and the treaty includes numerous others) imposed reciprocal duties on both rulers. The formulaic nature of Hittite defensive/offensive treaties is evident when, around fifty years after the aforementioned Kizzuwatna treaty was created, Hatti and its long-time enemy Mitanni came to create an alliance:

> In the future the Hittites and the Mittannians shall not look upon one another with a malevolent eye. The Hittites shall not do evil to the Mitannians; the Mitannians shall not do evil to the Hittites. When the King of Hatti goes to war, the king of the land of Mittanni shall attack any enemy of Hatti. As someone is the enemy of the land of Mitanni, he shall be the enemy of Hatti. The friend of the King of Hatti shall be the friend of the king of the land of Mitanni.[73]

Up until the end of the New Kingdom, defensive and offensive treaties made between Hatti and its vassals adopted almost identical demands,

72 'No. 2: Treaty between Tudhaliya II of Hatti and Sunashshura of Kizzuwatna', §§20–22, 25, 28, in Beckman, *Hittite Diplomatic Texts*, 20–1.

73 'No. 6a: Šuppiluliuma I and Shattiwaza of Mittanni', §8, in Beckman, *Hittite Diplomatic Texts*, 45.

commitments, and language.[74] This includes the famous treaty made between Hattušili III and Ramses II of Egypt: a diplomatic instrument made between the two superpowers of the ancient Near East. It clearly expresses an assumption that defence – whether self-defence or defence of allies – was a legitimate reason to go to war. An attack on a formal ally was equated with an attack on oneself. In light of the extensive oaths taken as part of treaty processes, to go to war for one's allies was not only justified, it was necessary: a consequence of the obligations that rulers had sworn to uphold.[75]

3.3 *Hittite Injustice*

An aspect of Hittite thought on war which was truly unique among their ancient Near Eastern contemporaries was an apparent willingness to countenance the possibility of their own crimes in the international arena. As such, there is evidence that the Hittites were the first ancient people to recognise that they themselves could wage unjust wars.

One of our most interesting Hittite sources is a series of 'Plague Prayers' composed by King Muršili II (reigned *c.*1330–*c.*1295 BCE) in response to a devasting plague that wracked Hatti for more than two decades. Believing that the gods were punishing the Hittites for some sin, the Plague Prayers demonstrate a forensic process whereby Muršili II and his advisers attempted to discover exactly what sin had been committed so that they could rectify it as soon as possible.

Having taken oracular enquiries, in the first of the prayers Muršili II believes that his father's (Šuppiluliuma I) usurpation of the former king, Tudhaliya the Younger, could be the cause of the gods' displeasure.[76] In the second Plague

---

74 For example: 'No. 7: Treaty between Šuppiluliuma I and Tette of Nuhashshi', §§4–6, in Beckman, *Hittite Diplomatic Texts*, 55–6; 'No 8: Treaty between Muršili II and Tuppi-Teshshup of Amurru', §§7–8, in Beckman, *Hittite Diplomatic Texts*, 60–1; 'No 9: Treaty between Muršili II and Niqmepa of Ugarit', §§2–5, in *ibid.*, 65–6; 'No. 10: Treaty between Muršili II of Hatti and Targasnalli of Hapalla', §§1–3, in *ibid.*, 69–70; 'No. 11: Treaty between Muršili II and Kupanta-Kurunta of Mira-Kuwaliya, §§12–19', in *ibid.*, 77–8; 'No. 12: Treaty between Muršili II of Hatti and Manapa-Tarhunta of the Land of the Seha River', §6, in *ibid.*, 84; 'No 13: Treaty between Muwattalli II and Alaksandu of Wilusa', §§5–12, in *ibid.*, 88–90; 'No 16: Treaty between Hattušili III and Benteshina of Amurru', §§10–13, in *ibid.*, 102–3; 'No 17: Treaty between Tudhaliya IV and Shaushga-muwa of Amurru', §§11–13, in *ibid.*, 106–7.

75 The Egyptian and Hittite versions of the treaty are translated in *Ancient Near Eastern Texts*, ed. Pritchard, 199–202, 202–3. See also the translations available in S. Langdon and Alan H. Gardiner, 'The Treaty of Alliance between Ḫattušili, King of the Hittites, and the Pharaoh Ramesses II of Egypt', *The Journal of Egyptian Archaeology* 6 (3) (1920): 179–205.

76 'No. 12: Muršili's "First" Plague Prayer to the Assembly of Gods and Goddesses', §§2–6, in Singer, *Hittite Prayers*, 61–2. For the same observation, see also 'No. 11: Muršili's "Second" Plague Prayer to Storm-god of Hatti', §1, Singer, *Hittite Prayers*, 57.

Prayer, a frantic Muršili laments that his people are still dying; so, searching the royal archive, his scribes discover 'two old tablets' which, he believes, explain why the gods are punishing his kingdom.[77] One of the tablets reveals how Šuppiluliuma I may have broken a treaty oath with Egypt and thus waged an unjust war in Syria-Palestine:

> The second tablet dealt with the town of Kurustamma: how the Storm-god of Hatti carried the men of Kurustamma to Egyptian territory and how the Storm-god of Hatti made a treaty between them and the men of Hatti, so that they were put under oath by the Storm-god of Hatti. Since the men of Hatti and the men of Egypt were bound by the oath of the Storm-god of Hatti, and the men of Hatti proceeded to get the upper hand, the men of Hatti thereby suddenly transgressed the oath of the gods. My father sent infantry and chariotry, and they attacked the border-land of Egypt, the land of Amqa. ...When the prisoners of war were carried off to Hatti, the prisoners of war brought the plague into Hatti. From that day on people have been dying in Hatti. When I found the aforementioned tablet dealing with Egypt, I inquired about it to the god through an oracle saying: 'Has this matter been brought about by the Storm-god of Hatti because the men of Egypt and the men of Hatti had been put under oath by the Storm-god of Hatti?' ... whereupon the men of Hatti themselves suddenly transgressed the word (of the oath), did this become the cause for the anger of the Storm-god of Hatti, my lord?'[78]

This is a fascinating and unique reflection from that Late Bronze Age on the possibility of one's own side committing sin and engaging in unjust war. The Hittites knew that the plague originated from the Egyptian prisoners-of-war, so it was natural enough to draw a connection between the prisoners and the cause of divine anger. The solution was to offer restitution for this sin:

> With regard to the problem of the oath of the gods which was established as a cause for the plague, I have offered the ritual of the oath for the Storm-god of Hatti ... I have confessed the sin of my father ... If there is some restitution to be made, then there has already been paid much for this plague caused by the prisoners of war who were brought back from Egyptian territory and by the civilian captives who were brought back.

77 'No. 11: Muršili's "Second" Plague Prayer to Storm-god of Hatti', §3, in Singer, *Hittite Prayers*, 58.

78 'No. 11: Muršili's "Second" Plague Prayer to Storm-god of Hatti', §§4–5, Singer, *Hittite Prayers*, 58–59.

> And since Hatti has made restitution though the plague, it has made restitution for it twenty-fold … Or if you want to require from me some additional restitution, specify it to me in a dream, and I shall give it to you.[79]

Note, however, that the compensation offered for Šuppiluliuma's sins was *not* offered to the Egyptians, nor to the captives taken during the campaign; rather, restitution was offered to the gods alone.

The capacity of a Hittite king to err is also intimated in a letter sent by Hattušili III (reigned *c.*1275–*c.*1245 BCE) to the king of Ahhiyawa (Achaea). In this letter, Hattušili III refers to previous hostility between the two kings over the kingdom of Wilusa (Troy):

> But my brother once wrote to me as follows: '… You have acted aggressively towards me.' But at that time, my brother, I was young; if at that time I wrote anything insulting, it was not done deliberately. We were at enmity … Over that matter concerning Wiluša we were hostile, because we have made peace, then what more is there? If one partner confesses his error/sin to the other, then because he confesses his error/sin to the partner, he will not reject him. Because therefore I have confessed my error/sin to my brother, let there be no more hostility me and my brother.[80]

In effect, Hattušili III admits culpability for the previous conflict between the two kingdoms. That a Great King of Hatti was prepared to 'confess his error' is really quite remarkable; it is unthinkable that an Egyptian or Assyrian king would have made a similar admission of guilt.

Taken together, the evidence suggests that the Hittites recognised that the possession of justice in war was not the sole monopoly of Hatti, and its kings countenanced the possibility (albeit only occasionally) that rival states could possess just cause. In sum, this was the first genuinely international and multipolar conception of just war.

4 A Hittite *Ius in Bello* Tradition? Prohibitions on Conduct

The Hittites conceptualised war in ethical and legal terms, developing what we would now term a *ius ad bellum* tradition. They believed in the importance of

79 Ibid., 59–60. Cf. 'No. 13: Muršili's "Fourth" Plague Prayer to assembly of gods (arranged by localities)', §5, ibid., 65.

80 'No. 101: From King Hattušili III to the King of Ahhiyawa ("Tawagalawa Letter")', in Hoffner, *Letters from Hittite Kingdom*, 311–12.

proper authority and held definite ideas about what constituted a just cause for war. Highly unusual for their historical context, they even admitted the possibility that Hittite kings – and thus the Hittite state – could commit injustices, rendering certain conflicts unjust. On the other hand, there was still conceptual space for permitting wars of conquest and aggrandisement.

Given that the Hittites devoted significant thought to the issue of war's legitimacy and justice prior to embarking on campaign, did they give equal attention to *how* war was conducted? Did they believe that the prosecution of war was an activity governed by rules, or that certain acts were prohibited? Were there norms regulating how certain persons should be treated during and after war? Put simply, was there a Hittite *ius in bello* tradition?

Hittites usually began their military conflicts with some formal declaration of hostilities. Letters demanding the satisfaction of specific grievances were dispatched to the opposing party; if refused, a further letter was sent, 'charging the enemy with having committed the first act of aggression and referring the affair to the judgement of heaven, to be settled by the ordeal of war'.[81] In its most basic sense, the declaration of war was an open challenge to battle. Šuppiluliuma I wrote to the king of Arzawa, 'Come, let us fight!'[82] His son, Muršili II, said much the same: 'I sent a messenger to Uhhaziti and I wrote to him: "My servants who have gone over to you that I requested back from you, you have not given the back to me … Now, come! We will battle! May the storm-god, my lord, judge our case."'[83]

As part of the legal and moral process of establishing a just war, Hittite kings would lay "charges" against their enemies – both human and divine – on the eve of a campaign, or at the point of entering enemy territory. This was explicitly stated in a grievance delivered on the northern-eastern frontier against the Kaška and the Kaškaean gods, citing injuries committed by them against the gods of Hatti and its people:

> [H]ear the charge we raise against you. The gods of the Hatti land have done nothing against you, the gods of the Kaškaean country. They have not put you under constraint. But you, the gods of the Kaškaean country, began war. You drove the gods of the Hatti land out of their realm and took over their realm for yourselves. The Kaškaean people also began war. From the Hittite you took away their cities and drive them out of their field and fallow and out of their vineyards. The gods of the Hatti land and

81 Gurney, *Hittites*, 114.

82 Güterbock, 'Deeds of Šuppiluliuma', 81.

83 'The Ten Year Annals of Muršili II: excerpts', §16, in *The Ancient Near East*, ed. Chavalas, 255. See also Liverani, *International Relations*, 110–12; Korošec, 'Warfare of the Hittites', 163.

> the Hittite people call for bloody vengeance. The vengeance of the Hatti gods and the vengeance of the Hittite people will be wrought on you, the gods of the Kaškaean country and the Kaškaean people.[84]

As David Bederman observes, the declaration of war between ancient states was 'a reaffirmation of nationalist impulses in religion … the ritual for opening hostilities was a celebration of exclusion and superiority.'[85] In the case of the Hittites, who managed international relations through the use of treaties and possessed a highly juridical understanding of war, conflict often resulted from one party violating specific treaty obligations. The transition from peace to war therefore involved a conceptual and legal shift in relations between Hatti and another state, and thus required a formal declaration.

Hittite warfare was a highly ritualized activity. Prior to the launching of any campaign, commanders and troops would undergo purification rituals while kings would make oracular enquiries to determine the favour of the gods and the wisdom of specific operations.[86] And though the Hittites took a very dim view of sorcery within the domestic sphere, magic was utilised against the state's enemies. Objects would be inscribed with the names of the enemy before being ritually destroyed, frequently by burning. Asking the gods to curse one's enemies was also considered perfectly acceptable. For example, Muršili II beseeched the gods to: 'Turn the plague, the hostility, the famine, and the severe fever towards Mitanni and Arzawa … To those enemy lands give severe fever, plague, and famine.'[87] Clearly, wielding magical and supernatural powers against the enemy was not prohibited.

---

84 *Ancient Near Eastern Texts*, ed. Pritchard, 354–5. See also Beal, 'Making Peace with the Hittite State', 91–2; Richard H. Beal, 'Hittite Military Rituals', in *Ancient Magic and Ritual Power*, edited by Marvin Meyer and Paul Mirecki (Leiden: E.J. Brill, 1995), 63–76, at 68; Liverani, *International Relations*, 104; Amnon Altman, 'Tracing the Earliest Recorded Concepts of International Law (5): The Near East 1200–330 BCE', *Journal of the History of International Law* 12 (2010), 101–54, at 138.

85 Bederman, *International Law in Antiquity*, 76.

86 Beal, 'Hittite Military Rituals', 63–7; Beal, 'Making Peace with the Hittite State', 91; Goetze, 'Warfare in Asia Minor', 126–9; Liverani, *International Relations*, 102; Sa-Moon Kang, *Divine War in the Old Testament and in the Ancient Near East* (Berlin and New York: Walter de Gruyter, 1989), 56–63.

87 'No 8, Muršili's Hymn and Prayer to Sun-goddess of Arinna', §7, §11, in Singer, *Hittite Prayers*, 52–3. See also 'No. 10, Muršili's "Third" Plague prayer to Sun-goddess of Arinna', §3, ibid., 57; 'No. 12, Muršili's "first" plague prayer to the assembly of Gods and Goddesses', §9, ibid., 63–4. On curse formulae in Hittite treaties, see Bederman, *International Law in Antiquity*, 144.

In the physical realm of battle, Hittite armies consisted of a core force of chariotry, so it is unsurprising that commanders often sought set-piece confrontations in which they could deploy their chariot forces to the best effect. The chariot, though a highly effective mobile platform to deliver shock troops to battle, was limited as to the terrain it could cover. Chariotry required terrain that was relatively flat and open, with little vegetation cover or topographical obstacles such as water courses or ditches. To deploy their chariotry, Hittite commanders sought pre-arranged battles on favourable sites, frequently on a flat area outside the walls of a city. At the city of Hahha, Hattušili I 'gave battle three times in the city gate.'[88] The *Deeds of Šuppiluliuma I* record how 'Karanni, king of Hayaša, came to meet him in battle below the town of Kummaha'.[89]

A preference for set-piece battles – and perhaps the existence of a norm encouraging their arrangement – is further suggested by pejorative descriptions of enemies, such as the nomadic Kaška, who resorted to 'dishonourable' tactics such as ambushes and night attacks.[90] But kingdoms such as Egypt could equally resort to identical tactics. A letter to the Hittite king from a regional commander in Syria describes the border struggles between the Hittite empire and New Kingdom Egypt:

> Now for five months the cold has been gnawing me, my chariots are broken, my horses are dead, and my troops are lost! *My men were attacked over and over again in the middle of the night*, and a battle was waged between them.[91]

A negative attitude toward ambush and surprise attacks in war can also be detected in letters sent from the royal capital to regional commanders. The king specifically advises his commanders to beware ambushes (*ši-na-ha*) when operating in enemy territory to the north, and, in another letter, we learn of a "cowardly" ambush on a Hittite chariot detachment. This resulted in the death of 'the Gold Chariot-Warrior': one of the highest military officers in the kingdom.[92] The killing so infuriated King Šuppiluliuma I that 'he mobilized

---

88 'Annals of Hattušili I', §10, §16, in *The Ancient Near East*, ed. Chavalas, 220–1.

89 Güterbock, 'Deeds of Šuppiluliuma', 76, 66.

90 For example, Güterbock, 'Deeds of Šuppiluliuma', 90–1, 92.

91 Bryce (ed.), *Letters of the Great Kings*, 173–4. For further examples of night attacks by Hittite enemies, see Beal, 'Organization of the Hittite Military', 30–1.

92 'Letter 22: from the king to Hulla, Kassu, and Zilapiya', in Hoffner, *Letters from Hittite Kingdom*, 124–5; cf. 'Letter 31: from King to Himmuili', ibid., 142. Hoffner believes that we should read this letter as implying that the Gold-charioteer was literally killed from *behind*, i.e. in an ambush: ibid., 144. On the Gold Chariot-Warrior, see Pechioli Daddi,

the troops and chariots of Hatti at once and went into the country of Arzawa', seeking revenge.[93]

Nevertheless, claiming the existence of a Hittite norm which absolutely prohibited night attacks and ambushes would be going too far. Šuppiluliuma I may have been furious about his forces being ambushed, but he himself resorted to surprise attacks in order to defeat Kaškaean armies,[94] and earlier Hittite kings also appear to have utilised night attacks against their enemies. Anitta of Kuššara (mid-eighteenth century BCE) used the cover of night to capture the city of Neša, although spared the civilian population: 'The king of Kuššara came down from the city with massed forces and *took Neša by storm at night*. He captured the king of Neša but in no way mistreated the inhabitants of Neša.'[95] Hattušili I, meanwhile, 'went to the city of Zippašna. Indeed, *at night I went up to Zippašna*, and I joined battle with them.'[96]

In the most famous battle fought by the Hittites, at Qadesh in 1274 BCE, the Egyptians later accused the Hittites of launching a surprise attack, catching Pharoah Ramses II's army as 'they were marching unaware and not prepared to fight'.[97] Unfortunately, we have no Hittite account of the battle and must rely on the Egyptian version of events, which seeks to cast the Hittites in a negative light.[98]

'Le cariche d'oro', in *Hittite Studies in Honor of Harry A. Hoffner, Jr. on the Occasion of His 65th Birthday*, ed. G.M. Beckman, R.H. Beal, and J.G. McMahon (Winona Lake, Ind.: Eisenbrauns, 2003), 83–92.

93 '[T]hey came after him out of ... and took him by surprise on the way and defeated him. When my father heard of the defeat of Himuili, his anger rose and he mobilized the troops and chariots of Hatti at once and went into the country of Arzawa.' Güterbock, 'Deeds of Šuppiluliuma', 80.

94 'My father set a trap for them and smote the Gašgaeans ... so that the Gašgaean troops and the auxiliary troops died in multitude.' Güterbock, 'Deeds of Šuppiluliuma', 63. Cf. ibid., 65, 67, 78.

95 'The Anitta Text', §2, in *The Ancient Near East*, ed. Chavalas, 217. My italics. Cf. slightly variant translations in Bryce, *Major Historical Texts of Early Hittite History*, 24–5; Güterbock, 'Hittite Historiography', 23.

96 'Annals of Hattušili I', in *The Ancient Near East*, ed. Chavalas, 221 (italics added); cf. Houwink ten Cate, 'Warfare according to Hittite Sources', 52.

97 *Kadesh Poem*, in *Ancient Egyptian Literature: A Book of Readings*, compiled and translated by Miriam Lichtheim, 3 vols. (Berkeley: University of California Press, 1973–1980), 2:64–6, quotation at 64. Cf. *Kadesh Bulletin*, in ibid., 2:60–2.

98 Egyptian sources claim that the Hittite army at Qadesh/Kadesh numbered 47,500 troops, including 3,500 chariotry. If these figures are even remotely accurate, one must wonder at the degree to which such massive forces were really capable of a 'surprise' attack. Liverani, for example, rejects the idea that the massive Hittite army could have 'surprised' the Egyptians: *International Relations*, 120–1. For an attempted coverage of the battle from the Hittite perspective, using Egyptian sources, see Bryce, *Kingdom of Hittites*, 234–41.

As a rule, it seems that tactics such as ambush and night-attacks were viewed as morally relative: damnable when utilised by enemies; lauded when successfully employed by one's own side. This trend is evident across all the cultures of the ancient Near East, and similar double standards can be found in most martial cultures, from the ancient world to the present day. It is a truism that we are inclined to look more favourably upon our own actions than upon those of our enemies.

In general, Hittite sources give an extraordinarily bloody impression of Hittite warfare. During battle, no restraints were dictated, observed, or expected between combatants. The phrase 'the enemy troops died in multitude', or derivatives, appears repeatedly in Hittite descriptions of military campaigns.[99] Such slaughter was presented as being achieved through divine aid: 'The gods helped my father, so that he slew the aforementioned Gašgaean enemy, the tribal troops, wherever he caught him.'[100] In other words, to smash one's enemy was a sign of martial and moral virtue, indicative of divine favour.

However, we must also bear in mind that the Hittite texts are deeply polemical and their claims cannot always be taken literally. Most of them should be regarded as propaganda of some stripe, and many contain contradictions. For example, descriptions of the enemy dying 'in multitudes' were also accompanied by claims that the number of captives 'were countless'. Indeed, significant numbers of combatants and non-combatants must have been captured rather than killed, and many more would have escaped by fleeing.[101] Moreover, it appears that enemy soldiers were frequently willing to surrender to the Hittites, suggesting that they expected to receive at least some degree of mercy and restraint (otherwise there would have been little incentive to surrender).[102]

Across the ancient Near East, there is no evidence of meaningful distinctions between combatants and non-combatants, and this is equally true of Hittite warfare.[103] Non-combatants were simply viewed as part of the enemy's movable property and were considered a valuable source of war booty. Combatant and non-combatant captives alike became the chattel property of the Hittite king, to be distributed among the troops and the temples of the gods. When recalling his conquest of Arzawa, Muršili II plainly stated that 'I have made the civilian captives whom I carried off to Hatti subject to the service obligation.'[104]

99 For example, Güterbock, 'Deeds of Šuppiluliuma', 60, 62–3, 68, 75–6, 111–18.

100 Güterbock, 'Deeds of Šuppiluliuma', 67.

101 Güterbock, 'Deeds of Šuppiluliuma', 63.

102 See Güterbock, 'Deeds of Šuppiluliuma', 65; Bryce (ed.), *Letters of the Great Kings*, 164.

103 For further discussion, see Cox, *Origins of the Just War*.

104 'No. 10: Treaty between Muršili II and Targasnalli of Hapalla', §13, in Beckman, *Hittite Diplomatic Texts*, 73.

Even elite non-combatants, such as the royal families of rival kingdoms, were liable to become prisoners-of-war. When the Hittites conquered the land of Nuhashshi, for example, its king escaped but Šuppiluliuma I 'captured his mother, his brothers, and his children, and I brought them to Hatti'.[105]

It is worth noting, however, that there is very little evidence of prisoners being summarily executed – testament, perhaps, to at least some degree of battlefield restraint. A chronic shortage of manpower in the lands of Hatti may partly explain this policy. Prisoners-of-war were highly valuable to the Hittite economy and defeated enemies must have been more attractive as slaves than as corpses.[106] The Hittite state also used hostages as diplomatic pawns, and such people could be ransomed or exchanged. Occasionally, arrangements for treating hostages could be formalised in treaties,[107] or they could be made on an ad hoc basis, dictated by the immediate circumstances.[108]

The federated nature of the empire may have further encouraged restraint in combat. Wars were often for the purpose of quelling rebellions or installing sympathetic client rulers, so waging wars of annihilation would have made little political or economic sense. Finally, the cosmological beliefs underlying the Hittite state lacked specific concepts or demands that encouraged wars of annihilation. Unlike the ancient Egyptians, Assyrians or Israelites, the Hittites were free from theological imperatives that called for the annihilation of certain peoples as cosmological rivals.

The most common fate of a prisoners-of-war, whether combatant or non-combatant, was enslavement. As the property of the king, the fate of captives was decided by the king or his representative, and seemingly on an ad hoc basis.[109] Some were gifted to individual soldiers as reward for their military service. Very large numbers could be relocated *en masse* across Hittite domains, often to supply much-needed manpower to the economy of a specific region.[110] Many of the Hittite treaties include stipulations to control the movement of slave and corvée labour, and the failure to return absconding slaves or to

105 'No. 6A: Treaty between Šuppiluliuma I of Hatti and Shattiwaza of Mittanni (Hittite version)', §5, in Beckman, *Hittite Diplomatic Texts*, 43.

106 Beckman, 'Foreigners in the Ancient Near East', 210.

107 'No 5: Treaty between Šuppiluliuma I and Aziru of Amurru', §5, in Beckman, *Hittite Diplomatic Texts*, 38.

108 'Early the following morning Nerikkaili, the man from Taphallu, awoke me and brought me the message: "What do I have in the way of hostages? The enemy who has already invaded Tarittara numbers 7,000!" 'Letter 49: To the King from Kaššu', in Hoffner, *Letters from the Hittite Kingdom*, 177.

109 Bryce (ed.), *Letters of the Great Kings*, 163.

110 See Letter No. 45, Hoffner, *Letters from Hittite Kingdom*, 169.

offer sanctuary to peoples 'claimed' by the Great King could be considered a *casus belli*.[111]

Some general distinctions between prisoners-of-war and domestic slaves existed. Captives who had been taken in war retained a higher social standing than ordinary slaves, being described by one scholar as *halbfrei* (semi- or half-free).[112] Many prisoners-of-war were integrated into the kingdom by recruiting them into the army: a practice common across the ancient Near East. Others were put to work as farmers, and Hittite laws indicate that such people were assigned fields and agricultural implements, and could even be exempted from taxes for the first three years.[113] This distinction in social standing among the unfree population may have been rooted in a perception that being captured in war bestowed an enslaved prisoner-of-war with greater honour or respect than a household slave born into servitude. Or perhaps it reflected a pragmatic realisation that warlike enemy populations had to be treated cautiously – offered a 'carrot' of some kind – if they were to be successfully and peaceably integrated into Hittite society.

Nevertheless, we can assume that some prisoners-of-war suffered significant physical and mental abuse. Prisoners-of-war had no rights, and undoubtedly physical violence was both threatened and deployed to enforce obedience. Women especially would have been vulnerable to sexual violence, and would have been distributed among the troops as a share of the booty, possibly becoming 'wives' or concubines. Forced to fulfil such roles, many of these women would have been integrated into Hittite society (whether willingly or unwillingly), and probably achieved a degree of personal liberty.

Yet it goes without saying that the humiliation of those taken into bondage must have been acute. After conquering Haššuwa and Hahha, King Hattušili I 'hitched the king of Haššuwa and the king of Hahha to a wagon', leading them in triumph back to the royal capital.[114] The abuse of prisoners could go beyond humiliation into the realms of torture and mutilation. A few Hittite sources

111 See also Beal, 'Peace with the Hittite State', 90.

112 Harry A. Hoffner Jr., 'The Treatment and Long-Term Use of Persons Captured in Battle According to the Masat Texts', in *Recent Developments in Hittite Archaeology and History: Papers in Memory of Hans G. Güterbock*, edited by K. Aslihan Yener and Harry A. Hoffner Jr. (Winona Lake, Indiana: Eisenbrauns, 2002), 61–2.

113 Hoffner, 'The Treatment and Long-Term Use of Persons Captured in Battle', 62–4; Beal, 'Peace with the Hittite State', 94. See Hittite Laws §40 and §112, *Laws of the Hittites*, Hoffner, 47–9, 107–8. Compare to similar Egyptian practices: Liverani, *International Relations*, 97–9.

114 'Annals of Hattušili I', §20, in *The Ancient Near East*, ed. Chavalas, 221; cf. 'Annals of Hattušili I', Houwink ten Cate, 'Warfare according to Hittite Sources', 53–4.

refer to 'interrogating' enemy prisoners to obtain military intelligence, and there's no reason to believe that such interrogations shied away from using torture.[115]

That being said, the mutilation of free or unfree persons was rare in Hatti. The relatively humane character of Hittite laws, and the lack of mutilation scenes in Hittite sculpture and material culture, has led some scholars to claim that the Hittites possessed an unusual respect for human life and individual "rights".[116] And yet there is evidence of prisoners-of-war suffering deliberate blinding at the hands of their Hittite captors. One text provides a list of captives, and specifically states whether they can see or not. As Hoffner observes: 'It would seem that a rather large proportion of the persons listed ... were "blinded" for this to be the accident of battle.' It seems more likely that the prisoners were 'blinded after capture, either in order to render them more controllable, as a punishment for the havoc they had wreaked on Hittite personnel, or to humiliate the enemy.'[117] It is also possible that these blinded prisoners included those who had taken oaths to serve in the Hittite army but had later rebelled, as blinding is mentioned as a punishment for soldiers who broke their military oath.[118] Kings could threaten even senior commanders with blinding or death as punishments for failure or insubordination.[119] As such, it is easy to imagine blinding being used as a means of punishment and intimidation among prisoner-of-war populations.

Hittite commanders were also willing to murder enemy captives. A regional governor, Kassu, reported to the king that: 'behind me the enemy attacked Zikkatta, and led away forty cattle and one hundred sheep. I expelled him. And sixteen men of the enemy – including captives and killed – I felled.'[120] When

---

115 Bryce (ed.), *Letters of the Great Kings*, 173; 'No. 2: Treaty between Tudhaliya II of Hatti and Sunashshura of Kizzuwatna', §§42–3, in Beckman, *Hittite Diplomatic Texts*, 22.

116 Hoffner, *Laws of the Hittites*, 4–11; Gurney, *Hittites*, 88, 115; see also Korošec, 'Warfare of the Hittites', 165.

117 Hoffner, 'Treatment and Long-Term Use of Persons Captured in Battle', 68; Bryce (ed.), *Letters of the Great Kings*, 164.

118 Hoffner, 'Treatment and Long-Term Use of Persons Captured in Battle', 68; Beal, 'Peace with the Hittite State', 95.

119 'Say to Kassu and Zilapiya: "As soon as this letter reaches you, come with all haste before His Majesty. If not, (my men) will come to you and blind you on the spot!"' HKM 16, cited Bryce (ed.), *Letters of the Great Kings*, 171; 'You Pipappa, bring the UKU.UŠ troops across as quickly as possible. Bring them here to the army. If not, you will come (and) you will die!' HKM 35, cited Bryce (ed.), *Letters of the Great Kings*, 171; cf. ibid, 164–5, 179.

120 'No. 16: From King to Kassu', in Hoffner, *Letters from Hittite Kingdom*, 114 (the quoted text is from Kassu's previous report sent to the king, which the king is reciting).

Šuppiluliuma I defeated a Kaškaean chief named Ariwašu in battle, he 'captured Ariwašu … and cut his head off.'[121]

The killing of prisoners may have been more likely when captured enemies were regarded as rebels. A treaty between Tudhaliya II and Sunashshura of Kizzuwatna includes five separate clauses detailing the terms of the two kingdoms' defensive alliance against revolt. In each clause, captured rebels are to be executed; furthermore, if either king failed to execute or turn over a rebellious vassal of their fellow monarch, this would result in the dissolution of the alliance and provided grounds for war:

> If the Hittites capture this enemy, they will kill him. If they give him into the custody of Sunashshura, he must kill him … If the Hittites do not kill that enemy or give him into the custody of Sunashshura so that he can kill him, Sunashshura must conduct hostilities against Hatti as far as he is able.[122]

5 Emerging Protections and Sanctions: Immunities

The vast majority of individuals enjoyed neither 'rights' nor protections during war. However, for a very select group of individuals, there did exist a handful of quasi-immunities that were generally regarded as normative. Principally, this included a recognition that envoys and ambassadors from foreign sovereigns should enjoy protection whilst engaged in official diplomatic business with a host nation.[123] As David Bederman observes, these protections were largely motivated by sheer pragmatism:

> The international law of diplomats and diplomatic protection was fundamental, because without it the simplest forms of negotiation between independent polities would have been impossible. The rules of diplomatic conduct were, therefore, motivated by the highest demands of necessity.[124]

---

121 Güterbock, 'Deeds of Šuppiluliuma', 118.

122 'No. 2: Treaty between Tudhaliya II of Hatti and Sunashshura of Kizzuwatna', §14, in Beckman, *Hittite Diplomatic Texts*, 20; see also §§13–17.

123 Ziskind, 'Aspects of International Law', 64–5; Beckman, 'Foreigners in the Ancient Near East', 207.

124 Bederman, *International Law in Antiquity*, 88. See also Liverani, *International Relations*, 71–6.

During peacetime, states did not maintain permanent residences or embassies, so envoys remained quite literally 'guests' within a host kingdom. Hospitality was an important cultural feature of the ancient Near East, and the private courtesies extended to guests were effectively ritualized at the level of interactions between state representatives. Nevertheless, ambassadors were obliged to obey the laws and the commands of the sovereign in whose country they resided, and kings retained the right to detain envoys for as long as they wished. This could amount to considerable periods of time; for example, a number of Assyrian envoys were detained in Hatti for three years.[125] In such cases, we must wonder where the line between honoured guest and imprisoned hostage lay, and it is likely that all ambassadors were viewed as both protected persons as well as potential bargaining chips.

As a major player in the geopolitics of the second millennium BCE, Hatti shared in these diplomatic conventions. Non-hostile interstate relations were defined by the relatively free coming-and-going of envoys. As Hattušili III pointedly remarked to the king of Babylon, 'Only if two kings are hostile do their messengers not travel continually between them. Why, my brother, have you cut off your messengers?'[126] Indeed, there is evidence that bilateral diplomacy could be re-established even quite soon after major military engagements.[127] However, as the above quote makes plain, there was also a recognition that *during* war normal diplomatic communication – and presumably any concomitant protections – ceased. In this sense, I would argue that it is difficult to classify diplomatic immunities as immunities of war *per se*.

Protections for diplomats were enshrined in treaty law, such as that agreed between Hantili II (*c.*1500 BCE) and Paddatissu of Kizzuwatna: 'If the Great King sends either his son or his subject to Paddatissu, Paddatissu shall not harm him. And if Paddatissu sends either his son or his subject to the Great King, the Great King shall not harm him.'[128] A later treaty with Kizzuwatna, created by Tudhaliya II (*c.*1400 BCE), formalised similar guarantees of immunity. However, the inherent suspicion underlying political interactions on the international stage – even between supposed allies – is colourfully illustrated:

125 Ziskind, 'Aspects of International Law', 66–7.

126 'No 23: Letter from Hattušili III to Kadashman-Enlil II of Babylon', §6, in Beckman, *Hittite Diplomatic Texts*, 140.

127 For example, Hittite-Assyrian correspondence following the battle of Nihriya (*c.*1237 BCE): Masamichi Yamada, 'The Second Military Conflict between "Assyria" and "Hatti" in the Reign of Tukulti-Ninurta I', *Revue d'Assyriologie et d'archéogie orientale* 105 (2011): 199–220, at 203.

128 'No. 1: Treaty between a King of Hatti (perhaps Hantili II) and Paddatissu of Kizzuwatna', §3, in Beckman, *Hittite Diplomatic Texts*, 12. Klengel, *Geschichte des Hethitischen*, 98 dates this treaty later, to Huzziya II (*c.*1450 BCE).

> If His Majesty sends his messenger to Sunashshura, Sunashshura must not harm him in any way. He must not ensnare him by means of a magical plant. If Sunashshura sends either his son or his messenger before His Majesty – or if Sunashshura himself comes – His Majesty must not harm them in any way. He must not ensnare them by means of a magical plant.[129]

One reading of these treaties could conclude that certain immunities for diplomatic personnel were widely recognised and attained something of the status of a universal norm. An alternative reading, however, might ask why, if such immunities were genuinely universal and widely recognised, was it necessary to repeatedly restate them in diplomatic instruments? If there were standardised and broadly enforced norms regulating the treatment of envoys and ambassadors, why would such protections have to be specified in individual treaties? One explanation could be that sovereigns were actually rather sceptical that their representatives would be immune from violence, *unless* a specific treaty oath had been sworn, binding other rulers to a particular code of conduct. In other words, diplomatic immunity may indeed have been widely practised between international actors, but it was *not* taken for granted and cannot be described as a universal norm.[130] Other treaty stipulations demanded the arrest and imprisonment of enemy envoys seeking to communicate with Hittite vassals (to undermine alliances): such messengers were to be intercepted and were not protected by any form of immunity.[131]

Ambiguity regarding the personal safety of individuals granted safe-conducts is revealed by the interactions between Hattušili III of Hatti, the king of Ahhiyawa, and a duplicitous warlord named Piyama-radu, who had formerly been a Hittite vassal but turned against his former masters.[132] Hattušili offered Piyama-radu safe-conduct to negotiate, but Piyama-radu rejected the overture,

129 'No. 2: Treaty between Tudhaliya II of Hatti and Sunashshura of Kizzuwatna', §§44–5, in Beckman, *Hittite Diplomatic Texts*, 22. The treaty also reveals that the trustworthiness of envoys was not taken for granted: 'In regard to a tablet which I, My Majesty, send you … and the words of the messenger, which he speaks … if the words of the messenger are in agreement with the words of the tablet, trust that messenger, O Sunashshura. But if the words of the speech of the messenger are not in agreement with the words of the tablet, you, Sunashshura, shall certainly not trust the messenger and shall certainly not take to heart the evil content of that report of his.' Ibid. §59, in Beckman, *Hittite Diplomatic Texts*, 24.

130 See also Bederman, *International Law in Antiquity*, 107.

131 For example, 'No. 27a: Indictment of Mita of Pahhuwa and Treaty with the Elders of several Anatolian communities', §§12, 16, in Beckman, *Hittite Diplomatic Texts*, 163–4.

132 For more on Piyama-radu, see Bryce (ed.), *Letters of the Great Kings*, 192–5; Bryce, *Kingdom of Hittites*, 224–7, 290–3.

presumably because he feared betrayal.[133] Hattušili III was so affronted by Piyama-radu's suspicion that he launched into an explanation to the king of Ahhiyawa, describing exactly how safe-conducts operated in Hatti:

> Have I not offered safe conduct to Piyama-radu? Now safe conduct works this way in Hatti: If they send ... to someone, they may not harm him. But with regard to the safe conduct I transported this message: "Come, make your case before me! Then I will put you on the road ... If you are satisfied with my proposals, let it be so. But if you are not satisfied, then my man will escort you back into the land of Ahhiyawa in the same manner as he came here with you. Otherwise, let this charioteer remain in his (i.e. Piyama-radu's) place, while he (Piyama-radu) is coming and while he comes back there."[134]

Not only does Hattušili III emphasise that the guarantee of safety is absolute, he also offers an "exchange": one of his closest courtiers will remain in Ahhiyawan territory as a hostage. Once again, this evidence contains interpretative contradictions. It suggests that safe-conducts and diplomatic immunity were commonly recognised mechanisms within the Hittite kingdom. Yet Piyama-radu (who himself had an impressive track record of flagrantly violating oaths) was obviously not willing to bet his life or his liberty on the promises of his former overlords.

In terms of immunities or protections pertaining to anyone other than individuals engaged in official state-level diplomacy, there is very little evidence. An exceedingly rare reference to the behaviour of an army *returning* from campaign contains fascinating instructions protecting non-combatants and their property: 'After the campaign no one shall steal a man, woman, son, daughter, slave, slave girl, ox, sheep, horse, mule, ass, silver, gold ... bronze, or copper implements.'[135] The same proclamation, issued to a number of Anatolian communities under Hittite control, is particularly concerned with the rape of women: 'And when you march ... after the campaign you shall not violate the wife or daughter of a man, nor shall you injure them.' It is notable, however, that these instructions pertain to behaviour *after* the cessation of hostilities. There is no evidence of rape being prohibited *during* a campaign. Given that this proclamation specifically refers to a returning army at the end of a

133 'No. 101: from King Hattušili III to the King of Ahhiyawa – "Tawagalawa Letter"', §5, in Hoffner, *Letters from Hittite Kingdom*, 305.

134 Ibid., §8, 307–8.

135 'No 27a: Indictment of Mita of Pahhuwa and Treaty with the Elders of several Anatolian communities', §18, in Beckman, *Hittite Diplomatic Texts*, 165.

campaign, the protections were probably designed to protect Hittite lands. Rape was illegal in the Hittite kingdom; with the conflict over and the army returning to the Hittite homeland, the pre-existing law of the land was simply being reasserted.[136] Consequently, this text cannot be taken as unequivocal evidence of prohibitions against rape or assault of non-combatants during war itself.

To illustrate the lack of *in bello* restraints in Hittite (and indeed, in all ancient Near Eastern) warfare, it is worth highlighting the important role played by plunder and destruction. While deception and ambushes were viewed somewhat ambiguously in terms of their martial honour and legitimacy, there were no qualms at all regarding the use of ravaging and burning. The Hittite Law Code may have explicitly prohibited the arson of agricultural lands and crops within the domestic sphere, but no such prohibitions carried over into the theatre of war.[137] King Hattušili I boasted that in the first year of his reign: 'I went to the city of Šanahuitta … I destroyed its countryside … Thereafter I went to the city of Zalpa and destroyed it.'[138] He performed almost identical deeds against the lands of other cities in following years, destroying their lands and plundering their goods.[139] He was most proud of a devastating campaign he led westwards, becoming the first Anatolian ruler to cross the Euphrates river, and razing the cites of Hahha and Haššuwa (among others):

> No one had crossed the Euphrates River, but I, the Great King, the Tabarna, crossed it on foot, and my army crossed it on foot behind me. Sargon [the Great of Akkad] also crossed it. He fought the troops of Hahha, but he did not do anything to Hahha … But I, the Great King, the Tabarna, destroyed Haššuwa and Hahha, and burned them down with fire.[140]

The records of Šuppiluliuma I, one of Hatti's most bellicose kings, are filled with references to arson and devastation. Over the course of several campaigns, Hittite armies burned cities and countryside all over Anatolia and Syria.[141] Only territories which were 'at peace' with the Hittites, or voluntarily offered

136 Hoffner, in *Law Collections*, ed. Roth, 237, §197. Cf. Deut. 22:25ff.

137 Hittite Laws: '§105 If anyone sets fire to a field, and the fire catches a fruit-bearing vineyard, if a vine, an apple tree, a pear tree or plum tree burns, he shall pay 6 shekels of silver for each tree. He shall re-plant the planting. And he shall look to his house for it. If it is a slave, he shall pay 3 shekels of silver for each tree.' *Laws of the Hittites*, Hoffner, 102.

138 'Annals of Hattušili I', §§1–2, in *The Ancient Near East*, ed. Chavalas, 219.

139 Annals of Hattušili I', §4, in *The Ancient Near East*, ed. Chavalas, 220; cf. Houwink ten Cate, 'Warfare according to Hittite Sources', 47–8.

140 'Annals of Hattušili I', §§19–20, in *The Ancient Near East*, ed. Chavalas, 221; Houwink ten Cate, 'Warfare according to Hittite Sources', 53–4.

141 Güterbock, 'Deeds of Šuppiluliuma', 60, 83, 108–9, 110.

them submission and hospitality, were spared.[142] Further examples could be provided *ad nauseam* from the military records of any of Hatti's kings – suffice to say that deliberate ravaging was a hallmark of Hittite warfare, just as it was a hallmark of all ancient, medieval, and early modern warfare. Indeed, there is little to differentiate Hittite tactics from those of General Sherman's infamous 'March to the Sea' in 1864.

In the agrarian economies of the pre-industrial era, the ravaging of agricultural land was a strategic ploy to cripple the enemy's financial resources. Equally, plundering enemy territories of their valuable movable goods was a crucial component of the Hittite military economy.[143] The vast majority of Hittite soldiers were unpaid, and performed their military duties as a form of quasi-feudal service. Booty was thus the principal remuneration for most soldiers, and taking plunder was widely understood as the right of the victor. This was simply how war was waged, and the Hittites displayed no sign of moral anxiety regarding it. But plunder could also be dedicated to the gods, and temples benefitted considerably from successful wars. In this regard, defeating one's enemies and acquiring plunder for religious dedication could be understood as a justifying process and a confirmation of Hittite piety. Winning plunder was indicative of divine approval, and could even be conceived as being 'demanded' by the gods: 'She [the Sun-goddess of Arinna] gave them the royal couple a battle-ready, valiant spear saying: "May the hostile foreign lands perish by the hand of the *labarna*, and let them take goods, silver and gold to Hattusa and Arinna, the cities of the gods!"[144]

Enemy attacks on Hittite religious property were roundly condemned as impious and justified the resort to war, but this did not prevent the Hittites themselves targeting valuable religious property.[145] Amidst this pattern of destruction, Hittite kings did at times extend protection to sites of religious importance. After Šuppiluliuma I's conquest of Carchemish, Hittite troops

142 Güterbock, 'Deeds of Šuppiluliuma', 109, 110ff; 'Letter 101: from King Hattušili III to the King of Ahhiyawa – "Tawagalawa Letter"', in Hoffner, *Letters from Hittite Kingdom*, 302–4. A similar process is evident in medieval European *chevauchée* campaigns: see Rory Cox, 'A Law of War? English Protection and Destruction of Ecclesiastical Property during the Fourteenth Century', *The English Historical Review* 128 (2013): 1381–1417.

143 Korošec referred to Hittite warfare as *Raubkrieg*, or 'war for plunder': *Hethitische Staatsverträge*, 62; cf. Korošec, 'The Warfare of the Hittites', 160.

144 'No. 3: Invocation of Sun-goddess of Arinna for protection of royal couple', §6, in Singer, *Hittite Prayers*, 26.

145 For example: 'No. 9: Muršili's hymn and prayer to Telipinu', in Singer, *Hittite Prayers*, 55–6. See also 'No. 5: Prayer of Arnuwanda and Asmunikal to the Sun-goddess of Arinna about ravages of Kaška tribes', in Singer, *Hittite Prayers*, 41–3; Gurney, 'Hittite prayers of Muršili II', *Annals of Archaeology and Anthropology* 27 (1940): 1–167, at 28–35; *Ancient Near Eastern Texts*, ed. Pritchard, 399–400.

took control of the lower town and 'removed the inhabitants, silver, gold, and bronze utensils and carried them to Hattuša.' However, since Šuppiluliuma 'feared the gods', he sectioned off the upper parts of the city where the palaces and temple precincts were located, and 'he let no one into the presence of the deity Kubaba and of the deity KAL, and he did not rush close to any one of the temples. Nay, he even bowed to them'.[146]

Šuppiluliuma showed similar restraint elsewhere, being careful to show due respect to the temples of the Storm-god: 'I destroyed the Land of Hurna, and the city of Hurna. But because there was a temple of the Storm God of Hurna behind the city of Hurna, I spared it and they did not plunder it. The servants of the god who were behind, I left alone, and they are still there'.[147] Some effort to provide a measure of religious immunity is also indicated within a vassal treaty between Muršili II and Kupanta-Kurunta of Mira-Kuwaliya:

> A single sacred city belonging to Mashuiluwa [the former king of Mira] himself is situated on the Siyanta River, and it shall be exempted from the oath. Protect for yourself this land which I, My Majesty, have given to you.[148]

Interestingly, two hundred years earlier, King Muršili I had been criticized for sacking Babylon – a city full of prestigious temples. This act 'made the gods sick', according to a text from the reign of Hantili.[149] However, Hantili had murdered Muršili I and usurped the throne shortly after the king returned from his Babylonian campaign. It seems more likely, therefore, that the new king was looking for any excuse to sully the name of his predecessor, rather than expressing a genuine condemnation of the destruction of religious property.

6 Conclusions

The Hittites developed a complex and sophisticated *ius ad bellum* tradition. The authority of the king as a representative of the gods was crucial, but

146 Güterbock, 'Deeds of Šuppiluliuma', 95.

147 Götze, *Die Annalen des Muršiliš*, 176–7; see also Beal, 'Making, Preserving, and Breaking the Peace with the Hittite State', 94.

148 'No. 11: Treaty between Muršili II and Kupanta-Kurunta of Mira-Kuwaliya', §10, in Beckman, *Hittite Diplomatic Texts*, 76.

149 Harry A. Hoffner, Jr., 'Propaganda and Political Justification in Hittite Historiography', in *Unity and Diversity: Essays in the History, Literature, and Religion of the Ancient Near East*, edited by Hans Goedicke and J.J.M. Roberts (Baltimore and London: Johns Hopkins University Press, 1975), 49–62, at 56–8.

wearing the crown did not necessarily make a king righteous or a war just. The Hittites recognised that to win the favour of the gods, wars must have just causes. Self-defence was the primary cause for war, but the restitution of property, vengeance for divine and mundane injuries (especially the violation of oaths), and the defence of allies all ranked as important reasons to go to war. In a sense, all of them were seen as extensions of the principle of self-defence. War was regarded as a form of legal process, prosecuted in the court of Hatti's gods. The recognition that even the Hittites could commit crimes against other states, and could thus engage in unjust wars, witnessed the first serious movement towards an ethical engagement with international justice as an objective concept. This was a remarkable and unique evolutionary step in the history of the ethics of war.

However, the substantial moral and legal dimensions of Hittite *ad bellum* thought did not generate a *ius in bello* tradition. Only the faintest outlines of what one could call *in bello* norms existed. Declarations of war were commonly issued and clearly regarded as the appropriate way to open hostilities: they were a declaration of intent, a chance to air grievances before the gods, and marked a shift in legal and diplomatic relations between Hatti and its antagonist. Certain tactics, such as night attacks and ambushes, were frowned upon when used by enemies but were lauded when successfully employed by Hittite commanders. Enemy combatants who surrendered were normally spared death, although many would have been enslaved. This form of "restraint" was largely motivated by the pragmatics of profit and politics rather than mercy or morals. No substantive immunities existed for combatants or non-combatants: all types of people were taken as prisoners-of-war, and kings boasted of enslaving 'civilian captives' as war booty. There is some evidence of occasional and ad hoc protection extended to temples and priests, as well as immunities offered to envoys and ambassadors – but these cannot be described as widely recognised "laws" of war.

In the final analysis, Hittite just war doctrine was self-reflective and highly original, but at heart their ethics of war were permissive rather than restrictive. They created an ethical framework in which the Hittites could interpret their military actions as legitimate, even righteous, when held against theological demands of right and wrong action. This framework mirrored jurisprudential norms that demanded retributive but, more importantly, restitutive justice for injuries against persons and property. Victory in war was taken as evidence of righteousness and divine favour, but the conduct of warfare was almost wholly determined by strategic, tactical, and economic imperatives.

CHAPTER 3

Jewish Ethics of War: the Middle Ages

Norman Solomon

1 Introduction

1.1 *Definitions, Sources*

"Ethics" in this essay is understood broadly as "norms of behaviour", whether formulated as laws, or as ethical or moral principles.

"Judaism" is the religion of the Jews, more properly called "Rabbinic Judaism". It is not to be identified with "Old Testament Theology". Judaism, like Christianity, has deep roots in the Hebrew scriptures ("Old Testament", "Bible"), but it interprets those scriptures along lines classically formulated by the Sages, or rabbis, of the Talmud. Talmud – there are two Talmudim, known respectively as Jerusalem and Babylonian – takes the form of commentary on the Mishna, a compilation of *halakha* (Jewish law) completed in early 3rd-century Galilee. It incorporates teachings of Jewish Sages (rabbis), mainly those of Palestine and Babylonia[1] from the late first century BCE to the final redaction of the Bavli (Babylonian) in the seventh century CE – about the time of, and in the much the same geographical area as, the rise of Islam. Talmud functions as a resource rather than a final statement; its laws and legends have been studied, interpreted and developed by generations of rabbis right up to the present time.

Jewish history is divided into three periods, which we may conveniently label as biblical, mediaeval and modern, though these terms do not carry precisely the same connotation as they might for European history.

The Bible (Hebrew scriptures) records the formation of the Israelite polity, briefly united under David and Solomon, subsequently divided into Judah (south) and Israel (10 northern tribes), constantly at war with neighbouring nations. Israel fell to Assyria; Judah was exiled to Babylon, subsequently returning home under Persian rule to face, after a brief respite, Alexander of Macedon and his successors and in 63 BCE annexation by Rome, by which time the Hebrew scriptures as we know them were complete. Throughout this period war was a constant reality, peace a distant, if fervently desired, prospect.

1 i.e., central Mesopotamia, now Iraq, then Sasanian Iran.

 | DOI:10.1163/9789004703094_005

Failed revolts against Rome in 66–70 CE and again in 131–135 confirmed the loss of Jewish independence, while the adoption by Rome (Byzantium) of Christianity in the fourth century and then, in the seventh, the spread of Islam to the east and south of the Mediterranean, reduced Jews to the status of barely tolerated minorities in both areas, in no position to develop significant military forces of their own.[2] These 'Middle Ages' constitute the period we shall focus on; when Jews in this period thought about the conduct of war it was in the context of eschatological vision rather than current reality.

The Middle Ages, at least for Western Jews, ended with the Enlightenment, emancipation, the rise of secularism and the consequent breakdown of religious authority. Some Jews became involved in European nationalist and revolutionary movements; some participated, whether voluntarily or as conscripts, in armed struggles for national independence; the notion grew in the nineteenth century that they might be called upon to fight for an independent territory of their own, perhaps even the ancestral land of Palestine. The traditional religious, by and large, distanced themselves from such initiatives; in their view, the collective return to the Land would come about only through miraculous intervention under the leadership of the Messiah. Advice was given to young men forcefully conscripted into the army of the Czar or participating in other armed conflicts, but this was concerned less with conduct of war, over which the rabbis had no control, more with how to maintain Jewish identity and religious observance in difficult situations.

The resigned attitude characteristic of the traditional religious is articulated in a homily attributed to the 3rd-century Palestinian sage Yosé bar Ḥanina:

> "I adjure you, O daughters of Jerusalem ... that you awaken not, nor stir up, love until it please" (Song of Songs 3:5). Rabbi Yosé bar Ḥanina said, Why these three[3] oaths? One: the Holy One, blessed be He, made Israel swear they would not go up (to the Land of Israel) in formation.[4] One: He made Israel swear that they would not rebel against the nations of the world. One: the Holy One, blessed be He, made the nations swear they would not oppress Israel unduly.[5]

2 The Berber princess and military leader Kahina Dihya, who in the early 700s held up the Arab advance across North Africa, may well have ruled a Jewish tribe as claimed by Ibn Khaldun. Unmentioned in Jewish sources, she is now celebrated both as a pioneer of Algerian independence and as a feminist hero.

3 The adjuration is repeated at 5:8 and 8:4.

4 Hebrew obscure. The term here translated 'formation' is *ḥoma* (literally 'wall').

5 Yalkut Shim'oni on Song of Songs, #986. Yalkut Shim'oni is thought to have been compiled *c.*1300 in Frankfurt-am-Main. There are parallel versions in other late midrashim, but not in earlier compilations; the attribution to Yosé bar Ḥanina is very doubtful.

The passivity and the sense of helplessness articulated here do not imply that the rabbis of the Middle Ages failed to comment on the rights and wrongs of war, only that they did not envisage being called upon to take personal or collective responsibility for its conduct. They continued to theorize, whether in biblical interpretation, in philosophical ethics, less often in codes of law, but with scant reference to current reality.

1.2 *On Reading the Bible*

The Bible (Old Testament, or Hebrew Scriptures) is a highly eclectic collection of literature compiled over more than a millennium; warfare was an inescapable feature of life throughout that period. At one extreme the Bible endorses ruthless wars waged by the Israelites against the Canaanites, at the other it embraces the vision that "nation shall not lift sword unto nation" (Isaiah 2:4; Micah 4:3).

However, more significant than the biblical text itself for understanding later Judaism is the way the Bible has been received and understood within the community. For that, we must turn to Talmud and other works of the rabbis – Bible commentaries, legal compilations, philosophical works. Genesis 35, for instance, reports that Jacob's sons slaughtered the inhabitants of Shechem on account of the rape of their sister, Dinah, by their leader's son. Are we to interpret this as a model of righteous zeal, a correct enactment of law, or as a grave aberration? From the text itself we would not know. Many later Jewish interpreters, however, regarded the massacre as a crime, or at best as an act requiring exceptional justification.[6] The Bible tells the story; it does not pass judgment.

2 The Rabbis on War

Within the Bible, the rabbis accorded privileged status to the "Torah of Moses," that is, to the first five books: Genesis, Exodus, Leviticus, Numbers and Deuteronomy. Laws receive their authority as "Torah law" from texts in these books, but not from elsewhere in scripture. Torah legislation, when rightly interpreted, is normative; the behaviour of, e.g., king David or even Moses himself, is not, and may indeed be open to criticism in the light of Torah legislation. Consequently, the legislation concerning warfare in Deuteronomy 20 and succeeding chapters assumes considerable significance in rabbinic thinking, as it was later to do amongst Christians.

6 Goren, *Combat Morality*, 223–6.

2.1 *Beginnings*

If we regard the revolts of Judea against Rome from 70 CE onwards[7] as wars of national liberation from tyranny, the last *offensive* war initiated by Jews against a foreign power was most probably the Hasmonean king Alexander Jannai's Transjordanian campaign *c.*75 BCE; even that campaign could, at a stretch, be regarded as defensive, though tarnished by Alexander's ruthless treatment of tribes who refused to accept Judaism.[8]

The *War Rule* ("War of the Sons of Light against the Sons of Darkness") of the Dead Sea Scrolls[9] illustrates sectarian apocalyptic thinking, or rather imagination, in the late first century BCE prior to the formation of rabbinic Judaism. Its adaptation of Deuteronomy to the wars against the "Kittim" (Romans), though utilising some Roman military terminology, has little to do with the conduct of any actual war.

Jewish contingents may well have supported both the Sasanian Emperor Shapur I (240–70) and somewhat later the Roman Emperor Julian (361–63), who had favoured rebuilding the Temple, and in 614 Jews of Palestine made a short-lived alliance with the Persians in the hope of regaining Jerusalem. Rabbinic sources on all these events are fragmentary at best. What are we to make, for instance, of a report in the Talmud (*Mo'ed Qatan* 26a) that Shmuel (Samuel) of Nehardea (sacked by the Palmyrenes in 261) refused to mourn for 12,000 Jews killed in a battle at Caesarea Mazaca by Shapur I because "it was their own fault" – perhaps they had sided with the Romans?[10]

By the time Talmud and associated formulations of rabbinic Judaism were redacted Jews had lost political independence; the sparse discussion of war in this literature accordingly lacks firm contact with contemporary reality. We come across rationalisations of biblical narrative, selective recollection of the revolts against Rome, and apocalyptic speculation, akin to that of the *War Rule*, about messianic wars. In the exposition of Deuteronomy 20 elements of legislation on warfare are present, but even this is historical reconstruction or messianic speculation rather than the operational law of an actual society.

7 Primarily 70 and 135, but restlessness simmered. The last recorded revolt took place at Sepphoris in 351 against Gallus Caesar, the tyrannical emperor Constantinus II. It was suppressed by the Roman general Ursicinus.

8 Josephus *Antiquities* 13:15.

9 Vermes, *Dead Sea Scrolls*, 161–189.

10 Talmud *Mo'ed Qatan* 26a.

2.2 *Military Heroes Downgraded*

A striking characteristic of rabbinic culture is the suppression of celebration of military personalities or achievements. There is of course no military caste akin to that of the Kshatriyas of India; even the hereditary priesthood is deemed of inferior status to the learned in Torah.[11] When the Talmud offers an account of the origin of the festival of Chanukah it refers only vaguely to the Hasmonean victory, and not at all to Judas Maccabeus, focusing instead on the otherwise unattested miracle of the oil.[12] Nor does any biblical festival celebrate an Israelite victory, but only the saving acts of God: Joshua's conquest of the Land is not celebrated, nor is David's victory over the Philistines. Any military success achieved by Israelites is attributed to God's intervention; any failure is due to Israelite sinfulness.

This downgrading of military prowess contrasts with the plain sense of scripture. The penultimate chapter of the Second Book of Samuel, for instance, lists the "names of the mighty men whom David had", starting with "Josheb-basshebbeth a Tahchemonite, the chief officer – he is Adino the Eznite; [he wielded his spear] against eight hundred and slew them on one occasion" (2 Samuel 23:8). The list of heroes, with some variation, is repeated in 1 Chronicles 11:11–41. Unlike Homeric heroes such as Hector and Lysander, Adino and the others are not recalled as national heroes. Their achievements are largely ignored by the rabbis, or else interpreted in such a way as to suggest that these men were primarily Torah sages; Adino, for instance, is said to have been a member, indeed the most learned, of the Sanhedrin: "when studying Torah he curled up tightly like a soft worm, but when he went to war he was like the [rigid] trunk of a tree".[13]

War is a consequence of sin, ultimately controlled not by humans but by God. When humans learn to obey God there will be no more war. At the pinnacle of society stand the scholars, or sages, not the generals or even the hereditary priesthood.

2.3 *Bearing Arms – Honour or Shame?*

Sometime between the Fall of Jerusalem in 70 CE and the Bar Kochba Revolt against Rome of 131–135, Eliezer ben Hyrcanus debated with the other sages (rabbis) whether a man might adorn himself with weapons in the public domain on the Sabbath even when not required for defence. This casuistic

11 "A learned bastard has priority over an ignorant High Priest" (Mishna *Horayot* 3:8).

12 Talmud *Shabbat* 21b. The omission of Judah's name may also reflect Pharisee disillusion with the Hasmonean dynasty.

13 Talmud *Moed Katan* 16b.

dispute on an obscure point in Sabbath law proceeds from a deep difference in attitude to the bearing of arms. To the majority sages the bearing of arms, though necessary for defence, disgraces the wearer; but Eliezer, who might in modern terms be described as a Jewish nationalist, regarded the bearing of arms as honourable.[14]

Almost a thousand years later the poet-philosopher Judah Halevi (1075–c.1141), in his philosophical dialogue The Kuzari, has the Rabbi ('Ḥaver') stress Jewish humility (non-aggressiveness) in contrast with the aggressiveness of Christians and Muslims. The Khazar king, considering conversion to Judaism, retorts, "This might be so, if your humility were voluntary; but it is involuntary, and if you had power you [too] would slay". The Rabbi concedes, "Thou has touched our weak spot …"[15]

There were rare exceptions. Shmuel (Samuel) ha-Nagid (993–1056), also known as Ismail ibn Nagrela, was vizier to kings Ḥabbus and Badis of Granada, and a Hebrew poet and scholar of distinction; he is probably unique among medieval Jews as military commander of a Muslim army. In a poem he composed in celebration of his victory over Seville in 1039, he wrote:

War at the outset is like a beautiful maid
With whom everyone wishes to flirt
At the end it is like a despised hag
Bringing tears and sadness to whomever she meets

To which Muslims as well as Jews (not to speak of others) might well respond Amen!

2.4 *Distancing from the World of the Bible*

Deuteronomy unequivocally calls for a *ḥerem* (war of extermination) against the inhabitants of the "promised land": "You shall annihilate them – Hittites, Amorites, Canaanites, Perizzites, Hivvites, Jebusites – as the Lord your God commanded you, so that they may not teach you to imitate all the abominable things that they have done for their gods and so cause you to sin against the Lord your God" (Deuteronomy 20:17, 18). What was to stop this verse becoming a general warrant for genocide?

14 Mishna *Shabbat* 6:4.

15 Judah Halevi, *The Kuzari*, ## 113–115, tr. Hartwig Hershfeld (New York: Shocken, 1964), pp. 78–9.

Boundaries are set within the text itself, which limits the *ḥerem* to the "seven nations".[16] But this would leave open the question of identification, and it would be only too easy to categorise a potential enemy as belonging to one or other of the despised nations. In fact the determination was made around the year 100 CE by a Palestinian rabbi, Joshua ben Ḥananiah, that "Sennacherib mixed up all the nations," that is to say, no-one can any longer be identified with the nations of earlier times; hence, the specific laws pertaining to those nations cannot be invoked.[17]

The rabbis restrict the severity of the superficial meaning of the biblical text of Deuteronomy in two ways:

1. They maintain that offers of peace were to be made even to the Canaanites.
2. They rule, rather impracticably, that in wars other than those of the original, divinely mandated conquest, if a town was placed under siege an escape route was always to be provided.[18]

This, at least, is what emerges from the halakhic, or legal, texts. Unfortunately, the waters are muddied by the symbolic or typological interpretation that occurs in aggadic (non-legal) texts.

Rabbinic texts refer to Rome, and later to Christendom generally, as "Edom";[19] Islam is (more plausibly) "Ishmael". It may well be that the early use of "Edom" for Rome was purely homiletic,[20] not intended as a literal assertion of Roman genealogy, let alone as a normative statement; at no time has it been suggested that Deuteronomy 23:7–8 should be applied to Romans, or to Christians.

Though rabbinic Judaism accepts the biblical vision that in time to come all humankind will recognize God and serve Him alone there is no suggestion of initiating any kind of 'holy war' to bring this about; the closest approach to such a proposal is Maimonides' statement[21] that an anointed king, with the backing of the Court of 71 Elders, might wage war to compel compliance with

16 Altogether ten nations are named in various verses, but they are conventionally referred to as seven.

17 Joshua's example concerned a self-proclaimed "Ammonite proselyte" who if not for Joshua's ruling would have been forbidden to marry a native-born Jewish woman. See Mishna *Yadayim* 4:4.

18 Rabbi Nathan in *Sifré* on Numbers 31:7. Perhaps he wants to explain how despite the annihilation of the Midianites alleged in Numbers, Midianite raids are reported in Judges 6. Meir Simcha Ha-Kohen of Dvinsk (Daugaupils, Latvia) (1843–1926), in his commentary *Meshekh Ḥokhma* (1927), notes that whereas Naḥmanides understands the requirement of an escape route as motivated by compassion, Maimonides regards it as merely tactical.

19 That is, Esau, the twin of Jacob (Genesis 25:25).

20 At a still earlier stage, reflected in the Dead Sea Scrolls, it may simply be a convenient ellipsis to avoid the political consequences of openly criticizing Rome.

21 Chapter 6 of *Hilkhot Melakhim*; see below.

the "Seven Commands of Noah", a basic code of human behaviour far short of the standard requirements of Judaism.[22]

At the polar opposite from conversionist war against other nations, the hasidic rabbi Yehuda Leib Alter of Gora Kalwaria (d. 1905) interpreted every statement about war in the Torah as symbolising the internal battle of the individual against the tendency to evil.[23]

Even so, extreme right wing rhetoric in modern Israel has sometimes identified the country's Palestinian enemies as "children of Esau" or even "Amalekites", contrary not only to the facts of history but to *halakha* itself.[24] Such talk underlay the ideology of Meir Kahane (1932–1990) and his "Kach" movement; it led Baruch Goldstein and his accomplices to shoot a number of Arabs at worship at Abraham's tomb in Hebron in February 1994, precisely on the festival of Purim which is linked with a reading about Amalek, and it inspired Yigal Amir to assassinate Israeli Prime Minister Yitzchak Rabin "as a traitor" on 4 November 1995.

Goldstein was denounced with shocked horror even by the mainstream Orthodox. Jonathan Sacks (1948–2020), for instance, then Chief Rabbi of the (Orthodox) British United Hebrew Congregations, vigorously denounced the attack as a travesty of Jewish values, and declared: "Violence is evil. Violence committed in the name of God is doubly evil. Violence against those engaged in worshipping God is unspeakably evil." The Chief Rabbis of Israel were equally forthcoming. Rabbis of all denominations of Judaism as well as Jews generally stress the distance between the world of the Bible and our contemporary world; the rules of war enjoined against the ancient Canaanites are inapplicable to the contemporary situation.

2.5 *Classification of Wars, and Competent Authority*

Reflecting on the text of Deuteronomy, the Talmud distinguishes between *milḥemet ḥova* (obligatory war) and *milḥemet reshut* (optional war):

> Rava said: All agree that Joshua's war of conquest was *ḥova* (obligatory) and the expansionist wars of David were *reshut* (optional). But they differ

22 On Noahide law, see e.g. Novak, David, *The Image of the Non-Jew in Judaism: An Historical and Constructive Study of the Noahide Laws*. New York: Edwin Mellen Press, 1983.

23 A condensed translation of his commentary *Sefat Emet* on the Pentateuch has been compiled by Arthur Green.

24 Ravitsky *Messianism* gives a penetrating analysis of Messianic Religious Zionism, in particular of the problematic resulting from Rav Kook's teaching as interpreted by his son, Zvi Yehuda Kook.

> with regard to [the status of] a pre-emptive war intended to prevent idolaters from attacking them.[25]

There is some resonance here with the Roman notion of *bellum justum*, though the rabbinic classification is into obligatory and optional rather than just and unjust.[26] A defensive war is obligatory (i.e., just); a pre-emptive war *might* be.[27] On the other hand, the "expansionist wars of David" are seen as more questionable, notwithstanding Psalm 18:48, "He has subdued nations beneath my feet".[28] Elsewhere the Talmud insists that the king would need to seek authorisation from the Great Court of 71 justices, as well as divine approval through the oracle[29] of the High Priest, before engaging in such a war.[30] As neither king nor Great Court has existed for thousands of years the definition of "competent authority" virtually rules out the possibility of non-defensive war. There is no Jewish equivalent to the process by which some 17th century English Puritans declared wars to be "commanded by God" simply because they were deemed by the religious leadership to be in conformity with God's will.[31]

The Talmudic distinction between *kibbush yaḥid* (individual conquest) and *kibbush rabim* (public conquest) may indicate the need for popular support in addition to the other requirements.[32]

---

25 Talmud *Sota* 44b.

26 The Puritan Henry Ainsworth, leader of the Separatist congregation in Amsterdam, in his *Annotations upon the Five Books of Moses* (London: John Bellarmine, 1627), leaning upon Maimonides, makes the same distinction. Johnson, *Ideology*, footnote p. 131, comments that "this distinction overrides any that might be attempted between offensive and defensive war"; he is incorrect.

27 Inbar 86, and n6 on 98, distinguishes between pre-emptive and preventive war. He cites the commentary *Leḥem Mishneh* whose author interprets Maimonides' expression "war to enlarge the borders of Israel" (*Mishneh Torah: Melakhim* 5:1) as preventive war, to deter potential aggressors. (Inbar incorrectly attributes *Leḥem Mishneh* to Joseph Karo; the author was the Salonika-born rabbi Abraham ben Moses di Boton, 1545?–1588).

28 That the rabbinic tradition is not entirely anti-imperialist is demonstrated by a midrash such as *Targum Sheni* on Esther (probably 8th century) that wildly exaggerates the extent of the dominions of Solomon and Ahab.

29 The Urim and Tumim (Exodus 28:30), the precise nature of which is a matter of debate. The oracular function assumed by the rabbis is hinted at in Ezra 2:62; Nehemiah 7:65. Compare the Roman practice of seeking guidance from auguries through the fetial priests.

30 Mishna *Sanhedrin* 1:5.

31 Johnson *Ideology*, 104, and 117 f., especially the section on Alexander Leighton 125 f.

32 Inbar 94 refers only to the later comments of Rashi (*Gittin* 8b and *Avoda Zara* 20b) and Maimonides (*Terumot* 1:2) for the consensus requirement.

2.6 *Maimonides' Codification of War Law*

The Talmud is a resource rather than itself a code of law; it is highly diffuse, setting out conflicting opinions without always deciding between them. From at least the 9th century rabbis in positions of authority began to compile thematic lists of decisions based on their reading and application of Talmudic norms. This process reached a climax in Moses Maimonides' (1138–1204) monumental *Mishneh Torah*, a systematic presentation in clear, precise Hebrew of the full range of *halakha* (law), including not only law currently in practice, but laws applicable "when the Temple is rebuilt", or in times when Israel will be "free of the yoke of the nations". The work concludes with a section entitled "Laws Concerning Kings and Their Wars", unique in the rabbinic corpus – no other code covers such topics, nor did Maimonides himself include it the revised list of commandments in his later, philosophical work, the *Guide for the Perplexed*.

In this final section of his Code Maimonides makes clear that he is dealing with eschatology rather than current realities; indeed, he concludes the work with a 'naturalistic' account of the Messiah and the "world to come" – the world will function as at present, but justice will prevail. However, the "law concerning kings" applies to any legitimate king of Israel, and since one of his functions is to act as leader in war, it is precisely here that Maimonides sets out the criteria for engaging in war. Here are some excerpts:

> 5:1 In the first instance the king must engage in obligatory war (*milḥemet mitzva*). What [constitutes] "obligatory war"? War against the seven nations (of Canaan), or defending Israel against attack by an invader. After that he may make war against other nations to enlarge the boundaries of Israel and increase his power and reputation.
>
> 5:2 He does not need to seek permission for obligatory war … but he may not lead the people to any other war, without authorisation from the Court of Seventy-One.[33]
>
> 5:4 He must completely destroy the seven nations … but all trace of them has [long ago] perished.
>
> 6:1 No war, obligatory or not, may be waged against anyone without first making an offer of peace

33 The supreme court of the land.

Clearly, this is consistent with the preceding account of the Talmudic classification of wars. Maimonides has firmly decided that "pre-emptive war intended to prevent idolaters from attacking" is permissible. However, neither he nor the Talmud envisages a situation like the present where there is no king, no body of 71 elders, and yet Israel collectively (or at least that part of it in the Holy Land) is faced with responsibility for defence. What emerges clearly from all the sources, however, is that Biblical precedents from the days of Moses, Joshua or David are not relevant; the 'seven nations', Amalekites and rest have long disappeared. Since there is no king, a war to "enhance his glory" is not relevant either. The only remaining possibility is the defensive war.

In sum, the Biblical provisions are maintained in principle, but interpreted in such a way as render them otiose in practice.

2.7 *Exemption from Military Service*

Given that some form of war, at least defensive, is envisioned under the rules of halakha and may even be obligatory, does the obligation to fight apply equally to all Israelites? Deuteronomy 20:5 has the officials address the troops: Whoever has built a house but not dedicated it, planted a vineyard and not harvested it, betrothed a wife but not married her, or who is 'afraid and disheartened' should return home. The Talmud (*Sota* 43b f.) expounds this passage in great detail – what constitutes a 'house' (as opposed to e.g. a cowshed), a 'vineyard' (inclusive of other plantations?), 'new wife' (virgin, widow etc.), or a 'disheartened' person – it is suggested that the 'disheartened' person is one who has sinned and who fears that this may lead to defeat. All these questions except the last have relevance in other areas of law and so are taken up in the Codes, but only Maimonides retains the war context; he also spells out that though members of these categories are exempt from combat service, they are expected to play a supporting role, for instance by providing supplies and repairing the highway (*Hilkhot M'lakhim* 7:9).

Scripture reports that King Asa of Judah (*c*.900 BCE) was inflicted with gout[34] (1 Kings 15:23). Rava, a fourth century Babylonian sage, speculated that this was a divine punishment because he had conscripted "disciples of the sages" into his army[35] – plausible, since scripture openly states that when enlisting the whole of Judah in war Asa "exempted none" (1 Kings 15:22). Rava's comment is a clear, if infrequently cited, precedent for the exemption of "clerics"

34 Other diagnoses are of course possible. Literal translation: "he was sick [in] his feet". Curiously in 2 Chronicles 2:16 he is criticized for going to the doctors with his complaint rather than "seeking the Lord".

35 Babylonian Talmud *Sota* 10a.

from military service;[36] it has been cited in modern Israel by those who wish to exempt yeshiva students from military service.

2.8 *Non-combatant Status; Hostages*

It is difficult to determine the meaning of 'non-combatant' outside the context of institutions of international law such as the Geneva Conventions and the existence of independent, international agencies such as the Red Cross, or of recognized, neutral institutions such as hospitals, none of which existed in the days of the Bible or for many centuries afterward.

Women and children were generally assumed to be non-combatants. This saved their lives, but not their husbands or fathers, and was of limited comfort, since they were regarded as legitimate booty. A captive female with whom the captor has sex and then decides not to marry her has some measure of protection and attains her freedom (Deuteronomy 21:10–14), but other women and children might be taken as slaves.

The question arises, especially but not only with weapons of mass destruction, of how in practice to avoid injury to those not directly involved in a conflict, even where the attacking force wishes to avoid such injury. The dilemma is even more acute where the defenders in effect use their own 'non-combatants' as hostages, for instance (to take a modern example) by using hospitals as military command centres or arms storage depots.

Finally, there is the issue of hostage taking, still practised by terrorist groups and authoritarian governments and with a history reaching back to the ancient world. Hostage taking is mentioned just twice in the Hebrew scriptures. 2 Kings 14:14 in parallel with 2 Chronicles 25:24 reports that king Jehoash of Israel took *bnei ta'aruvot* (lit. "sons of exchange") in a conflict with Amaziah of Judah; this is generally understood to refer to hostages. But "Jehoash was sinful and did evil in the eyes of the Lord" (2 Kings 13:11), certainly not an example for emulation.

Many instances are recorded in the Talmud and later of Jews having been captured or taken hostage by others, and the obligation to "redeem captives" is frequently stressed. One of the most notable medieval Jewish hostages was Rabbi Meir ('Maharam') of Rothenburg (*c.*1215–93) imprisoned by Rudolf I in a fortress in Alsace against a huge ransom; though the ransom was collected, Meir refused to allow it to be paid, arguing that payment would simply encourage the rulers to take more hostages and increase the ransom; he died while still incarcerated.[37]

---

36 For an example of this application see *Crossroads* 199.

37 For a statistical treatment see Arin K.P., Feess E., Kuhlenkasper T., Reich O.F.M. (2019). Negotiating with terrorists: The costs of compliance. *Southern Economic Journal*, 86(1),

Halakha does not permit the taking of innocent hostages; at the very least it constitutes kidnapping, a capital offence.

2.9 *Environment*

> When you are at war, and lay siege to a city ... do not destroy its trees by taking the axe to them, for they provide you with food (Deuteronomy 20:19)

In its biblical context this is a counsel of prudence rather than a principle of conservation; Israelites are enjoined to use only 'non-productive', that is, non-fruit-bearing trees, for their siege works. However, rabbinic tradition has applied it generally as a prohibition of waste, and modern Jewish environmentalists have quarried this tradition in support of their pleas for conservation.

It does provide an additional argument against warfare and raises the question of whether there is some limit to the amount of environmental degradation that might be legitimately caused even in pursuit of a permitted war. Was the defoliation of the forests of Vietnam acceptable even if the war aims were agreed? Irrespective of the human suffering caused, could it ever be acceptable to have recourse to nuclear weapons, seeing that their use would severely damage the environment? The works of Artson and Landes give some indication of the range of Jewish views on these matters; while the duty of conserving nature is universally acknowledged, there is disagreement over how this duty should be balanced against the duty of defence of human life.

2.10 *Self-Defence and Proportionality*

Genesis 32 relates how Jacob, a fugitive for many years in the house of Laban, returns home with his family, and as he reaches the border meets his brother Esau with 400 men. "And Jacob feared greatly and was distressed" (Genesis 32:7).

> Said Rabbi Judah bar Ilai: fear and distress are not the same thing. He was afraid lest he be killed, and distressed that he might have to kill someone.[38]

Jacob, on this reading, does not doubt that in self-defence, including the defence of his family, it might be his duty to kill even his own brother, however much it might distress him.

305–317. They conclude that "although moderate rates of negotiation increase the number of future terror events, higher negotiation rates tend to have the opposite effect".

38 *Genesis Rabba* 76:2.

This homily is supported in the legal system of the *halakha*. Defence, including self-defence, is not so much a *right* as a *duty*. The principle of self-defence is derived from Exodus 22:1, understood by the rabbis as referring to a thief who breaks in with intent to kill should he be discovered; *ha-ba l'horg'kha hashkem l'horgo* "If someone comes to kill you, kill him first". Proportionality follows from Exodus 22:2: "If the sun has risen on him, there shall be blood-guilt for him ..."; as the rabbis express it, "Does the sun rise only on him? [Surely not. But the verse teaches:] if it is as clear as day to you that he does not come in peace (i.e. that he is ready to kill), kill him, but otherwise not".[39]

The duty to defend a threatened victim, even at the expense of the life of the aggressor, is derived somewhat more tortuously from the case of the betrothed victim of rape (Deuteronomy 22:25–27). Scripture itself compares rape to murder, and implies that if anyone heard the victim cry out he should have defended her, if need be by slaying the rapist. The same would apply to any other *rodef* (pursuer), for instance someone intent on murdering another person. But what, asks the Talmud, if the victim could be saved by "one of his limbs," i.e., without killing him? Then the saviour would himself be guilty of murder if he killed the attacker.[40] This last caveat establishes a principle of proportionality.

These texts are set in the criminal code, not among the laws pertaining to war. Later authorities extrapolate from personal to collective self-defence, that is, war designed to defend society as a whole, or its most cherished values. This is analogous to the way in which Christians such as Ambrose and Augustine argued that "Christian love" mandated not only personal defence of individual Christians but military defence of Christian society.[41]

2.11 *Prohibited Conduct*

Deuteronomy 20, a "military oration,"[42] is concerned with what jurists would later refer to as *jus in bello* rather than *jus ad bellum*; it regulates conduct in war but does not specify conditions under which it is appropriate to engage in war. It distinguishes between (a) the war directly mandated by God against the Canaanites and (b) other wars. This is something like the distinction made in early modern Europe between religious wars (wars of the Church) and wars of the Prince.[43]

---

39 Talmud *Sanhedrin* 72a.

40 Babylonian Talmud *Sanhedrin* 74a.

41 Ambrose, *De Officiis* 1.41.201. Augustine Letter 185 (to Boniface) and *Contra Faustum* 22.74, 78.

42 Weinfeld, 45.

43 On this distinction *see* Johnson, *Ideology*, 53.

As indicated above, Deuteronomy's *jus in bello* is of two kinds. War against the Canaanites is based on the *ḥerem*, or holy ban; it is a war of extermination that knows no bounds (verses 15–18). Justification – *jus ad bellum* – is offered, on the grounds that these nations might teach Israel "abominations" and lead them to sin (verse 18).[44] No restraints are indicated.

However, "normal" war is subject to several restraints:

- The war is to be fought only by those who are courageous, possessing faith in God, and who do not have a commitment such as a new house, vineyard or wife (verses 1–10).
- An offer of peace is to be made to any city which is besieged, conditional on the acceptance of terms of tribute (10, 11).
- Should the city refuse the offer of peace the males are put to the sword, the females and small children are taken captive, and the city plundered.
- Food trees may not be cut down in prosecution of the siege (19, 20).
- 21:10–14 offers some amelioration of the status of the female captive.

According to a rabbinic observation, based on Joshua 11:19, "No city made peace with the Israelites, save the Hivites who lived in Gibeon", though an offer of peace was made to the Canaanites, too.[45]

We must be careful not to read later concepts into the text. For instance, someone might read the commandment to spare the lives of women and children as a primitive form of non-combatant immunity, all adult males being regarded by default as combatants. Read in context, however, Deuteronomy is not about the human rights of citizens of an opposing state, but about whether Israelites might retain heathen women and children as booty, or whether, in war against the Canaanites, women too come under the *ḥerem* ban and must be killed.

Likewise, the commandment not to cut down fruit trees has been utilised as a "proof-text" for environmental responsibility in time of war; in its context, however, it is a counsel of prudence, that the conquering army should not destroy its own potential food sources.

Moreover, the distinction often taken for granted between defensive and offensive wars may be inappropriate in the context of the Ancient Near East and much of pre-modern (and sadly some modern) society, just as it would be inappropriate if we were speaking of animal societies in which territorial

---

44 Compare Deuteronomy 9:5. Dan Jacobson explored the Bible's ambivalence about the conquest in *The Story of the Stories: The Chosen People and its God*, New York: Harper & Row, 1982. Michael Walzer ('Idea of Holy War,' 215) aptly observes that no biblical author "undertakes to construct an argument on behalf of the seven Canaanite nations comparable to Abraham's argument on behalf of the Canaanite cities of Sodom and Gomorrah".

45 Jerusalem Talmud *Shevi'it* 6:1.

or sexual competition reigns. If you do not take the initiative, someone else will; you eat, or you are eaten. Offensive merges into preventive, preventive into defensive.

As to *jus ad bellum*, many biblical passages indicate the need for a *casus belli*; Jephthah's argument with the Ammonites (Judges 11), for instance, hinges on the validity of an Ammonite territorial claim. However, the Bible does not articulate principles from which we might judge whether a particular cause was justified. If God issued explicit instructions, that would constitute adequate justification. However, God conspicuously does *not* rely on divine fiat alone when he commands the Israelites to conquer the "promised land" but vindicates it with the claims that (a) He has condemned the Canaanites on account of their immorality[46] and (b) if left, they might "contaminate" the Israelites. Who is to judge?

Here again, extrapolation is dangerous. Malachi prophesies "The Lord will rule the whole earth" (Malachi 14:9), but nowhere in the Bible or in rabbinic[47] tradition does this translate into a general "holy war" against idolaters beyond the borders of Israel.[48] When Christians and subsequently Muslims abandoned Jewish "particularism" they extended the concept of "holy war" to the international level; a nation might initiate war against another in order to bring it to the "true faith", or at least to keep it within the true faith.

As against this tendency, the Dominican theologian Franciscus de Victoria (1492–1546) supports his "natural law" arguments against war for religion by a direct appeal to the Hebrew scriptures:

> [E]ven in the Old Testament, where much was done by force of arms, the people of Israel never seized the land of unbelievers either because they were unbelievers or idolaters or because they were guilty of other sins ... but because of either a special gift from God or because their enemies had hindered their passage or had attacked them.[49]

At least one biblical scholar has argued that the provisions of Deuteronomy were the "radicalism of the writing desk," a retrojection by authors attempting

46 "For the sin of the Amorites will not be total until then" (Genesis 15:16) is a justification of the Israelite conquest on the grounds that God would not have permitted the Canaanites to be destroyed unless and until their evil justified it.

47 Those outside the rabbinic tradition, as Alexander Yannai (see below), may have taken a different view.

48 There is no indication that David's rather limited "expansionist" wars were religiously motivated.

49 *De Indis*, sect. II, 16, cited by Johnson, *Ideology*, 156/7.

to bolster the covenantal consciousness of Israel.[50] Two kings – Saul and Ahab – were reprimanded by prophets for challenging the ruthlessness of the Deuteronomic position,[51] while the prophet Amos (chapter 1) condemns several nations for atrocities committed in wars against each other.[52]

But how were such matters interpreted within rabbinic Judaism? The rabbis would not criticise Deuteronomy, for they regarded it as the authentic word of God; rather, they expressed their unease with the plain meaning of its words by interpreting in a different sense. Likewise, they would not exonerate Saul for his remissness in failing to destroy the Amalekites, since the Bible states that he was deservedly punished; but they retell the story in way that is sympathetic to Saul and articulates their own perplexity at the command to destroy Amalek:

> "And he strove[53] in the valley (1 Samuel 15:5)." Rabbi Mani says, "Concerning the inheritance.[54] For when the Holy One, blessed be He, said to Saul, "Go, smite Amalek …" (15:3) he said, Surely, if the Torah says that if someone kills even one person a calf's neck must be broken,[55] how much more so for all these people, and if the adults have sinned, what about the children! A heavenly voice issued forth and said, "Do not be over-righteous" (Ecclesiastes 7:16).[56]

The "heavenly voice" here is put on the defensive; it is Saul whose moral reasoning is made to appear correct.

---

50 Weinfeld (51) compares Deuteronomy's military orations with those to be found in Herodotus and Thucydides; they are "literary programmatic creations and do not convey the actual content of speeches delivered in concrete circumstances". He attributes them to the scribes of Josiah's Reform (158 f.).

51 1 Samuel 15; 1 Kings 20. Whether Deuteronomy in the form we know it existed at that time is irrelevant.

52 Amos may nevertheless have held that Israel had an exceptional covenantal obligation to "cleanse" the land of idolaters; perhaps he hints at that in 2:9, though the "destroying" is there attributed to God.

53 Some English translations have "lay in wait".

54 The Hebrew *naḥal* may be translated "valley" or "inheritance"; Rabbi Mani interprets the verse as hinting that Saul was troubled about the means by which he was to secure possession of the land for Israel.

55 The allusion is to the atonement ceremony to be performed by representatives of the town nearest to where a slain person was found (Deuteronomy 21:1–9, immediately following the section on war).

56 Talmud *Yoma* 22b. *Midrash Rabba* Deuteronomy 5:12 ascribes to Moses the initiative, confirmed and praised by God, to seek peace with Sihon; Midrash Tehillim on Psalm 120:7 ascribes a similar initiative to the Messiah.

2.12 *Arms Trade*

The Mishna ruled, "One may not sell bears or lions, nor anything that may harm the public, to [gentiles]".[57] A discussion in the Talmud on whether iron lamps may be sold to gentiles, seeing that the material could be reworked into weapons "that harm the public," is cut short by the interjection "But nowadays that we sell them …" to which Rav Ashi replies: "To the Persians, who protect us".[58] Evidently fourth century Babylonian Jews felt it appropriate to sell arms to their Persian overlords; the remark of the Tosafists that "It would seem that nowadays we are permitted for the same reason …" shows that comparable trade was afoot in 13th century Lotharingia. These are among precedents cited by Chaim David Halevi (1924–98), then Sefardi Chief Rabbi of Tel Aviv/Jaffa, in his responsum, published shortly after the Yom Kippur War of 1973, on whether the sale of arms by Israel to friendly countries is permissible under halakhic law.[59]

Jews in the Middle Ages were rarely if ever involved as principals in war, but they often played a subsidiary role in finance and supply. Isaac Abarbanel (1437–1509) is said to have loaned 1½ million gold ducats to the 'Reyes Cristianos' Ferdinand and Isabella to pursue the war against Muslim Granada (1491–92). Jewish immigrants, including refugees from Spain, are said to have introduced significant military technology to their new Ottoman, Muslim overlords.[60] More recently, in the 17th and 18th centuries, several Jews functioned as purveyors of livestock, fodder, food, uniforms, etc. across Europe. Among the most famous army contractors for pay and supplies in 18th century England were Sir Solomon de Medina, the associate of Marlborough, and Abraham Prado. In all these cases it is impossible to assess the extent to which Jews were acting under duress, or in the perceived interest of their own communities, rather than on the basis of some freely embraced religious principle.

3 In Conclusion

3.1 *Compassion*

Ben-Hadad, king of Syria, after a crushing defeat, sought refuge with the victor Ahab, king of Israel; his advisers had counselled him that Israelite kings

57 Mishna *Avoda Zara* 1:7.

58 Talmud *Avoda Zara* 16a.

59 Halevi Vol. 1 #19. See also *Shulḥan 'Arukh: Yore De'a* 151 and *Ḥoshen Mishpat* 409. Some more recent responsa are reviewed in Bleich, 'Sale of Arms'.

60 Bernard Lewis, *The Jews of Islam*, Princeton NJ: Princeton University Press, 1984, 134/5.

were *malkhei ḥesed* "merciful kings" (1 Kings 20:31). Ahab was reprimanded by the prophet for affording refuge to Ben-Hadad; the consequences, *pace* the author of Kings, proved disastrous. In more recent times, however, the reputation of the Israelite kings for showing compassion became a source of pride. You may be relieved at the downfall of enemies, but from God's point of view they, too, are his creatures. R. Yoḥanan observed that the expression "for He is good" that normally follows "give thanks to the Lord" (cf Psalm 136) is omitted after the identical phrase in the instructions to the army in 1 Chronicles 16:41, for the Lord takes no delight in the downfall of the wicked; likewise, observed R. Jonathan, He forbade the angels to sing psalms of triumph when He drowned the Egyptian pursuers in the sea at the Exodus: "The work of My hands drowns in the sea, yet you sing songs of praise!"[61]

Earlier still Philo of Alexandria, with an eye to gentile as well as Jewish readership, refers the provisions for non-Canaanite war in Deuteronomy 20 to those who revolt from an alliance, implying that wars of conquest or aggression are never sanctioned; he stresses the restraint to be shown by Israel in first offering peace. The women are in any event to be spared "as in virtue of their natural weakness they have the privilege of exemption from war service". He writes:

> All this shows clearly that the Jewish nation is ready for agreement and friendship with all like-minded nations whose intentions are peaceful, yet is not of the contemptible kind which surrenders through cowardice to wrongful aggression.[62]

Some medieval rabbis, for instance the thirteenth century author of *Sefer ha-Ḥinukh*, argued that the rationale of less-than-total war against the "other nations" was to instil compassion, for "it is fitting for us, the holy seed, to act [with compassion] in all matters, even towards our idolatrous enemies".[63]

Amongst those exempted from participation in *milḥemet ha-reshut* is "he who is afraid or of tender heart" (Deuteronomy 20:8). Tosefta attributes to José of Galilee (second century) the interpretation "Even if he is mightiest of the mighty and strongest of the strong, but compassionate (*raḥaman*), he should return from the lines".[64] Of course, by *raḥaman* José may mean no more than

61 Yalkut Shim'oni on 2 Chronicles #985.

62 Philo *The Special Laws* 219–224.

63 *Sefer ha-Ḥinukh* No. 527. The work is of unknown authorship, though commonly ascribed to Aaron ha-Levi of Barcelona (c.1235–1300). Philo's work was unknown to medieval Jews.

64 Tosefta *Sota* 7:14. (Tosefta is conventionally thought to be a third-century supplement to Mishna.)

"soft-hearted," and considers it a defect rather than a virtue; it is incorrect to use his words, as some have done, to argue for compassion in the conduct of war.

We conclude with the fine words of Isaac Abarbanel, the most experienced statesman of medieval Jewry, in his commentary on Deuteronomy 20:10, "When you approach a town to attack it, you shall offer it terms of peace":

> The highest aim in war is to seek peace, to make efforts to achieve it, to flee from conflict and the intensity of war, and this for three sound reasons:
>
> First, those who aim at perfection should walk in the ways of God, may He be blessed, as it is written, "Walk in His ways" (Deuteronomy 28:9), and it is known that God does not desire death or destruction, but that the sinner should repent of his ways and live; forgiveness is with Him, and His right hand is extended to welcome the penitent. This is appropriate too for mortal kings and all people: they should not seek strife and quarrel but forgive offence and make peace with all who will make peace with them. This is what the servants of Ben Hadad the king of Syria advised him: "We have heard that the kings of Israel are magnanimous ..." (1 Kings 20:31).

Strong words indeed from the man who in his early years, after serving king Afonso v of Portugal as treasurer, fled to Castile, who then faithfully served Ferdinand and Isabella and was present when Torquemada, head of the Inquisition, persuaded them to expel the Jews,[65] who served again in high office in Naples and ended his days in the republic of Venice, where he was involved in an attempt to negotiate a commercial treaty between Portugal and the Venetian republic. Few can have surpassed the efforts of this medieval rabbi to replace war by peaceful negotiation.

Bibliography

Bleich, David J., "Sale of Arms," in *Tradition* 20 (1982), 358–9.

Cohen-Almagor, Raphael, *The Boundaries of Liberty and Tolerance: The Struggle against Kahanism in Israel.* Gainsville: University Press of Florida, 1994.

65 His firsthand account is preserved in the Introduction to his commentary on Kings.

Crossroads: Halakha and the Modern World. Jerusalem: Zomet, 1987 (5747). The volumes of Crossroads contain select material based on articles in the Hebrew journal *Teḥumin*.

Goren, Shlomo, *Meshiv Milḥama: Sh'elot ut-shuvot b'-inyané tzava, milḥama u-vitaḥon* (Hebrew). 4 vols. Jerusalem: Ha-Idra Rabah, 5743–5752 (1983–1992).

Goren, Shlomo, "Combat Morality and the Halakha," in *Crossroads* 1 (1987), 211–31.

Halevi, Chaim David, *Responsa: Aseh L'kha Rav* (Hebrew).

Inbar, Efraim, "War in the Jewish Tradition," in *Jerusalem Journal of International Relations* 9/2 (1987), 83–99.

Jacobson, Dan, *The Story of the Stories: The Chosen People and its God*, New York: Harper & Row, 1982.

Johnson, J.T., *Ideology, Reason and the Limitation of War: Religious and Secular Concepts 1200–1749*. Princeton NJ: Princeton University Press, 1977.

Johnson, J.T., *The Just War Tradition and the Restraint of War*. Princeton, NJ: Princeton University Press, 1981.

Josephus Flavius, *Antiquities*.

Lewis, Bernard, *The Jews of Islam*, Princeton, NJ: Princeton University Press, 1984.

Nardin, Terry (ed.), *The Ethics of War and Peace: Religious and Secular Perspectives*. Princeton, NJ: Princeton University Press, 1998.

Philo of Alexandria. *The Special Laws*.

Ravitsky, Aviezer, *Messianism, Zionism and Jewish Religious Radicalism*, tr. M. Zwirsky and J. Chipman. Chicago: University of Chicago Press, 1996.

Ravitsky, Aviezer, "Prohibited Wars in the Jewish Tradition," in Nardin, *Ethics*, 115–127.

Ravitsky, Aviezer, "The Roots of Kahanism." *Jerusalem Quarterly* 39 (1986), 98–118.

Vermes, G., *The Complete Dead Sea Scrolls in English*. London: Penguin Press, 1997.

Walzer, Michael, *Deuteronomy and the Deuteronomic School*. Oxford: Clarendon Press, 1972.

Walzer, Michael, *Just and Unjust Wars: A Moral Argument with Historical Illustrations*. New York: Basic Books, 1977. Second edition. 1992.

Walzer, Michael, "War and Peace in the Jewish Tradition," in Nardin, *Ethics*, 95–112.

Walzer, Michael, "The Idea of Holy War in Ancient Israel," in *Journal of Religious Ethics* 20/2 (Fall 1992).

Weinfeld, Moshe, *Deuteronomy and the Deuteronomic School*. Winona Lake: Eisenbrauns, 1992.

CHAPTER 4

Traditional Somali Laws of War

Ayan Abdirashid Ali

> The white man ... desires the world and wants it for himself alone. He considers himself predestined to rule the world. He has made it useful to himself. But here are values which do not submit to his rule.[1]
>
> FRANZ FANON

1 A Word on the Methodology

This research seeks to explore the Pre-Colonial Somali Laws of War which assists in answering and addressing the question of how truly international Modern International Humanitarian Law (IHL) is, with the aim of challenging and abrogating certain apparent and problematic Eurocentric paradigms.

The international legal order and by extension, IHL carries a deep Eurocentric history. This proposition becomes apparent upon the observation the inception and germination of IHL, from the 1860s until today.[2] In the simplest of forms, one need only look to the names of modern IHL protagonists: Grotius, Dunant, Dufour, Lieber or the Battle of Solferino being *the* motivation for drawing up such laws.[3] Modern laws of armed conflict have paid little heed to alternative traditional laws present in diverging civilisations. As a corollary, the argument that IHL is potentially exclusive and impenetrable to a majority as it diminishes a large portion of humanity's conceptions, eventuates. A

1 All Somali translations are by the author except where otherwise indicated. In Somali x is a deep H sound and C is a deep A sound from the middle of the throat. Franz Fanon, *Black Skin, White Masks*, tr Charles Lam Markmann (Pluto Press, 2017) 27.

2 International Committee of the Red Cross, 'What are the origins of International Humanitarian Law?' *ICRC* (online 7 August 2017) <https://blogs.icrc.org/ilot/2017/08/07/origins-international-humanitarian-law/#:~:text=The%20Swiss%20government%2C%20at%20the,the%20birth%20of%20modern%20IHL>.

3 Ibid.

 | DOI:10.1163/9789004703094_006

more critical translation of this quandary would recognise a disjunction of kinds between IHL and the social realities it seeks to regulate.[4] A product of neglecting morally and practically useful principles. It is the case then, that such demurrals may work to the detriment of humanity. This scholarship seeks to counteract the forcefulness of this Eurocentricity by surfacing Somali Pre-colonial laws of war.

The starting point in this scholarship is to position the exact nature of the said Eurocentrism. To do so would require revisiting the drafting and production of IHL with reference to the broader international legal order. 'Professional' international law is said to have emerged in the 1860s as classical liberalism gains traction. It presented itself with objectives to progress the universe sociologically, economically, technologically, and most notably, 'to "civilize" the behaviour of their nations, including in the colonies.'[5] This objective is delineated precisely by Kant in his 'Idea for a Universal history with a Cosmopolitan Purpose.'[6] On his account, humanity is led to this entrancing 'cosmopolitan existence' where Europe 'will probably legislate eventually for all other continents,'[7] and that this is where humanity teleologically reaches its benevolent and utopian end.[8] These are the kind of intentions we see underpinning the production of international law and IHL. In taking this premise a step further, some have argued this is no longer the case and that on a normative level international laws have especially progressed as a platform for cooperatively advancing humanity socially, economically, and environmentally, as a guardian of human rights and global security.[9] There is truth to such a proposition. It remains minimal, however, as its injurious history and practices expunge altruistic themes it may possess. 'The law between European sovereigns was constructed largely in opposition to the law applicable overseas ... broad notions such as Christianity, civilisation ... direct even universal international law in a particular direction.'[10]

This is where it becomes distinctly possible to categorise the said Eurocentrism as part of the on-going neo-colonial regime. PLO Lumumba (citing

4 Nicholas Lamp, 'Conceptions of War and Paradigms of Compliance: The "New War" Challenge to International Humanitarian Law' (2011) 16(2) *Journal of Conflict and Security Law* 225, 238.

5 Martti Koskenniemi, 'Histories of International Law: Dealing with Eurocentrism' (Treaty of Utrecht Lecture, Utrecht University, 16 November 2011) 5.

6 Immanuel Kant, *Idea for a Universal History with a Cosmopolitan Purpose*, ed Hans Reiss (Cambridge University Press, 1991) 52.

7 Ibid.

8 Ibid; Koskenniemi (n 5) 8.

9 Antonio Cassese, *International Law* (Oxford University Press, 2005) 45.

10 Koskenniemi (n 5) 16.

Kwame Nkrumah) turns our attention to the ubiquity of the colonial enterprise. He articulates this proposition adroitly where he speaks of a particular timeline – when slavery lost value, the regime scrambled for the continents, when colonisation lost all desirability, independence ensued, but most fallaciously.[11] Pseudo-emancipation emanates onto the neo-colonial project (for which it is at its most diabolical stage).[12] The inference here is that the international legal order and by extension, IHL is part of this ongoing neo-colonial project, and that it has been from its inception. 'Whatever the contrasts and transitions *imperialism is constant*'[13] and once this accepted, one is distinctly capable of countering this parochialism through the integration of alternative principles. This scholarship attempts to do so through the appraisal of Pre-Colonial Somali Laws of War.

In examining the Pre-Colonial Somali Laws of War, my aim was to address a few core questions derived from the structure of the book series. These included exploring the Somali people, their systems of governance, their objectives in warfare, their methods of regulation, and their traditional prohibitions. However, given the compound nature of Somali society and history, the analysis naturally diverged from a strictly structured approach. Instead, it embraced a more organic, free-flowing method in order to capture the depth and fluidity of Somali traditions, ensuring the findings remained true to their unique context.

The scarcity of written sources on Somali history and the enduring oral culture of the Somali people necessitated the use of interviews for this research. The need to conduct interviews became both evident and unavoidable due to the unique historical and cultural context of Somalia, especially the paucity of written material on Somali history. My initial approach involved researching purely through secondary sources, books, journal articles, pictures, and videos/documentaries available online. However, the degree of limitations was unworkable.

Similarly, most of the available research was authored by foreign scholars, such as Richard Burton, Enrico Cerulli, Ioan Lewis, Georgi Kapchits, and Bogumil Andrzejewski, whose work often reflects the colonial mindset or the orientalist gaze. These scholars, while valuable in their own right, wrote from

---

11 Kwame Nkrumah, *Neo-Colonialism: The Last Stage of Imperialism* (Nelson, 1965) 15–31; Kigali Today, 'Prof Lumumba: There is a new scramble for Africa || A discussion on foreign interference in Africa' (YouTube, 19 May 2023) 00:00:00–00:05:30 <https://www.youtube.com/watch?v=76hLdREQ-bE>.

12 Ibid.

13 Antony Anghie, *Imperialism, Sovereignty and the Making of International Law* (Cambridge University Press 2004) 315.

perspectives shaped by their positions within colonial administrations, or with an inherent sense of distance and difference that often misrepresented or oversimplified Somali traditions, cultures, and legal systems. Much of the scholarship on Somali society, including its legal frameworks, governance systems, and cultural practices, has been shaped by foreign observers and during the colonial era, these studies were often conducted within the framework of imperial domination, where the intent was less about genuine understanding and more about exploiting and controlling. Somali traditions and laws were frequently mischaracterised, oversimplified, or presented as inferior to Western systems, reinforcing colonial hierarchies and narratives of supremacy. Many foreign scholars approached Somali society with the orientalist gaze, a perspective steeped in exoticism and othering, where the Somali people and their customs were studied as objects of curiosity rather than as equals. Such scholarship often carried a paternalistic tone, focusing on differences to perpetuate stereotypes rather than seeking to understand the intricacies and logic of Somali systems on their own terms. Richard Burton and I.M. Lewis are examples of this. It was imperative for me to then foreground the voices of Somalis themselves when exploring the Somali Laws of War, rather than relying solely on the interpretations of foreign scholars. This decision underscores a methodological and ethical commitment to authenticity and self-representation in understanding Somali history and legal traditions.

Given this fraught legacy, relying on the work of these scholars risked perpetuating outdated and harmful narratives, and in even simpler terms an uneasy feeling came with the engagement of such materials. To counter this, I prioritised conducting interviews with Somalis themselves, whose lived experiences, cultural insights, and oral traditions provide a far more authentic and nuanced understanding of Somali legal principles. By engaging directly with Somali individuals, I was able to access interpretations of the Laws of War that authentically portray the cultural, historical, and moral composition of Somali society, most of which is arguably absent in foreign accounts.

Furthermore, the oral tradition remains central to Somali identity, functioning as a dynamic repository for the preservation and transmission of knowledge. Unlike the often static accounts produced by external observers, the oral narratives of Somalis are imbued with contextual richness, linked with the lived realities and collective memory of the community. Hearing directly from Somalis allowed me to capture this dynamism, ensuring that the study was grounded in the voices of those whose ancestors created and upheld these laws.

This approach not only elevates Somali voices but also challenges the historical imbalance in the production of knowledge about Somali society. It reflects a deliberate effort to centre the agency of Somalis in defining and interpreting their own history and legal traditions, rather than allowing external narratives to dominate. By prioritising interviews with Somalis themselves, this research aligns with a broader commitment to decolonising knowledge production and ensuring that the study of Somali laws and customs is guided by the perspectives of those who live and embody them.

If we return to the influence of the Somali oral tradition, it became apparent quite quickly that it was not merely a method of storytelling, but rather a dynamic and adaptable means of transmitting cultural knowledge and even legal principles. By conducting interviews, I was able to access a wealth of knowledge that exists outside the confines of written records and explore the nuanced understandings of Somali legal traditions that could not be captured in secondary resources.

It was also the case that when considering Somali history, many of the historical records had been lost in the Somali Bibliocaust, which resulted from the civil war and the subsequent collapse of the Somali state in 1991. The destruction of libraries, government archives, and other cultural institutions during the conflict erased much of the written documentation that had been produced in both the colonial and post-colonial periods.

Although the Somali people did possess written documentation, particularly in Arabic for communication with trade partners, this was peripheral to the dominant oral culture that has long served as the cornerstone of Somali knowledge transmission. Somalis have historically relied on oral traditions to preserve their history, genealogies, and legal principles, methods that do not fit neatly into written records or Western frameworks of scholarship. The Somali oral tradition has, for centuries, been the lifeline of Somali identity, sustaining a living, dynamic repository of history and legal principles that cannot be captured through written documents alone.

It was this confluence of historical challenges, the paucity of written sources and the significant loss of materials in the Somali Bibliocaust, that made it clear I had to shift my research approach. Given the limitations of existing secondary sources and the overwhelming dominance of foreign voices in the available literature, interviews with Somalis themselves became an indispensable method for this research.

The interviews also allowed me to address gaps in existing scholarship. Much of the work on Somali traditional laws, particularly the famed study by the ICRC in the 1990s, has been disproportionately focused on northern Somali tribes such as the Darood and Isaaq with only brief mentions of southern Somali groups. By conducting interviews with members of the Hawiye clan based in Mogadishu, I was able to contribute to a more balanced representation of Somali legal traditions on warfare, specifically those from the southern regions, which had been overlooked in much of the previous research. The findings were of course, not considerably different, but noticeable to the Somali.

I also acknowledge that most of my interviewees were from the Hawiye clan. This was partially a deliberate focus and a result of logistical and personal constraints, as I was only able to conduct interviews in Mogadishu, where many Hawiye reside.

As a Somali researcher, I am acutely aware that much of the existing scholarship disproportionately centres on northern tribes. Therefore, this study also serves as a contribution to the relatively sparse academic discourse on the traditions and perspectives of southern Somali communities. My intention is to enrich the broader understanding of Somali laws of war by including these often-overlooked voices, while maintaining an ethnohistorical lens devoid of political representations.

This chapter draws on 14 interviews, two of which were conducted in Australia and the remainder in Mogadishu, Somalia, where I gathered substantial material. While the core questions I asked remained consistent, they were tailored to the specific expertise of each interviewee. It is also important to note that the interviews are ongoing, forming part of a larger research project focused on exploring Somali history, warfare, and literature.

2 A Word on the Use of Certain Sources and Their Relevant Historical Periods

The initial intention for this scholarship was to focus on obtaining the traditional laws of war from an approximate period of the 7th–17th century. Around the time Islam came to the Horn of Africa and then right before any colonial impositions. However, during my research, I noticed a difficulty in discussing historical periods and sources as it was important to recognise that certain sources do not always fit neatly into Western-established historical periods. The use of certain poetry was the central concern here. For example, the poetry of Sayid Mahamed Abdulle Hassan, who was active during the late 19th and early 20th centuries as part of the Dervish Movement clearly fits outside of the 17th century. However, this did not invalidate its relevance and there was compelling reason to include Sayid Hassan's poetry as a source.

Poetry in Somali society holds a unique and essential place. It is not just an art form but an inheritance, *daxal*, passed down through generations. Although

Somali society often believes that poets are born with their talents, gifted by God, the methods and structure of Somali poetry are culturally consistent. The style, themes, and methods employed by poets like Sayid Mahamed Abdulle Hassan are not fundamentally different from those used by earlier Somali figures, such as Imam Axmed Gurey who in this instance concerns the relevant historical time period. While the content of the poetry may differ, reflecting different social, political, and emotional contexts, the essence of the craft remains the same. Both poets, despite the different historical circumstances, were products of Somali literary tradition (*sugaanta*) and the way they used language, symbolism, and rhythm to communicate their ideas can be seen as part of a long-standing tradition.

The same can be said for not including the history of the Sayyid and including the history of the Imam as Somali figures involved in warfare. Both fought against colonialism and foreign expansion, albeit in different contexts, Sayid Hassan against the British and Italians, and Imam Gurey against Ethiopian and Portuguese forces. While it has been argued that the warfare tactics of Sayid Hassan differed from traditional Somali laws of war, this perspective becomes problematic when comparing him to earlier figures like Imam Gurey, whose approach to warfare was also distinct but still fundamentally Somali. Both leaders were engaged in resistance movements that were deeply embedded in Somali identity and culture, and their methods, while perhaps differing in their specifics, cannot be entirely divorced from the broader Somali context of resistance.

Thus, attempting to draw rigid lines between historical periods in Somali scholarship is a challenging task. The fluidity of Somali history, with its oral traditions and evolving cultural practices, means that the boundaries between different historical moments are often less defined than those in Western historical frameworks. The use of sources like poetry is invaluable, as it helps bridge these gaps, offering insights into Somali culture, identity, and historical continuity that are not bound by strict chronological categories.

> Of all the races of Africa there cannot be one better to live among than the most difficult, the proudest, the bravest, the vainest, the most merciless, the friendliest; the Somalis.[14]
>
> GERALD HANLEY (1971)

---

14 Gerald Hanley, Warriors: Life and Death among the Somalis (Indiana University Press, 2004) 29.

3 Who Are the Somali People?

3.1 *Geo-ethnographics*

Ethnically, the Somali people are generally represented to be homogenous with a vastly similar ethnic composition, a uniform language (inclusive of the various dialects), a single religion (Islam), an alike culture and a traceable heritage to common ancestor(s). A common national identity has also formed from the profusion of various ethnic groups and more accurately, from the conjunction of clans, sub-clans and or clan-federations. These (agnatic) kinship-based communities constitute the basic political units responsible for social, political and legal governance, as well as conflict resolution.

Somalis are also considered to be part of the Afro-Asiatic family, inhabiting the Eastern horn of Africa. From the Red Sea Coast and the Gulf of Aden, until the regions of three adjoining states – modern day Ethiopia, Djibouti and Kenya. This geographical positioning was historically known as Greater Somalia as Somalis lived and inhabited the Ogaden region (Ethiopia), the Northern Frontier District in Kenya and the Djibouti region. It was in the late 19th century when these three regions were affected by the arbitrary borders drawn up by French, English and Italian colonialists. The colonial partitions are, and have provoked nationalistic questions modern Somali history and politics. This scholarship is only concerned with mapping of Greater Somalia during the Pre-Colonial period.

Somalis have a long history of nomadic pastoralism, primarily herding camels, goats, and sheep. Their nomadic lifestyle required constant movement to find grazing lands and water. In more fertile regions across southern Somalia, they practiced agro-pastoralism where farming with livestock rearing was combined.

The land has also been attributed many titles – The Land of Punt (Land of the Gods by the Egyptians), or of the Barbaroi (Berbera[15] by the Greeks), Terra Aromatica (by the Romans due to the incense produced by native gum resins), Regio Cinnamafore (Land of the Cinnamon, also by the Romans) and the Land of the Milk and Myrrh.[16] It is also the nation that 'teems with poets, poetasters,

---

15 Berber being the previous term for the Somali. Berbera is also a region in the North of Somalia.

16 Gerald Reece, 'The Horn of Africa' (1954) 30(4), *Royal Institute of International Affairs* 440; Abdurahman Abdullahi Baadiyow, *Making Sense of Somali History: Volume 1* (Adonis and Abbey Publishers, 2017) 45–47.

poetitos, poetaccios.'[17] Linguistically, the official spoken language is Somali, a recognised Lowland East Cushitic language.[18]

3.2 *Governance*

Beyond such exciting descriptions and whilst there are numerous articulations one might make in explaining Somalia and the Somali, this scholarship is sufficed through an understanding of the dialectic or triangular relationship between Xeer (law(s)), Tol (the clan) and the Sharia all of which arguably form the (natural) traditional system of governance. Each component plays a crucial role in maintaining order, peace, justice and social cohesion. The three systems complement one another and interact in such a manner that a balance is produced between customary practices, clan rights and responsibilities and religious principles. A cohesive system of governance is then produced.

3.3 *Tol – the Clan Genealogy*

3.3.1 Tol Waa Tolane – the Clan Is Woven

The Somalis are a clan-centric people, strictly fashioned by a rather extensive system of segmented groups which produces Somalia (the nation-state), the family of clans (the Hawiye, Dir, Darood, and the Digil and Mirifle (Rahanweyn), confederations, sub-confederations, the singular (basic) clan which might also be understood as the most basic political unit, and finally the immediate family. The singular clan is in this regard, the basic political and jural unit whereby each function with distinct names, tribal markings (*sumaad*), traditions and histories. Both pre-colonial Somalia and modern-day Somalia is formed in the order of this clan-based kinship. Kinship for Somalis is a fundamental source of agency, identification, and political and social organisation.[19]

The clan is structurally formed through agnatic or patrilineal relations, and these have existed for centuries. The entire Somali genealogy is said to originate from two progenitors, brothers Soomaal (also known as Samaale) and Sab.[20] The Soomaals led a pastoral-nomadic lifestyle and the Dir, Darood and Hawiye clans are said to be his descendants.[21] Comparatively, the Sabs

17 Richard F. Burton, *First Footsteps in East Africa* (Longman, Brown, Green and Longmans, 1856) 115.

18 Raymond G. Gordon Jr., *Languages of the world* (SIL International, 15th ed, 2005).

19 See for example, Samatar's characterisation; Abdi Ismail Samatar, 'Destruction of State and Society in Somalia: Beyond the Tribal Convention' (1992) 30(4) *Journal of Modern African Studies* 626.

20 Although there are a number of stories to the contrary, however, this is the most widely accepted.

21 "Again, there are conflicting modern accounts on this history."

led an agro-nomadic lifestyle and the Rahanweyn and Digil clans are of his descendance.

It is also historically understood that a clan generally forms after the successful continuance of about 20 or 30 generations; the birth of a son extends the patrilineal line.[22] It is the kind of belonging that emerges from the common ancestor a group of people hail from. What one owes to one another based on patrilineal descendance from a common ancestor.[23] The clan relations importantly produce certain rights, responsibilities and liabilities that binds members at the individual and at the collective level.[24] At the individual level, each clan member is entitled to certain protections and provisions from their kin. For instance, a member has the right to be cared for in times of need, fed, housed, or given property when necessary. That is a collective duty of the clan to offer a safety net. The individual member is also expected to contribute to the collective, whether through labor, resources, or knowledge which reinforced this cycle of collective duty and responsibility.

At the collective level, clan membership creates broader obligations that extend to the group as a whole. These include responsibilities to defend the clan's honor, its territory or its resources and to contribute and defend the clan during times of war or smaller conflicts. It is also the collective responsibility of the clan to contribute to blood compensation (*diya*) if a member harms someone from another clan, and the clan will generally function as the independent third-party managing disputes through customary mechanisms like Xeer. It is the collective responsibility to stand together in the delivery of justice, protection, and restitution. These shared responsibilities advance a sense of unity and collective identity, as each person's fate is tied to that of the group.

Therefore, in this context, 'clan-lines and loyalty to one's lineage are the defining characteristics of Somali politics and social life.'[25] In this context, clan relations determine many aspects of warfare. It is the clan that determines alliances, loyalties, conflicts and aggression. The upper limit of the structure is known as the clan family (the Dir, Darood, Hawiye) and the 'lower limit'

22 Joakim Gundel, 'Clans in Somalia' (Austrian Centre for Country of Origin & Asylum Research and Documentation Lecture, 15 May 2009) 7–8; Jama Mohamed, 'Kinship and Contract in Somali Politics' *Africa: Journal of the International African Institute*, (2007) 77(2) 226, 226.

23 Abdi Ismail Samatar, 'Destruction of State and Society in Somalia: Beyond the Tribal Convention' (1992) 30(4) *Journal of Modern African Studies* 626.

24 See for example, Joakim Gundel, 'Clans in Somalia' (Austrian Centre for Country of Origin & Asylum Research and Documentation Lecture, 15 May 2009) 7–8.

25 Abdi Ismail Samatar, 'Destruction of State and Society in Somalia: Beyond the Tribal Convention' (1992) 30(4) *Journal of Modern African Studies* 627.

of the structure is the singular basic clan which is also the mag or diya paying group.[26] Generally, the diya or mag paying group is the essential political unit of clans as it is this group that is responsible for paying compensation for the loss of lives, is responsible for the mutual defence of groups and mutual defence of the unit.[27] It is also at this level that interclan warfare consistently occurs. For example, it is very uncommon (historically) for the entire Isaaq clan to go to war with the entire Hawiye clan and instead, it is the singular basic clan that often goes to war with another singular basic clan. As the unit that enters into war with other clans, it is also the unit that instates or enters into peace treaties.

As the social structure of clans is such that Somali society is complexly organised along patrilineal clan lines, it serves as a primary axis of interpersonal and inter-clan relations. In the milieu of warfare, these clan affiliations become pivotal in the dictation of formation of alliances and in the delineation of adversaries. The obligations to one's clan, which is manufactured upon a shared ancestry, encompass not only loyalty but also the imperative to defend the clan's honor and collective interests.

3.3.2 Nin xukunkisa saxda ah, waxeey la heshiiysa kitaabka Alle A Man's Sound Judgement/Rule Concurs with That of the Book of Allah

Politically, the clan is led by a head known in Somali as the Suldaan (Sultan or Ruler), Ugaas (the authentic Somali term for Sultan), Garaad, Imaam (Paramount religious leader) or Boqor (King). The diverging titles are attributable to minor dialect differences which are present in the major regions. For example, in the north he may be known as the Suldaan. Conversely in the center-south region for instance, the Abgaal clan attributes the title of Imaam. The Imaam would then lead his Imaamate and the Suldaan, his Sultanate.

26 Jama Mohamed, 'Kinship and Contract in Somali Politics' *Africa: Journal of the International African Institute*, (2007) 77(2) 226, 226.

27 Interview conducted with Sheikh Mohamed Dau'ud via telephone, on 3 December 2023 at Mumbai, India and at Adelaide, South Australia; Sheikh Mohamed Dau'ud is a traditional and religious scholar and judge who hails and governs from the Abgaal, Waceysle, Abdirahman Saleebaan clan; Interview conducted with Imaam Daahir Imaam Mohamud Imaam Omar in person on 10 June 2024 at Shangani, Mogadishu, Somalia; Imaam Daahir is the current Imaam (Head) of the Abgaal Clan who hails from the Harti Abgaal Clan, the eldest of the Abgaal Clan; Interview conducted with Boqor Abdullahi Geedi Shadoor in person on 10 June 2024 at Shangani, Mogadishu, Somalia; Abdullahi is the current King of the Waceysle clan, which is the youngest subclan of the Abgaal Clan.

A Somali (male) clan leader generally obtains his position through two means. First, he may be nominated and recommended for the position, or he may naturally retain the position through an inheritance. Historically, there was a tendency for a candidate's father or grandfather, and of his agnatic lineage to have retained the position. The position is then capable of reaching him through inherited means. The rationale behind this is that the traits a clan leader exhibits are in fact innate and passed down intergenerationally. Although inheritance is one avenue, the starting point is that the candidate is nominated and elected by clan elders and the clan's managing party. The managing party which of course consists of the responsible, the council of jurors (xeer beegti), the peace-seeker (nabaddoon), the religious elders (the ulema) and so forth, the candidate is assessed by the group in accordance with questions of the following nature:

(a) Whether he is capable of greatly benefitting the clan (by maintaining the clan economically, legally, politically, socially and militarily).
(b) Whether he is and has maintained a favourable position within the clan.
(c) Whether he possesses an exemplary character and the traits which are usually exhibited by a clan leader.
(d) Whether he is knowledgeable (in the traditional law (xeer), the Sharia and the tradition), and whether he is an intelligent, insightful, pious, charismatic individual.
(e) And whether he is capable of maintaining peace, justice, rightful military campaigns etc.

Imaam Daahir Imaam Mohamud, the current clan leader (Imaam) of the Abgaal clan explains that the clan as a family, gathers to assess the eldest of the current leader for his ability to lead (hogaan), whether he is fair, blessed, lucky, and an individual close to God who might then have his prayers answered on the clan's behalf.[28]

Once an agreement is reached between the clan elders, he is awarded the position, and a marking ceremony is initiated (caleemad saar) which affirms his election. He is enshrouded and draped in grand clothing which will distinguish him from ordinary members of the clan and even the managing party of the clan. Tahliil[29] is spat on over 1000 times, tawfiiq (prosperity or success) emerges and from that moment onwards, he is then known as the leader of the

28 Interview conducted with Imaam Daahir.

29 Tahliil is produced at traditional religious events where the Holy Quran is read extensively over a bowl or bottles of water. A key element of this ritual involves blowing or lightly spitting over the water after the recitation of the Quran. The idea is that the words of the Quran infuse the water with barakah (blessings) through the breath of those reciting.

clan and will only be approached and dealt with as the clan head.[30] The position is of importance as it carries with it, various duties and responsibilities. His duties extend from maintaining the mundane items such as the wellbeing of the clan (literally access to water, food, livestock etc) and until declarations of war and military campaigns. He for example, possesses the ability to order a conflict to a halt and may subsequently call for peace, or he may encourage the military pursuit to continue and for it take a certain direction. His word is of course, the last word.[31]

Sheikh Mohamed Dau'ud[32] expands on the clan leader's duties and responsibilities to include to the following:

1. 'When members of the tribe are in dispute and matters cannot be solved in between the parties in conflict, he assumes the role of a mediator. Whatever he says and orders is taken, and it is the last word.'[33]
2. 'When there are external concerns or matters that affect the tribe and or its interests, he will speak on such matters and encourage a particular course of action. The Sultan or Garaad or Imaam will declare that a particular action shall be taken, or no action shall be taken at all. As 'he possesses the traits of intelligence and insight, whatever he orders in the name of the clan is then treated as that which is most beneficial and must then be accepted, supported and followed.'[34]
3. 'If the clan is at war with another clan or with an external aggressor, the course of the conflict is in the hand of the clan head. The clan head may order for the conflict to halt, or he may encourage the conflict to continue in a certain manner.'[35]
4. 'If for example, the clan has been transgressed against by another clan and there is justice or a kind of revenge to be pursued, the clan head encourages for the conflict to continue until the conflict has reached a

30 Interview conducted with Imaam Daahir.

31 To indicate the extent of his authority: there is the anecdote of the Waceysle King being told to be quiet whilst the Abgaal Imaam sought to speak while he was speaking. There is also a significant age gap between the two where the Waceysle King is significantly elder than the Abgaal Imaam. However, out of the respect for the rank and position of the Imaam, the King allowed for the interruption and this is something that would otherwise be disallowed in Somali society.

32 Interview conducted with Sheikh Mohamed Dau'ud via telephone, on 3 December 2023 at Mumbai, India and at Adelaide, South Australia; Sheikh Mohamed Dau'ud is a traditional and religious scholar and judge who hails and governs from the Abgaal, Waceysle, Abdirahman Saleebaan clan.

33 Interview conducted with Sheikh Mohamed Dau'ud.

34 Interview conducted with Sheikh Mohamed Dau'ud.

35 Interview conducted with Sheikh Mohamed Dau'ud.

noble and just point. In some instances where this is still the case, but the condition of the clan does not allow for the conflict to continue (for example, where there is a drought) the clan head will act int the interest of the entire clan and order the conflict to halt or cease. Even where there is justice or revenge or a kind of nobility to be sought.'[36]

5. 'Where he chooses to halt the conflict, he calls together all affected parties and lays out his decree. He usually opines that the conflict will not continue, that parties are to reach a peaceful agreement, where lives have been lost, he orders for the calculation of the diya (blood compensation), the restoration of certain rights and entitlements (for example, livestock ownership).'[37]

Certainly, as some of the praises in Burranbur[38] of the north might go,

garta uu gooyo na, gadaal, loma laabaan jirin,	the judgment he gives is irreversible and once decided, is never overturned
maa beentay baa? Alley lehe mayaa	is this a lie? By God, it is not a lie
maa beentay baa? Alley lehe mayaa	is this a lie? By God it is not a lie
Miyuusan aheyn? Alley leh haa	is he not as such? By God he is
Miyaanuu oran? Alley leh haa	did I not say so? By God you did

3.4 *The Council of Elders*

Whilst the clan head is in possession of considerable authority, he certainly does not rule on his own and power is not so individualised. He instead rules through the consent and harmony of the clan. He is supported by and advised by much of the clan's elders (odeyaal) and the religious scholars (ulema).[39]

36 Interview conducted with Sheikh Mohamed Dau'ud.

37 Interview conducted with Sheikh Mohamed Dau'ud.

38 The female form/medium in poetry.

39 Interview conducted with Sheikh Ali Waajiis in person on 10 June 2024 at Mogadishu Somalia; Sheikh Ali Waajiis is an Islamic Scholar and an advisor on Islamic affairs to the current Federal Somali government.

They produce a council, and the council is the clan's entire depository of knowledge. For example, the elder(s) of the Holy book (ulema)[40] might advise on the Islamic legality of a military campaign or what kind of fate awaits them in the hereafter should a certain action be pursued, the general group of male elders (odeyaal)[41] might advise and recite history that exists between two clans who are about to engage in conflict (in order to know how relations have been and how they might then manifest), the poet (who might be an ulema or even the clan leader or simply a poet)[42] might recite poetry invoking certain emotions in favour or against the military campaign and there is also the peace-seeker/keeper (nabaddoon)[43] who might particularly advise on the value of amity and peace.

40 The Ulema (religious scholars) are tasked with providing moral and religious guidance, ensuring that Islamic principles are upheld in times of conflict. In Somali society, where Islam plays a central role, the Ulema will condemn unjust warfare and will emphasise the ethical rules of war as required by the sharia. They may intervene to remind on of the importance of protecting non-combatants and respecting the property and dignity of civilians, as dictated by Islamic teachings. Their spiritual authority can also serve to justify or delegitimise a conflict, giving weight to decisions about whether a war is justified or whether peace must be sought.

41 During times of warfare, the Odey (singular. elder) or Odeyaal (plural. elders) serve a vital role in mediating conflicts and facilitating peace negotiations. Every elderly man is considered a politician and is vested with a right to deliberate at 'shirar' (political council meetings) or xeer beegti (legal council meetings). The extent of an elder's right to deliberate or influence, after their right as a male is generally contingent on his gift in poetry, political acumen, eloquence in speech, intellectual depth, devoutness, wisdom, hospitality, bravery, strategic brilliance in battle and strength. During war or in the post-conflict stage, Odeyaal often act as neutral parties, and they advance dialogue between warring parties. They rely on their understanding of Xeer (the customary law) and strive to ensure that warfare adheres to traditional codes of conduct, particularly on the protection of the Bir Ma Geydo (civilians, women, children and all of the exempt from warfare). They may advocate for ceasefires or organise compensation agreements, such as diya (blood compensation), to mitigate the risk of escalating violence. Although they do not hold real military authority like the clan head, their influence is crucial in breaking cycles of conflict and promoting reconciliation following hostilities.

42 The oratory ability is an innate one and so the role of the poet is not exclusive, it is rather interchangeable.

43 The Nabaddoon are specialists in peacekeeping and conflict resolution. They assume a pivotal role both before and after warfare. Their primary mission is to prevent conflicts by mediating disputes at an early stage ensuring that minor tensions do not escalate into full-blown hostilities. By addressing issues proactively, they contribute to a more stable environment and reduce the likelihood of violence. In times of war, the Nabaddoon become intermediaries, and they work diligently to broker temporary peace agreements or truce negotiations between rival clans. Their presence often helps de-escalate tensions and once the fighting subsides, the Nabaddoon play a role in establishing lasting peace. They oversee the negotiation of peace settlements, ensuring that reparations

In any given clan, there is a managing party who alongside the clan leader, govern and oversee disputes on behalf of the entire clan, in accordance with the Sharia and Xeer. They are known either for their legal role, where the Xeer Beegti (a council of jurors) is formed, or for their participation in shirar (political council meetings).[44] In their political capacity, they frequently assess the significance of inter-clan relations, weighing the merits of going to war, and provide counsel on such decisions. In their legal capacity, they act as mediators, judges, and arbitrators in conflict resolution, and they are responsible for the administration of justice, reconciliation and cohesion amongst their own clans and on occasion act as a council for other clan disputes in a neutral third-party capacity. Their role is fundamental to the functioning of Xeer, the customary law system that governs interpersonal, inter-clan, relations that are relevant in terms of social, political, economic and military relations. The Xeer Beegti serve as custodians of oral law and tradition, ensuring disputes are settled according to the long-established principles. They offer legal expertise that complements the political leadership of the clan leader.

Women historically hold restricted influence within clan councils and their responsibilities in this context is generally limited to being roobdoon (the seekers of rain)[45] or ziyaarad (the one who brings prosperity and nourishment).[46] There is, however, an exception present in for example the Reer Mataan clan where women who reach the age of 40, marking the onset of menopause and the completion of childbearing, are granted a distinctive status.[47] At this juncture, these women transition into a matriarchal role, thereby becoming integral

(non-monetary compensation) or compensation (monetary) are discussed and agreed upon. They actively monitor the adherence to these settlements, holding both parties accountable to uphold their commitments. By focusing on active peace-making, the Nabaddoon contribute significantly to reconciliation efforts and help build a foundation for enduring stability in the aftermath of conflict.

44 Jama Mohamed, 'Kinship and Contract in Somali Politics' *Africa: Journal of the International African Institute*, (2007) 77(2) 226, 228.

45 Roobdoon, the term refers to women as pivotal figures in the quest for sustenance and vitality. Traditionally, women are seen as the custodians of agricultural knowledge and practices intimately connected to the cycles of nature. Their expertise in these domains is paramount during periods of aridity and ecological distress. As they engage in rituals and practices to invoke rain, they embody a profound connection to the cyclical nature of life, illustrating their significance as both nurturers and sustainers of their environment.

46 Conversely, the concept of ziyaarad encompasses the broader responsibilities that women assume in promoting the community's well-being and prosperity. In a society that values hospitality and communal ties, women are often the architects of social cohesion.

47 Interview conducted with Professor Yahya Amir in person on 11 June 2024 at Xamar Weyne, Mogadishu, Somalia; Professor Yahya Amir is a public intellectual, academic and customary tradition and law expert.

members of the clan council, where their voices are vested with authority and significance. This transformation elevates them to a position of prominence where their decisions carry considerable weight. This shift in dynamics can lead to some men relinquishing their decision-making capacities, allowing women to assume leadership roles. These matriarchs are recognised as adept administrators, fully capable of steering significant decisions that impact the clan's welfare.[48] As matriarchs, they emerge as custodians of wisdom, embodying a wealth of life experience and knowledge that uniquely qualifies them to navigate matters of governance and community welfare.[49]

3.5 *The Pre-colonial Clan*

A clan also inhabits a particular region. The different regions also present with divergent ecologies which pre-supposes the different economic conditions. For example, much of the Isaaq and Darood inhabit the northern (west and east respectively) regions, and the Hawiye inhabit the Central and Southern regions. The different regions also present with divergent ecologies which pre-supposes the different economic conditions, traits and interlocutions. Pastoral and agricultural differences are attributed to this diverging condition of the land. For example, the arid land would not allow for much cultivation of agriculture in the North, so they naturally resort to pastoralism. This is also some etymological congruence as the word Somali is a derivative of the word Soomaal meaning in its literal – Soo maal (go and milk).[50]

Historically the Somalis, through an extension of these clan structures, established kingdoms or sultanates across various parts of Greater Somalia. The following table indicates the names, geographical coverage, and duration of the most important of these kingdoms and sultanates.

Name	Historic time period	Geographic location
Sultanate of Ifat or the Kingdom of Zeila (Saylac)	13th Century-15th Century[a]	Northern Somalia around the Saylac region
Warsangeli Sultanate	13th Century–20th Century	Northern Somalia

48 Interview conducted with Professor Yahya Amir.

49 Interview conducted with Professor Yahya Amir.

50 Said Sheikh Samatar, *Oral Poetry and Somali Nationalism: The Case of Sayyid Mahammad Abdille Hasan* (Cambridge University Press, 1982) 10.

(*cont.*)

Name	Historic time period	Geographic location
Ajuran Imamate	13th Century–17th Century	Southern Somalia (Kismayo to Hobyo)
Sultanate of Adal	15th Century–16th Century	Across the Harar Plateau moving into the Gulf of Tadjourah
Geledi Sultanate	17th Century–20th Century	Southern Somalia (along the interior of the Banadir region (Afgoye), across the Juba and Shabelle Rivers)
Majeerteen Sultanate	16th Century–20th Century	Easternmost of Somalia where the 'Horn' forms
Hiraab Imamate	17th Century–early 19th Century	Southern Somalia, including Mogadishu, Marka, and Afgooye

a Abdurahman Abdullahi (Baadiyow), *Making Sense of Somali History: Volume 1* (Adonis and Abbey Publishers, 2017) 64.

> *Xeerla'aan wa xukun iyo xolo la'aan*
>
> Without law is without rule and property
>
> *Xeer Alle dhigo aya no dhigan*
>
> The law God has passed is the law laid out for us

The clan structure is the primary mode of social organisation, and it is complemented in terms of governance by the xeer system. Abdi explains that the xeer system ought to be observed as a 'regime,' noting that 'social order may be obtained without formal authority' as seen in the European contexts.[51] 'Society is characterized by [the] feasibility of collective action and [with a] uniformity of shared beliefs.'[52] This 'regime' is thus understood as a system

51 Jamal Abdi, 'Social Order: Voluntary Agreement and Constent in Pre-Colonial Somali Society' (2021) 21(15) *Bildhaan: An International Journal of Somali Studies* 166, 167.

52 Jamal Abdi, 'Social Order: Voluntary Agreement and Constent in Pre-Colonial Somali Society' (2021) 21(15) *Bildhaan: An International Journal of Somali Studies* 166, 167.

of governance because of the 'conformity of shared beliefs.'[53] The uniformity of these shared beliefs results in the necessary normative legitimacy. These shared beliefs within the xeer system include the law and rules, principles, and norms and values which are universally understood as necessary by the Somali. It is the system that 'issues command and demands obedience.'[54] A prime example of the universal rules within traditional Somali society is the Bir Ma Geydo, referring to those exempt from warfare or those who are 'spared from the spear'. This is the traditional set of laws that protect non-combatants in war, and they are acknowledged universally throughout Greater Somalia.

Without the influence of individual or unilateral decision-making,[55] all decisions, sanctions, and matters of importance were settled through collective consensus. Abdi rightly observes this process as being facilitated by a comprehensive framework of publicly negotiated and universally embraced laws, values, norms, regulations, social standards and customs, and codes of conduct which are collectively known as Xeer.[56] Xeer in the literal might be translated as a custom or as a contract and both attributes contribute to traditional Somali law.[57] Xeer can be understood as a manifestation of custom in so far that it is a collection of the understood cultural values and norms which are contingent on Islam. It profiles behaviour or conduct which is socially acceptable and capable of regulating society. It is simultaneously a kind of social contract as the question of what is fair, reasonable and just, is answered by collectively negotiated and universally recognised moral and normative frameworks. This is the same law that regulates war, war crimes, crimes and all kinds of social transgressions. Decisions made by xeer are also as in any legal system, legally binding.

Importantly, there might also be exclusive Xeer which is drawn up, known and entered into by two or more particular clans.[58] It is manifold as specific

53 Jamal Abdi, 'Social Order: Voluntary Agreement and Constent in Pre-Colonial Somali Society' (2021) 21(15) *Bildhaan: An International Journal of Somali Studies* 166, 167, 173.

54 Jamal Abdi, 'Social Order: Voluntary Agreement and Constent in Pre-Colonial Somali Society' (2021) 21(15) *Bildhaan: An International Journal of Somali Studies* 166, 167.

55 See Jamal Abdi who distinguishes this concept from other social structures where for example, a chief leads and where his decision-making capacity is paramount and exclusive.

56 Jamal Abdi, 'Social Order: Voluntary Agreement and Constent in Pre-Colonial Somali Society' (2021) 21(15) *Bildhaan: An International Journal of Somali Studies* 166, 170.

57 Jamal Abdi, 'Social Order: Voluntary Agreement and Constent in Pre-Colonial Somali Society' (2021) 21(15) *Bildhaan: An International Journal of Somali Studies* 166, 170.

58 Interview conducted with Boqor Abdullahi Geedi Shadoor; Interview conducted with Sheikh Ali Waajiis; Interview conducted with Haji Maroco in person on 10 June 2024 at

clans may have xeer in between them and then there is that which is generally understood by each clan as xeer. Both have developed over time and with history. Where there is exclusive xeer between two or more clans, it is considered long-standing law that governs them both in conflict and in peace, and it is well known by both clans, usually carried down intergenerationally. The current Waceysle king, Abdullahi Geedi Shadoor notes that that this latter category of xeer is of course in this regard, only ever entered into by the greater diya paying clan like the Waceysle of the Abgaal and the Abakar of the Mursade, or the Waceysle and the Sacad of the Habargidir.[59]

This bilateral or multilateral manifestation of xeer can be understood as treaties between clans.[60] It explicates the rights and duties particular clans will have in the case of conflict and or resolution.[61] For instance, some clans might have a xeer laid out between them that disallows the killing of any clan member whatsoever.[62] Instead, the preference would be to as a first, resolve matters at the initial stages of 'colaad' (adverse relations) and to 'drink water together' which safeguards against any transgressions.[63] These treaties might also stipulate relatively low diya payments, especially for clans that have history or tendency for adverse relations. Professor Camir and the current Waceysle King, Abdullahi Geedi Shadoor indicate that historically, some clans will reduce the required diya so that the tendency for conflict might be 'assuaged or eliminated, it is a conscious decision from both warring clans to reduce their entitlements by the sharia so that for the sake of peace, relations may improve.'[64] The required diya payment for the death of one male is 100 camels and may be reduced to 30 or 20 camels so as to reduce any hardship on the relevant clan. In other circumstances, 'a clan might be asked after the disaster to emphasise or accentuate the xeer between them, (xeerka xooji).[65]

Xamar Weyne, Mogadishu, Somalia; Haji Maroco is a religious scholar, family and civil lawyer and customary law and traditional expert.

Interview conducted with Professor Yahya Amir; Interview conducted with Imaam Daahir.

59 Interview conducted with Boqor Abdullahi Geedi Shadoor.

60 Interview conducted with Boqor Abdullahi Geedi Shadoor; Interview conducted with Haji Maroco.

61 Interview conducted with Haji Maroco.

62 Interview conducted with Haji Maroco.

63 Interview conducted with Haji Maroco.

64 Interview conducted with Professor Yahya Amir; See also Interview conducted with Boqor Abdullahi Geedi Shadoor.

65 Interview conducted with Boqor Abdullahi Geedi Shadoor.

Xeer has also historically remained unwritten. It "is not learnt in the ordinary manner of learning things nor is it originally found in books."[66] On one account, it emerges as legal precedent following certain conflicts. There are some notable conflicts amongst the clans and so the manner in which they are resolved or navigated develops as xeer passed down by elders. As Sheikh Mohamed Da'uud explains, "the depository of such knowledge is born by the elders of tradition who have been sitting under the tree."[67] He further states, "when a judgement is handed down and it experiences much acquiescence from the clan, or where it exhibits practicality, it becomes xeer and the precedent" becomes binding and common knowledge.[68] Xeer is also not static in that it evolves as the clan navigates new challenges and experiences, remembering that at its core, xeer operates on principles of consensus and communal agreement, allowing it to be fluid and responsive.[69] The word maslaxad has been used to describe xeer here and it suggests that xeer is a tool at the dispense or interest of the clan.[70]

Xeer is employed both prior to conflict and at times of conflict resolution.[71] This section explains xeer at the stage of conflict resolution and reconciliation. In the aftermath of a conflict or even where there has been a wrong committed and the parties prefer to conciliate rather than pursue a full-blown war, the involved parties will conciliate based on existing Xeer. Conciliation traditionally occurs at shiraar (council meetings) which resembles typical peace-making circles. Affected or interested parties present grievances in front of the Odeyaal (male elders), the Nabaddoon (the established peace seeker), the clan leader (Ugaas, Suldaan, Imaam, Boqor etc), the Ulema (religious scholars) where a circle assembles for deliberations to commence. The main effort behind such an assembly is for the administration of justice (xaqq). Any agreement entered into at the shir (council meeting) was also treated as legally binding.

3.6 *Xeer as an Emulation of the Sharia*

Xeer is of course, apace with the Sharia as in the Holy Quran, the Sunna or practice of the Prophet peace be upon him (which is found in Ahdith) and Fiqh (Islamic jurisprudence) which in the (historic) Somali case is the Shaafi'i

66 Interview conducted with Sheikh Mohamed Dau'ud; Interview conducted with Boqor Abdullahi Geedi Shadoor.

67 Interview conducted with Sheikh Mohamed Dau'ud.

68 Interview conducted with Sheikh Mohamed Dau'ud.

69 Odeyaal daqmeed 135.

70 Odeyaal daqmeed 135.

71 A discussion on Xeer regulating warfare and the stage prior to war, is had below.

school of thought. For a full historical image, it is worth mentioning the pre-Islamic religious beliefs Somalis held.

Prior to Islam's arrival to the Horn, Somalis along with other Cushitic groups in the region (Oromo and Afar) worshiped the God of Waaq.[72] Waaq was considered the monotheistic God of the sky, and he was associated with agricultural and pastoral abundance, peace and harmony. This God was worshiped alongside his angels and spirits. This is consistent with the etymology of Somali words, clans and townships. For instance, the word barwaaqo means prosperity or bountifulness, there are also clans named Jidwaaq (in the path of God) who are of the Absame Darood family and, many townships including Abuudwaaq (the worshiper) and Ceelwaaq (the Well of God).[73]

At some point during the seventh century, Islam reaches the Horn, and the premise is approximate as the exact arrival is a cite of contestation. Professor Baadiyow in his assessment first observes one hagiological submission that argues Islam's arrival occurred during the first Hijrah (migration) of Islam. As the Muslim persecution in Mecca increased, the Prophet (peace be upon him) sent a delegation of his companions, led by Ja'far ibn Abi Talib to Abyssinia, 'the land of truth.'[74] The group requested and received asylum from the then Abyssinian king, Najashi for about 13 years (615–628 AD).[75] Here, it is argued that Somalis accepted Islam through the Muslim presence in Aksum and the active preaching of Islam in the region. This is in some order plausible. However, this would mean Islam reached the Horn before it even reached Medina. Baadiyow takes issue with this position as he submits the distance between Aksum and Saylac (or Zeila, the capital of the Adal Sultanate) to be more than 1000 kilometers and even further by sea.[76] Another possibility is attributed to the Yemeni Muslims who in their travels to Medina, disembarked at Abyssinia and may have encountered the companions there and potentially spread Islam from there.[77] There is also the telling evidence of the Qibla change at the Masjid Al-Qiblatayn (the Mosque of two Mihrabs) in Saylac, northern Awdal where the prayer orientation changed from Jerusalem to Mecca. Baadiyow continues

72 See Mohamed Haji Mukhtar, *Historical Dictionary of Somalia, New Edition* (Scarecrow Press: 2003), 258–259.

73 See Mohamed Haji Mukhtar, *Historical Dictionary of Somalia, New Edition* (Scarecrow Press: 2003), 258–259.

74 See Baadiyow, Making Sense of Somali History Vol. 1, 48–49 ('Baadiyow vol. 1').

75 Baadiyow vol 1, 49.

76 Baadiyow vol 1, 49.

77 Baadiyow vol 1, 49, 50; Ismael Mukhtar, 'Milestones in the History of Islam in Eritrea' (Eritrean Muslim Council's 6th Annual Convention Lecture, July 2008) 2.

to explore various Somali opinions on the matter especially where unambiguous and precise evidence appears from Arab-Somali commercial relations.[78]

It can be surmised that the Islamisation of Somalia transpired at some juncture during the seventh century; however, of greater significance is that the enmeshing of the two enables an analysis of the degree in which the Sharia informs and shapes traditional Somali warfare.

A pivotal inquiry arises regarding the extent to which xeer emulates sharia and the degree to which sharia informs xeer. Primarily, it is evident that xeer has adeptly adapted to incorporate and reflect Islamic principles. However, the depth of this adaptation poses a historical conundrum, as scant records exist to substantiate any definitive argument. The nuances surrounding how Somalis received sharia, the methodologies of its instruction, the interpretations they gleaned, and the extent to which pre-existing xeer necessitated modification to align with sharia remain largely enigmatic.

A consensus indicates that historically, xeer and the sharia coexist harmoniously and 'they do not refute each other', they are apace with each other and 'much of what is regulated by xeer emerges from the sharia.'[79] As the elders currently leading the National Peace and Reconciliation Council explain, 'xeer comes from the deen [religion]', 'what is outside of the deen [religion] is not xeer' and certainly, 'ma iss qilaafaan' (they are in agreement).[80] At the same time, it is essential to acknowledge that there is no definitive way to ascertain the extent to which the embrace of Islam altered xeer or whether xeer originally mirrored sharia. This uncertainty is compounded by the traditional understanding that xeer inherently aligns with sharia; indeed, it is posited that there can be no xeer that does not correspond with Islamic principles. Consequently, it is necessary to confront this entrenched belief that individuals engage xeer (an inheritance cultivated through generations) often without realising the extent in which their governance is entangled with sharia.[81] This divergence invites critical exploration into the relationship between traditional warfare and sharia especially seeing as there is a foundational belief that Somalinimo (the state or essence of being Somali) inherently aligns with being Muslim and adhering to sharia.

78 For a further discussion on this, see Baadiyow vol. 1, 50 and onwards.

79 Odeyaal daqmeed.

80 Odeyaal daqmeed 135; Interview conducted with Sheikh Mohamed Dau'ud.

81 This is contrasted with the position of the ulema who possess a more nuanced understanding as their expertise in Islamic principles significantly surpasses that of the general populace.

As such, any examination of traditional warfare ought to consider how these elements coalesce, which this scholarship attempts to do where appropriate.

A reconciliatory stance would assert that xeer is distinctive in its own right, and that the extent of a clan's knowledge of Islam serves to clarify the position and manifestation of sharia throughout Somali history.

4 Conflict and Resolution Process and Diya

Dhibaato, Dhibaato laguma saxo

A disaster is not solved with futher disaster

Conciliation traditionally occurs at shiraar (council meetings) which resemble typical peace-making circles.

The odeyaal (male elders), the Nabaddoon (established peace seeker) which is present in every clan), the clan leader (Ugaas, Suldaan, Imaam, Boqor etc), the Ulema (religious scholars) and the affected or interested parties will assemble a circle, usually under a tree (geedka) where deliberations commence. The setting under the tree is a symbolic space known for negotiation and reconciliation.

There is also no particular schedule for when the shir (council meeting) occurs, they simply occur as required. A shir often occurs for weeks or months and sometimes over years as it is rare for conflict to resolve with one or two rounds of talks. The rationale behind this rather lengthy consultation is so that the exact or the root cause of the conflict or hostilities may be ascertained.

It is worth noting the role of these odeyaal at the circle so that one may imagine the exchange of words occasioning the resolution.

The clan leader is present, with his Islamic duty to end hostilities and he beings with 'the task of softening the hearts and softening the feelings of enmity' and this is generally in the form of words, poetry, proverbs, a verse from the Quran or even a recitation of the relevant history between the parties.[82]

The Nabaddoon (peace seeker) is vested with the authority to initially seek peace at the earlier stages of conflict on behalf of each clan. He usually engages with the conflict with a few other odeyaal ula gaduud (lit. elderly men with red sticks which means elderly men of wisdom and experience, capable of providing counsel) and they attempt to deliberate on the methods to end hostilities. Where there is no badbadis (extrication or release), the matter escalates to a

82 Interview conducted with Sheikh Mohamed Dau'ud.

shir. At the shir, the Nabadoon will address the council with such gravitas that attendees will be reminded of the true value of peace.

The Ulema, positioned at the periphery of the assembly, are vigilant custodians of the dialogue, ensuring that the discourse never strays beyond the limits of Sharia. Their presence, while secondary, serves as a theological safeguard, though rarely do participants stray beyond the permissible limits of the Sharia, given the overwhelming religiosity of the clan members.[83] The Ulema are typically consulted only when complex jurisprudential issues arise, necessitating a fatwa (religious decree). Yet, when negotiations falter or tensions reach an impasse, their intervention becomes the final recourse, stepping in to mediate when xeer fails. Xeer is here regarded as the "Sulux[84] As-Sayyid Al-Axkaam" (the master of agreements), a system that operates in harmony with Islamic principles, serving as the first point of resolution.

However, once the dispute escalates to the level of Sharia, and xeer proves inadequate, there is no room for further debate (dood kama furno). The Ulema, at this juncture, issue binding declarations: either the right unequivocally belongs to one party, or the transgression of another is pronounced. Unlike the negotiable nature of xeer, the rulings of Sharia are unyielding (Sharicadda laa laab malahan), offering no space for appeals or further deliberation. The finality of these decisions stands in stark contrast to the fluidity of xeer, where compromise is still possible.

This represents the pinnacle and most legitimate form of conflict resolution, where the authority of the process ensures mutual respect between the clans. Once the matter is resolved, colaadaha (hostilities) come to an unequivocal end, restoring not just relations, but trust.[85] The clans regain the ability to coexist in peace, free from lingering grievances or hidden resentments. Most significantly, no bitterness remains harbored within, caloosha wax kuma herin which signifies true reconciliation where nothing festers beneath the surface, and harmony is fully restored.[86]

In their broader role, the Ulema act as the moral compass of the gathering, consistently reinforcing Islam's divine stance on justice, fairness, and the consequences in the afterlife for those who transgress. They enrich the proceedings by reciting relevant Quranic verses that lend authority to specific decisions

---

83 Interview conducted with Sheikh Mohamed Dau'ud; Interview conducted with Professor Yahya Amir; Interview conducted with Sheikh Ali Waajiis; Odeyaal 135.

84 Sulux meaning reconcilliation or settlement.

85 Interview conducted with Sheikh Mohamed Dau'ud; Interview conducted with Professor Yahya Amir; Interview conducted with Sheikh Ali Waajiis; Odeyaal 135.

86 Odeyaal 135.

and actions, as well as recounting the Seerah of the Prophet (peace be upon him) and the wisdom of the four caliphs and so the assembly is grounded the Shaira and the tradition.

There is also the Guudi or Waafti, the neutral third-party clan who is employed where two opposing parties find themselves entrenched in a conflict that eludes resolution, and the customary avenues of reconciliation through internal dialogue prove ineffective, they are compelled to seek the intervention of a neutral third-party clan, a practice well known and available with xeer.[87] This third-party clan, selected with meticulous care for its impartiality and distance from the immediate tensions, is often regarded as the embodiment of equitable judgment and moral authority, capable of transcending tribal allegiances to ensure fairness in the reconciliation process. To unequivocally demonstrate their impartiality, the neutral party intentionally refrains from partaking in any sustenance offered by either disputing faction on the day of negotiations, embodying a profound commitment to objectivity.[88] By refraining from indulging in the victuals of either faction, the mediator not only signals his detachment from their respective interests but also embodies the principles of fairness and equity that underpin xeer.

4.1 *The Diya System*

> It is 'the loss of life and or property [that] is then reinstated through the diya system'.[89]

As previously detailed, Somali clans are taxonomically structured in a complex, tiered hierarchy, descending from the broader clan, through sub-clans and primary lineages, down to the most operative kinship entity, the diya or mag paying group.[90] This unit functions to compensate which in turn restores balance between groups or individuals after an offence or war crime has been committed.

By paying (traditionally in the form of livestock like camels), the offending party or their clan offers restitution to the aggrieved party, thereby preventing further conflict or escalation. Importantly, responsibility is collective rather than individual. Comprised of several interconnected lineages, these groups

87 Interview conducted with Professor Yahya Amir; Interview conducted with Boqor Abdullahi Geedi Shadoor; Odeyaal 135; Interview conducted with Haji Maroco.

88 Interview conducted with Boqor Abdullahi Geedi Shadoor.

89 Interview conducted with Sheikh Mohamed Dau'ud.

90 Diya means blood compensation.

trace their shared ancestry to a common progenitor spanning approximately four to ten generations. Their numerical strength, typically ranging from several hundred to a few thousand men, renders them capable of discharging the requisite diya payments mandated under the Sharia, traditionally quantified as 100 camels in cases of a male death. Consequently, every man's social standing and political affiliations are inextricably bound to his membership in such a group.

The compensatory scheme is employed to address two distinct categories of injury: xaal (restitution) and diya (blood compensation). Typically, xaal compensations are rendered in modest amounts and are aimed at rectifying non-fatal injuries and moral transgressions that might otherwise lead to escalation or prolonged conflict.

This category is usually reserved for the misuse of one's tongue as indicated in the following proverbs:

> Af caaytamay ninkiisa ayeey ku taal – The insult belongs to the one who utters it.[91]
> Af daboolan waa dahab – A covered mouth is a mouth of gold
> Afkaaga iyo adinkaagaba waa la dhawrta – Your mouth and your limbs are to be protected.[92]
> Afkaaga kun ayuu ka celiyaa, addinkaagana hal nin – Your mouth protects you from a thousand men and your limbs protect you from one.[93]
> Afkaagoo aadan ku cad goosan waa cadow kugu yaal – A tongue that does not speak up for itself is like an enemy lodged within you.[94]
> Aflagaado waa astaan dagaal – Slander is a symbol of war.
> Afxumo nabadna waa ka kaxeysa, colaadna wax kaagama tarto – Bad mouthing deprives you of peace nor does it benefit you during war.
> Afxumo rag waya kala dishaa – Bad mouthing kills men.
> Carrabkaaga ka adkaaw intuusan kaa adkaanin – Restrain your tongue before it becomes unrestrainable / before it overpowers you.
> Carrabkaaga waa faraskaaga, hadaad sii deeyso, wuu kula tagiidonna – Your tongue is your horse, if you set it free, it will uncontrollably lead you astray.

91 The proverb especially speaks of the unfounded insult here and that it only returns to the one insulting.

92 As much as a person is naturally inclined to protect their body parts, they are encouraged to protect their mouth from ill speech.

93 If you are eloquent, a man can fight a thousand people but with his limbs, can only fight one.

94 The tongue that does not defend you is an enemy inside you.

Conversely, diya is reserved for the most grievous offenses, most notably, homicide. The severity of the offense dictates the application of diya. For instance, the death of each male is a cost of 100 camels and the rare death of a female is 50 camels and this is predicated upon the Sharia, which stipulates specific reparative measures for the loss of life. The transactional nature of the diya system mandates that compensation flows from the transgressing clan to the aggrieved clan. This inter-clan financial exchange aims to restore balance and harmony following the wrongful act, particularly in cases of homicide or serious injury.

Notably, the dynamics of this compensation may be influenced by historical agreements forged between clans, which can stipulate diya amounts that deviate from the Islamic norm. Such negotiated amounts may range from 20 to 40 to 50 camels which is often a reflection of the prevailing economic circumstances or the cordiality of inter-clan relations. In instances where historically antagonistic clans' endeavor to ameliorate their fraught relations, they may engage in treaties that delineate significantly reduced diya payments. Such concessions are deliberate, and they aim to mend longstanding grievances which paves the way for improved inter-clan relations. As Abdullahi Geedi Shadoor explains that words of the following nature are regularly exchanged …

> Qolo[95] hebel waa cafis
>
> Those people are forgiven,
>
> Qolo hebel waa xeer sidaas,
>
> There is that xeer among those people,
>
> Qolo hebel waa aargosi ama qisaas intaas,
>
> Those people are to be revenged or equal punishment for the crime.[96]

Moreover, once a diya amount is publicly articulated and embraced by both parties, it attains an intergenerational permanence. An enduring expectation is created which stipulates that subsequent descendants will honor this now stablished xeer.[97]

95 Qolo can also mean a clan in this context.

96 Retributive justice or retaliation in kind.

97 Interview conducted with Professor Yahya Amir.

The diya system also stands as a time-honored concept. It functions as a mechanism for restoring harmony after grievances, particularly in cases of homicide. However, when diya obligations are not honored or fulfilled, it can precipitate animosity and conflict, igniting tensions between clans. The failure to recognise and uphold these reparative commitments often leads to cycles of retribution, transforming what could be a conciliatory process into a catalyst for renewed warfare and clan hostilities. Otherwise, it is at the diya stage that conflict is expected to truly resolve. Diya is certainly, 'complete and self-sufficient and … waa wixi dadki daqijiray.'[98]

The resolution of any conflict, whether of great magnitude or lesser consequence, is traditionally marked by symbolic ceremonies that embody reconciliation, unity, and collective restoration. At these ritualistic gatherings, formal apologies and acknowledgments of transgressions are delivered. Livestock, a symbol of wealth and peace, is presented as an offering. Poetic praises, extolling the virtues of the wronged clan, are solemnly recited.[99] These acts are accompanied by the performance of traditional dances and the shared consumption of milk and camel meat, emblematic of the re-establishment of harmony and the mending of fractured relations between clans. To example this, there is the shirib nabadeed (peace Shirib) present in the central-south region of Somalia.[100]

4.2 *Suugaanta Somaliyeed – Somali Literature*

> A Somali has two aces in the hole
> His Faith in Islam and
> his Lyrical Poetry[101]
> [*Somaalidu been wey sheegta, lakin ma maahmaahdo* – Somalis could tell lies but lies are not told in proverbs.]

The proverb Somaalidu been wey sheegtaa, laakiin ma maahmaahdo encapsulates the cultural reverence for oral traditions as sacrosanct vessels of truth, wisdom, and moral authority. Suugaanta, the Somali term for literature, transcends mere artful expression; it constitutes the heartbeat of a society where words embody governance, history, and social regulation. In a culture shaped

98 Interview conducted with Sheikh Ali Waajiis.

99 Interview conducted with Imaam Daahir.

100 Odeyaal 135; Interview conducted with Imaam Daahir; See explanation below.

101 Mahmud Siad Togane, 'The Poet's Death is His Life' (2006) 6(10) *Bildaan: An International Journal of Somali Studies*, 86, 86.

by its nomadic heritage and decentralised structures of governance, suugaanta endures as an archival force, resilient through upheaval and loss.

Prior to delving into the oral culture of the Somali people, it must be recognised that there is a dearth of traditional historical accounts that troubles this scholarship. The paucity is attributed to two central reasons. First, the absence of the Weberian model of statehood,[102] a framework ingrained in European governance but absent in the Somali context, has resulted in the lack of centralised governance and accompanying bureaucratic registers. Historically, Somalis demonstrated limited inclination toward conventional statehood or the establishment of a formal administrative apparatus, leaving little room for written records or official annals.

The second factor is tied to the catastrophic disintegration of public administration following the collapse of the Somali state in 1991. The ensuing civil war wrought unparalleled devastation, ushering in protracted conflict and acute lawlessness. Among its many tragedies was the Somali Bibliocaust,[103] the obliteration of historical, literary, and artistic records. This obliteration has left a void in tangible records, but not an unfillable one. The oral tradition, long before and long after the collapse, has been the lifeline of Somali culture. It has preserved history, genealogies, and even legal philosophies and so it is suugaanta that subsists as a living repository of memory and identity.

The spoken word carries with it history on folkloric narratives, poetry and proses, hagiographies and hymns, traditional dances and dance songs. It is the instrument that sustains the culture and the instrument that preserves the truths of the Somali people, the anchor that steadies the Somali identity in an ever-shifting world.

4.3 *Words as Weapons and Peacemakers*

The power of poetry as a tool for conflict resolution was particularly crucial in Somalia's fragmented social landscape, where no centralised authority could effectively enforce peace. In such a system, oral traditions became not only the repository of collective memory but also the mechanism for mediating disputes. Somali poets, known as the 'abwaan' (*m*) and 'abwaanad' (*f*) in the context of poetic forms, could sway the course of a conflict through strategic verses, offering both counsel and condemnation through their carefully crafted words.

---

102 Mohammed Haji Ingriis, 'From Pre-Colonial Past to the Post-Colonial Present: The Contemporary Clan-Based Configurations of Statebuilding in Somalia' (2018) 61(2) *African Studies Review* 55, 60.

103 Marian Nur Goni, 'Repairing (With) The Archive? Re-Collecting Dispersed Somali Photographs' (2018) 12(2) *Journal of African Art History and Visual Culture* 170.

For instance, during periods of clan conflict, the poet would be called upon to deliver a 'gabay' or 'geeraar' or other poetic forms to negotiate peace between warring clans. This could include invoking historical precedents, moral teachings, and the common values shared by the clans. Poet Abdullahi Sultan Timacadde was very well known for employing geeraar to urge clans to embrace reconciliation, is a prime example of how Somali poetry has been used to de-escalate violent conflict. His poetic plea called on the memory of past unity and the values that underpinned Somali society, emphasizing peace as a vital principle more powerful than bloodshed.

4.4 *Ethics and Suugaanta*

The ethical underpinnings of Somali oral literature are embedded in the culture, shaping not only how conflicts are resolved but also how they are prevented.

Central to this framework is 'xeer,' the customary law system that has been passed down through generations. Suugaanta is arguably an integral component of xeer as it functions as both a codifier and a clarifier of these rules.

The ethical teachings found in Somali poetry are centered on values that are universal yet ones that resonate with Somali identity. The protection of life, the sanctity of human dignity, and the importance of social cohesion are central tenets of Somali oral literature. These values align with the principles enshrined in International Humanitarian Law (IHL), such as the protection of civilians in armed conflict, the prohibition of indiscriminate violence, and the treatment of prisoners of war with dignity.

Suugaanta's ability to communicate these ideals is rooted in its capacity to evoke deep emotional responses and to resonate with the lived experiences of Somalis. The use of proverbs, poetry, and oral storytelling not only conveys ethical teachings but also reinforces them through repetition and communal participation. As a result, suugaanta becomes more than just a medium for expression – it is a mechanism for social regulation, an ever-present reminder of the moral boundaries that govern individual and collective behavior.

4.5 *The Poet as Arbiter of Conflict and Agent of Peace*

The Somali poet's role as an arbiter and influencer is a storied tradition. In pre-colonial times, poets served as spokesmen for clans, wielding words as tools of diplomacy and weapons of war. Their poetry was a double-edged sword, 'seef laba afalaha, mar na dinac oo wax uu goya marna dinac kale', a sword of two mouths, cutting one side and then the other.[104] Sheikh Mohamed

104 Interview conducted with Sheikh Mohamed Dau'ud.

Dau'ud explains this to mean their verses could either heal or harm, incite violence or bring peace. This dual capacity positioned poets at the epicenter of Somali communal life, their words revered as much for their beauty as for their power to influence events.

Referred to as Gabayaal[105] or, when their words were especially impactful, Af-maal, 'the mouth of wealth', the poet's speech was seen as a treasure when it benefited the clan or supported a noble cause. Yet, when misused, it could devastate the delicate balance of peace, escalating tensions and inciting conflict. 'They can recite poetry to exacerbate, aggravate and inflame the war,' Sheikh Mohamed Dau'ud notes, while simultaneously wielding the power to mediate, inspire, and reconcile.

4.6 *Poetry as a Catalyst for War*

> *Nabad iyo Colaad, Carab ba keno*
>
> Peace and Conflict is brought about by the Tongue

The destructive potential of poetry is vividly illustrated in moments of inter-clan disputes. Consider a scenario where a clan has chosen restraint after losing men in conflict, seeking their Islamic and traditional right to blood compensation rather than pursuing revenge. The poet of the adversary clan, however, crafts verses mocking their decision, accusing them of cowardice, military incompetence, and weakness. His words stir the embers of hostility, reigniting the flames of conflict. The poet's verses act as provocations, undermining peace efforts and sowing discord.

On the battlefield, the poet's power is equally evident. Sometimes, he physically enters the fray, reciting his poetry aloud to embolden warriors. As Sheikh Mohamed Dau'ud describes, 'his poem is then read amongst the clan in the battlefield, the gabay has composed the following verses, and the war must continue.[106] His poem of encouragement then intensifies the war. The combatants are even more encouraged, diiga kacda, wadnaha aa kacda (their blood raises, their hearts beat).'[107] His words drive combatants to greater ferocity, solidifying their resolve. Even when the poet is absent, his verses, passed along to be read aloud, hold the same galvanizing effect.

105 Otherwise broadly known as Abwaan.
106 Interview conducted with Sheikh Mohamed Dau'ud.
107 Interview conducted with Sheikh Mohamed Dau'ud.

The power of poetry is not always benevolent. As Professor Yahya Caamir aptly states, poetry is 'an absolute instigator', historically provoking both conflict and reconciliation.[108]

Similarly, Sheikh Ali Waajiis explains that 'poetry, proverbs, stories, and buraanbur, have severe repercussions. This is a phenomenon that holcis' war. It torches or inflames the conflict even further. It plays a significant role in causing war and conflict ... [it] carries much power in Somali society' and must be shielded from misuse. In some regions, the potency of poetry in warfare had led to its deliberate suppression. Professor Yahya Caamir recounts the teachings of his father, Sheikh Caamir, a customary law expert, who advised against the recitation of poetry during conflict. His reasoning was based on its purely destabilisng impact. Poetry could exacerbate the hatred and animosity (colaad) between warring factions, 'it induces and becomes a separate cause for war or a prolongation of the conflict,' Caamir explains.[109] Sheikh Camiir, understanding the incendiary power of poetry, disallowed its recitation during times of war.

This category of poetry is known as 'guubaabo'. When misused, guubaabo can become a source of vexation and provocation, leading to heightened animosity between clans. Sheikh Ali Wajis recounts a historical example involving the Xawaadle and two subclans of the Agoon Yare Gaaban (Buraale, Iloodhi) of the Harti-Abgaal clans around the Middle Shabelle region.[110] After the Agoon Yare (Iloodhi) refrained from avenging the deaths of their men against the Xawadle, another subclan of the Agoon Yare (Buraale) expressed their frustration through poetry:

> 'Iloodhi Muuse aarsanma [yo] iri na beerka aali maa [yo].'[111]
>
> This translates to: *The Iloodhi clan does not revenge when they need to; they are miskeen (weak), and their goats are eaten without repercussion.*[112]

The poetry escalated tensions by questioning the Iloodhi's honor and implying their inability to defend themselves. Another line, 'beertoodi mar walbo laga cunayo', meaning their land and property are repeatedly exploited without

108 Interview conducted with Professor Yahya Amir.
109 Interview conducted with Professor Yahya Amir.
110 Interview conducted with Sheikh Ali Waajiis.
111 Interview conducted with Sheikh Ali Waajiis.
112 Expansive translation of this Shirib offered by interviewee.

retaliation, further aggravated the situation.[113] This shirib[114] oo kicin ah (inciting poetry) demonstrates how guubaabo can provoke war by attacking a clan's sense of pride and justice.

4.7 *Poetry as a Force for Peace*

Conversely, the poet wields an unparalleled ability to mediate and inspire peace. When the Sultan, Imam, elders, and nabaddoon (peaceseekers) convene to resolve a conflict, the poet lends his voice to their cause. Through his verses, he brings to light the arag-xumo – the ugliness and futility of prolonged conflict. His words stir emotions, invoking a sense of collective regret and yearning for peace. 'When the Sultan and Imaam and the elders, the nabaddoon, organise to bring the conflict to an end, he recites poetry in support of this,' Sheikh Mohamed Dau'ud explains.[115] "He speaks of the horror of the conflict, the little benefit there is in continuing it, and he brings this to light through his words. He speaks with such wisdom and emotion that anyone in opposition to this is led to change his position."[116]

The poet's influence extends even into the heat of battle. Just as his words can inflame combatants, they can also quell their fury. In the midst of the battlefield, he might compose verses discouraging the continuance of war. His words are so cajiib (extraordinary) and yaab (awe-inspiring) that the warriors, gripped by his eloquence, listen.[117] Whether present on the battlefield or distant, the poet's words resonate with equal power, delivered through emissaries or recited aloud to the warriors.

Sheikh Ali Wajis highlights that poetry has a waajib (obligation) to promote peace, 'in nabadda loo adeegsada, it is employed in bringing about peace.'[118] He explains that, under sharia, the misuse of poetry is equivalent to the misuse of normal speech and is punishable in the sight of Allah (SWT).[119] Just as spreading hatred or inflammatory information is forbidden, a Somali is similarly disallowed from employing poetry to inflame relations between clans or individuals.

To example both poetry as a weapon of war and as a force for peace, one can look to the poetic expression employed by the Abgaal clan known as Shirb. The

113 Interview conducted with Sheikh Ali Waajiis.
Interview conducted with Sheikh Ali Waajiis.

114 The form of poetic expression employed by the Abgaal clan.

115 Interview conducted with Sheikh Mohamed Dau'ud.

116 Interview conducted with Sheikh Mohamed Dau'ud.

117 Interview conducted with Sheikh Mohamed Dau'ud.

118 Interview conducted with Sheikh Ali Waajiis.

119 Interview conducted with Sheikh Ali Waajiis.

Shirib can be separated as Shirib Dagaleed (War Poetry) and Shirib Nabadeed (Peace Poetry).

Shiriib Dagaal refers to poetry that is composed during times of war. This type of poetry is designed to rally the clan, boost the morale of its warriors, and fuel the fire of battle. It is often aggressive and provocative, calling for the defense of the clan's honor and land. Through vivid and forceful language, the poet inspires warriors to take up arms and fight for their people. The content of shiriib dagaal often includes insults directed at the enemy, mocking their strength or valor, thus escalating tensions between clans. The poetry can also glorify the warriors, portraying them as heroic figures in the battle for survival and clan pride. This form of poetry functions as both a psychological weapon and a means of rallying the community, making the warriors feel invincible and the enemy weak.

For instance, there is the warning like poetry like Weershe Xussein's[120] 'Hadaan ley dooran dagaal iyo waxaan ridaa' who recited the following verses …

> Hoo Hooo Hoo hooo Helay wayaaaa Helay wayaaaaa
> [prolonged recitation of these literary filler words which are used in the opening and close]
>
> Aniga hadaan, aniga ley doorahaayn leyna dabajoogin deg deg na aan ciiyoow leygu siin derajo iyo gar Dagaal iyo waxaan kici ha weerar dhabadheer haddi uu aduunki yiraada …
>
> If I am not stood behind by and am not chosen, and I am not quickly granted respect and rank, and the right, I will wake up an attack that prolonged and chronic if the universe allows.
>
> Dadna wuxu heeshiiyaa hadu kala dhambeeya …
>
> People are in agreement when there is concessions and surrender
>
> Sad miya in leys dila raggana raggana doorka laga socodo dan miyaa?
>
> Is it in our interest to kill men and to lose the role played by men, is it in our interest?

120 Shaciye TV, 'Shirib Hadaan ley dooran dagaal iyo waxaan ridaa' (YouTube, 21 February 2013) 00:00:00–00:02:45 <https://www.youtube.com/watch?v=DzBZkfB5SD0>.

Dagaalkaan batte dhabada dheereyay dan miyaa?

Is this prolonged conflict in our interest?

Ee dan miya in leys dila, raggana doorka laga socodo, dar xumo na layse, waxan illaah la duceysanaya

Is it in our interest to kill men and to lose the role played by men, is it in our interest, misery has killed us, and we seek refuge in God

Magaaladda dab aa lagu gubay, ee daxal madoobaatay

The city has been burnt with fire and our inheritance has been darkened

Magaladda ninki lugu dilay ba diya la qaada … waxna la toogahayn aya dib loo raadsha …

A man killed in the city is administered with the Diya.. and where no person is shot or stabbed is the condition that we seek

ee iss dugaansho somaliyeey nabadda uu duuba dhabeel caafimaad aan helnay ee dawo nabadeed …

Somali familiarity is woven at times of peace, and we have received winds of health and the medicine of peace

Dadna wuxuw heeshiiyaa hadu kala dhambeeya

People are in agreement when there is concessions and surrender

4.8 *The Moral Authority of the Poet*

The duality of the poet's role as a seef laba afala, underscores his moral authority in Somali society. Poetry served as a means of accountability, with poets critiquing governance, exposing injustices, and demanding rectitude from leaders. As Professor Yahya Aamir aptly states, poetry is 'an absolute instigator', historically provoking both conflict and reconciliation.[121] Similarly, Sheikh Ali

121 Interview conducted with Professor Yahya Amir.

Waajiis underscores that "poetry carries much power in Somali society" and must be shielded from misuse.

In Somali tradition, the poet is more than an artist, he is an arbiter, a historian, a diplomat, and a moral compass. Whether urging peace or stirring conflict, the poet's words shape the trajectories of Somali clans, reflecting the profound respect Somalis have for the power of the spoken word. As Sheikh Mohamed Dau'ud reminds us, the poet's tongue is mightier than any weapon, it is the true double-edged sword of Somali society.

5 Sababaha iyo Horumarka Dagaalka
The Causes and Developments in Warfare

This section will explore the numerous causes and motivations that have historically compelled Somalis to engage in warfare, both among the clans and externally, against non-Somali adversaries. This non-linear inquiry will investigate the social, political, economic, and cultural dimensions that have traditionally catalysed conflict. From the relentless competition for resources and contentious land and border disputes to the preservation of honor and the unyielding quest for justice, this examination aims to illuminate the complex interplay of factors that have historically spurred Somalis to take up arms.

6 Resource Competition and Territory Disputes

Resource competition stands as one of the most prominent and enduring catalysts for conflict within traditional Somali warfare, a reality intricately tied to the region's challenging ecological conditions. The Somali territories, predominantly characterised by arid and semi-arid landscapes, experience scant and irregular rainfall, rendering water a rare and fiercely contested resource. The nomadic pastoralist and semi-sedentary agriculturalist livelihoods that sustain the Somali people have always been contingent upon access to these limited water sources. As a result, competition for water wells for drinking (*ceelasha*), livestock, and crop cultivation inevitably becomes a flashpoint for conflict.

During the long, dry seasons, both people and their herds would converge upon natural water sources known as the *ceel* (well) or some cases, along the Juba and Shabelle rivers. The very act of congregation around these scarce water points often induced tensions, with disputes emerging over the scheduling of access and prioritisation. The scarcity water intensified these disputes, leading to frequent clashes between clans or lineages as they vied for control over these life-sustaining resources. In some cases, these disputes escalated into full-scale armed confrontations, as the stakes were nothing short of survival.

Likewise, the most fertile grazing lands became the epicenter of intense competition, as clans vied to monopolise these vital resources exclusively for their own herds. This rivalry escalated particularly during and after arid seasons, when rains were unevenly distributed across the region, compelling clans to drive their livestock en masse toward areas that had been rejuvenated with fresh grass. The sudden influx of people and animals into these pockets of abundance inevitably bred friction.

Resource competition not only incited conflict but also led to the inevitable migration of clans into each other's territories in search of sustenance and survival. The nomadic and semi-nomadic nature of Somali pastoralism, coupled with the erratic distribution of resources, often necessitated such movement. At times, this migration occurred amicably, particularly when the migrating clan shared lineage ties or maintained historically good relations with the resident clan. In these instances, the relationship between the clans facilitated peaceful negotiations, allowing access to water and grazing lands as a gesture of generosity or mutual obligation.

However, in many cases, the movement of a clan into another's territory occurred forcibly, driven by sheer desperation for survival. When the rains were scarce, and water points were few, or when fertile grazing lands were isolated to a single region, clans had little choice but to infringe upon the territories of others, often without prior consent. The urgency of maintaining their herds and securing food led to territorial encroachments that could quickly escalate into violent confrontations. While some clans forged lasting alliances through resource sharing, others deepened their historical animosities, as the pressure of resource scarcity became a relentless driver of both cooperation and conflict.

As articulated by Professor Yaxya Camir, in certain regions 'every conflict revolves around the *tub iyo ceel*,' the well and the path leading to it' or '*soo dintaa reer hebel*', the territory/border demarcation of so and so clan.[122] Territorial encroachments are a notorious and recurrent cause of conflict, regarded as an egregious '*xadgudbin*' or transgression. The boundaries delineating each clan's domain are entrenched, often codified through formal or even historical declarations of ownership, known and respected across generations. To breach these borders without explicit '*fasax*,' or permission, is to invite inevitable and

122 Interview conducted with Professor Yahya Amir; Interview conducted with Boqor Abdullahi Geedi Shadoor.

bitter warfare.[123] Indeed, one must approach the clan endowed with abundant resources, humbly seeking reprieve during times of drought, certainly, the infringement sows the seeds of enduring animosity and conflict.

In situations where a clan has been held responsible for paying diya (blood compensation) as a result of a conflict, yet finds itself unable to meet the required payment, the repercussions can escalate beyond the original peace settlement. Rather than continuing to wait for compensation that may never arrive, the creditor clan may assert control in a more direct and forceful manner. This often involves assuming ownership of a portion of the indebted clan's land as a tangible form of compensation.[124] For example, they might lay claim to an area of 2 or 4 kilometers of land, establishing their presence and marking it as their own in lieu of the agreed monetary or livestock payment.[125]

While this resolution might appear functional in the short term, it often sows the seeds for future discord. The indebted clan may harbor deep resentment, perceiving the arrangement as coercive and unjust. On the other hand, the creditor clan views the land as rightful and proper compensation and lingering grievances are not heeded. Without genuine reconciliation or mutual agreement, the bitterness beneath the surface remains unresolved. This festering tension not only strains relations but also lays the groundwork for future disputes. It remains a point for re-agitation as the descendants of the original indebted clan may seek to reclaim the lost territory.

7 Geelka, the Camel

Elders, intellectuals and Somali society have held a consensus that it is pastoralism which offered a far more advantageous and economically viable mode of subsistence for the Somali people rather than the pursuits of fishing or agriculture. It is this prevailing view that explains why most Somalis embraced the herding of livestock as the primary vocation. The climatic conditions, as well as the unique ecological characteristics of the land, further nurtured this proclivity towards animal husbandry. With its mostly hot and dry conditions, minimal rainfall, and short rainy seasons, much of Greater Somalia did not easily lend itself to agricultural or fishing endeavours. It was livestock herding that offered a mobility that farming did not; while the farmer was tethered to his land, the herdsmen possessed the freedom to roam vast distances in search

123 Interview conducted with Boqor Abdullahi Geedi Shadoor.
124 Interview conducted with Professor Yahya Amir.
125 Interview conducted with Professor Yahya Amir.

of water and pasture, ensuring the continued survival of their animals even in the face of drought.

Among the animals reared by the Somali people, camels, cattle, sheep, goats, horses, and mules, there exists a hierarchy of value, with camels reigning supreme. Horses and mules, while important for transportation, do not provide the vital sustenance that camels, cattle, sheep, and goats offered in the form of milk and meat, upon which the livelihood of the herdsmen depends. Yet, it is the camel, with its unmatched utility, stamina, and ability to thrive in the harshest of environments, that stands as the most treasured and valuable of all livestock.

Prior to the introduction of a monetary economy, the barter system governed trade in Somali society, and the camel, as the most prized possession, served as the fundamental unit of exchange. The value of a single camel equaled that of five cattle or thirty sheep and goats, with only horses occasionally surpassing camels in worth due to their role in transportation.[126]

To the Somali man, the camel transcends mere utility, it embodies an irreplaceable symbol of wealth, endurance, and cultural pride. The camel is also the centerpiece of dowries, the source of blessings in Somali poetry, and a sign of divine favor. It is celebrated in the oral traditions passed down through generations, immortalised in proverbs and verses that extol its virtues.

For instance, Sayyid Maxamed Cabdulle Xasan asserts that a comparison between the donkey and the camel is inherently meaningless, as the two cannot be meaningfully equate:

> a donkey with two tiny vessels on it
> in the hot sun driven
> of this little load it thinks
> as though a mountain huge it carries the truth the donkey should be told
> equal it never could be to the powerful burden camel.[127]

He further categorises the relative values of livestock as:

> He who has goats has a garment full of corn:
> A milch cow is a temporary vanity;
> A he-camel is the muscle that sustains life:

126 Axmed Cali Abokor, *The Camel in Somali Oral Traditions*, (Nordic Africa Institute, 1987) 2.
127 Axmed Cali Abokor, *The Camel in Somali Oral Traditions*, (Nordic Africa Institute, 1987) 16.

> A she-camel, whoever may have her, is the mother of men.[128]

The 'garment full of corn' insinuates the possession of a goat is akin to the fleeting nature of grains. Certainly, the cultivation of corn relies on the unpredictable seasonal rains and so too is the transient cow. In contrast, the he-camel is depicted as the muscle that supports life, while the she-camel is revered as the mother of men, highlighting her position as paramount.

The camel is also there to assuage during the drought:

> ever-ready are camels for milking sessions
> even if from the heavens no rains come
> in seasons of plenty as in droughts severe
> their milk all and sundry satisfies[129]

The camel's emblematic value in wealth and social status has also rendered it not only a coveted asset, but also a catalyst for conflict. Conventionally, a man devoid of a considerable herd of camels wielded minimal influence or authority within the clan. This circumstance often incited individuals or smaller clans to embark on expeditions or raids against neighbouring clans with the intent of appropriating their camel stocks. This was treated as a serious crime and consequently, such endeavors frequently culminated in violent altercations between those raiding and those defending, leading to casualties and injuries on both fronts. This often escalated into protracted hostilities between the factions involved.

Camel raiding was valorised in Somali society and it was a virtuous pursuit. Although this tradition opposed the Sharia, the law Somalis professed to follow and the law which categorically forbade such actions, the cultural reality was embraced camel raiding was embraced as an honorable endeavour. It was celebrated, and the warriors who engaged in it were hailed as paragons of courage and heroism. There are songs sung which speak of the men who would steal camels, hobeey raggi geela dhicin jiray. Men of the same lineage would rally together, daring one another to demonstrate their martial prowess by capturing camels from rival clans. This practice bestowed honor upon the raiders, while failure to retaliate against such raids brought shame and public scorn, often memorialised in poetry. The clan that successfully executed a raid

---

128 Said S. Samatar, Oral Poetry and Somali Nationalism – The case of Sayyid Mahammad Abdille Hasan (Cambridge University Press, 1982) 12.

129 Axmed Cali Abokor, *The Camel in Somali Oral Traditions*, (Nordic Africa Institute, 1987) 6.

gained prestige and social elevation in contrast to the victimised lineage who faced ignominy unless they were to avenge the theft and reclaim their camels.

In one such poem on this matter, there is Faarax Laanjeer's poem '*Have I Seized Some Skinny Sheep and Goats?*' who was imprisoned for camel raiding. He composes that camel raiding is not as an act of theft but is a noble enterprise and that the one who targets camels, is viewed not as a transgressor but as a hero who reinforces his lineage's pride and prestige.[130]

He composes:

> Fierce war, anger, enmity, cunning and thieving
> The man who would deceive Xiis[131] will go beyond these ways
> The parties of allies in the past took their share from each other Xasan and Xuseen[132] knew the law [regarding camels]
> If Dheeho[133] is slaughtered out of spite and the crisis remains
> To keep them to yourself needs a killer and a group of brothers
> An old man who milks on his own cannot care for Xiito[134]
> Strength is needed in the place where the enclosures are put up
> That religious leader of the Dervishes[135] who settled in Xadeed and Xalin[136]
> Who used to bring them [camels] to the headquarters having saddled Xamar[137]
> He knew the Qur'aan by heart and had made the hajj a number of times
> For him right and wrong were both clearly separated
> If it [camel raiding] were forbidden he wouldn't have used horses
> How the account, the truth and the balance for the next world stand today
> Whether good is written or whether it will be bad
> This has been set on the loox maxfuud;[138] and the Judge [God] will tell

130 Rashiid Sheekh Cabdillaahi 'Gadhweyne', *War and Peace: An anthology of Somali literature Suugaanta Nabadda iyo Colaadda* (Progressio and Ponte Invisibile, 2009) 148–149.

131 The northern term for a milkable camel.

132 The grandchildren of the Prophet Muhamad (peace be upon him).

133 The northern term for a milkable camel.

134 The northern term for a milkable camel.

135 A reference to the Sayyid Maxamed Abdulle Xassan.

136 Two regions in Sanaag, north eastern Somalia.

137 A chestnut coloured horse.

138 The preserved tablet which connotes the divine record where the deeds of all creatures are recorded, and which will indicate the destination of the creature in the afterlife.

In this world the man who attacks for Xiito in a raid cannot be punished
as if it's unlawful
Since Adam and Eve, everyone has had a fever for
Watering, grazing, camel ghee and the fattened male camel
Oh Xiirey[139] the soul loves the valuable livestock
Even if I've been imprisoned are not camels still a part of being a man?
Are you all slandering me in Burco[140] as if I had raided some skinny goats?

Of the many songs used in the maintenance of camels, there is this song which is used in fetching water for the camel:

O black-statued camels
no fence is strong enough
to contain you secure
but the strength of my tribe
and men united in your defence[141]

And in another song:

unless relatives
and brothers loving
with spears sharp
camels defend not
quarrels on camels end
through concord temporary
they may somehow achieve[142]

As camels are considered the ultimate form of wealth, they are used as the primary currency in settling diya claims. As indicated above, the death of a single male warrants 100 camels and 50 for the very unusual death of a female. As poet Omal Xuseein Istelliye composes:

when relatives close quarrel and fight
in the fray men are murdered
elders wise and men of religion
as mediators are appointed

139 This poet's companion.

140 The township in Toogdheer where the poet was imprisoned.

141 Axmed Cali Abokor, *The Camel in Somali Oral Traditions*, (Nordic Africa Institute, 1987) 34.

142 Axmed Cali Abokor, *The Camel in Somali Oral Traditions*, (Nordic Africa Institute, 1987) 34.

heated debate conducting
where justice lies to find
they finally decision make
to the grieved party
camels selected in compensation pay
then from the camel pen are chosen
lactating she-camels graceful
those that but once calved
black-headed virgin ones pregnant camels beautious
along with Seeri and Luuli[143]
burden camel fat and strong
the best calves in the herd
when all this wealth in good faith
to the grieved party paid
men shake hands to promise
peace and harmony
among them to observe henceforth[144]

On this matter, professor Yaxya Camir elucidates that in certain cases where a man has been killed under circumstances deemed 'xeer kabax,' meaning a breach of customary law that brings dishonor, the act is considered both unlawful and dishonorable.[145] In such situations, the transgressor is obligated to pay double diya. This entails not only compensating for the man's death with the standard diya payment but also addressing the disgraceful nature of the killing. As a result, 200 camels are required. 100 for the life taken and 100 for the dishonor inflicted and for the restoration of honour, peace and in settling the dispute.[146]

8 Haweenka, Women

Naagla'aan waa nafla'aan – Without women is to be without a soul

Naag waa balaayo loo baahan yahaay – A woman is a needed disaster

143 Two names for female camels.
144 Axmed Cali Abokor, *The Camel in Somali Oral Traditions*, (Nordic Africa Institute, 1987) 39.
145 See explanation below on this category of xeer kabax.
146 Interview conducted with Professor Yahya Amir.

> Naag iyo xoolo was kii reerka uu horeeya – To have a woman and animals is the one who is first in the family

In traditional Somali society, women at times emerged as key figures in the onset of warfare. As the embodiment of lineage and clan prestige, conflicts often erupted over matters concerning women. Disputes surrounding clan alliances, and the protection of the women often ignited tensions that could escalate into violent confrontations. The protection of women especially was not merely a familial concern but a matter of collective honor for clans.

The interplay between honor, kinship, and gendered roles in Somali society has historically shaped the motives behind conflicts involving women. These wars were not solely about individuals but about collective identities, where the protection and control over women became a reflection of a clan's status, influence, and future continuity. There are several nuanced reasons men historically engaged in warfare over women.

When a woman was forcibly taken without her consent or that of her family, or where she was subjected to sexual violence, and even her mere mistreatment (especially where she has married into another clan, seperate from her own),[147] signified not only a personal affront to the affected woman, but also an existential threat to the clan's honor. Inflicting harm upon a woman was tantamount to a declaration of war, compelling the aggrieved clan to resort to violent reprisals. 'The response is extra-ordinary because they [women] are off the table.'[148]

The abduction, sexual violence, or murder of a woman constituted a grievous transgression against her personal autonomy and the honor of her clan, provoking a response marked by extraordinary violence.[149] When a woman was forcibly taken without her consent or that of her family, or subjected to sexual violence, even mere mistreatment, especially if she had married into another clan, this signified not only a personal affront to the affected woman but also an existential threat to the clan's honor. Inflicting harm upon a woman was tantamount to a declaration of war, compelling the aggrieved clan to resort

---

147 This is mistreatment might be in the form of physical abuse but also any violation, real or perceived, of a woman's dignity whether through insult, slander, or harassment was an existential threat to the clan's collective honor. Women, as bearers of familial prestige, could not be disgraced without igniting a fierce need for vengeance. In this context, honor was something to be violently defended, with the perpetrator's blood often demanded to expiate the offence.

148 Interview conducted with Haji Maroco.

149 Interview conducted with Haji Maroco.

to violent reprisals. 'The response is extraordinary because they [women] are off the table.'[150]

Even when a woman had married into a separate or unrelated clan, she was still defended fiercely. The relevant xeer mandated an aggressive response to restore honor or administer diya where required, rendering the defense of women and their honor a sacred and inviolable obligation. In these circumstances, warfare transcended the mere reclamation of an individual; it became a fervent endeavor to preserve the integrity of the clan and to venerate its women. Certainly, 'no person will sit idle with a degradation of honor,' and 'the one who kills a woman is shamed and asked are you a woman when you are killing a woman?'[151]

Elopement was another source of conflict where marriage was treated as strategically constructed alliances which bound clans. Remembering the individual responsibility of the collective of the clan, there was a web of obligations and expectations. When a couple absconded without familial approval, they disrupt the maintained socio-political order and the defiance was emblematic of transgression, often requiring retribution, igniting inter-clan violence as a means to reassert dominance and in order to recover the woman. The underlying impetus for this conflict lies in the primacy of clan prestige and there is an overshadowing of individual agency and autonomy.

There are also the consequences of the folkloric dances[152] like *shirib*,[153] *wiliqiso*,[154] *diisow*,[155] *dhaanto*, *saar*,[156] *jaandheer*, *gibliyo*, and *sacab botor*[157] which are more than just artistic performances, they are potent expressions of clan pride, personal valor, and social standing. These gatherings, though festive and celebratory, have often served as stages where intense rivalries are showcased and at times, fanned into conflict, particularly when performed before women whose presence heightens the stakes of competition.

150 Interview conducted with Haji Maroco.

151 Interview conducted with Haji Maroco.

152 See Somali Folk Dances, Ministry of Culture and Higher Education (Somali Democratic Republic, Mogadishu) 1977, available here, https://arcadia.sba.uniroma3.it/bitstream/2307/2949/1/Somali%20folk-dances.pdf.

153 Native to the central-southern regions.

154 Native to the central region, particularly Hiraan.

155 Native to the most southern region, now known as Jubaland.

156 Native to the western regions.

157 The Shirib is a southern folkloric dance, dhaanto, gibliyo and sacab botor being of the northern regions.

Shirib,[158] a popular tradition in the southern regions of Somalia, is a form of oral poetry that when performed, often transforms into competitive displays of wit, pride, bravado and verbal dexterity. Men, through their carefully crafted verses, would sing the praises of their clan's power, their own valor, and romantic endeavors, engaging in subtle or overt challenges to their rival participants. The presence of women lent an added dimension to these exchanges; their reactions, admiration, approval or laughter served as a powerful motivator, pushing men to outdo one another. When a man's performance fell short or was outdone by a rival, especially under the watchful eyes of women, it could become a matter of personal and clan honor. What began as a poetic duel could quickly spiral into simmering tension and, in more extreme cases, provoke physical conflict.

It may be appropriate to mention inter-clan activities under this heading where at particular events like at xusas,[159] bootin[160] or fardhaha[161] can quickly devolve into hostility. What begins as a celebration of skill and prowess may ultimately spiral into violence and warfare. The competitiveness is usually fueled by the flames of pride and honor and where there to be a death or injury, this is certainly a cause for conflict.

This category in some order also connects with the issues of interclan activities whereby colaadaha dhalinyarada beesha (where they are competing in interclan actitivites at *xusas, bootin, ama fardhaho lagu tartamayo*) goes sour and physical conflict erupts. The competitiveness could result in animosity and then in *laga aar goosto* (partaking in revenge) which could become war.

9 Hadal iyo Xumaan, Words and Wickedness

The Somali language is often one where verbal exchanges and social interactions transcend the conventional function of mere communication. It embodies a unique phonetic and linguistic essence that can only be fully appreciated by those who speak it and grasping its revered meanings and subtleties is an experience reserved for its speakers. In this context, words wield the power to incite discord, misunderstandings, and animosities, particularly when imbued with derogatory undertones or hostile connotations, especially where pride

158 Hankoolaale Channel, 'Shirib Hiddo iyo Dhaqan' (YouTube, 19 May 2023) 00:00:00–00:18:37 <https://www.youtube.com/watch?v=2UfQB3lY3t4>.

159 Remembrance or anniversary events.

160 Dancing events or traditional games.

161 Horse competitions.

and honor are at stake. The implications of language extend far beyond mere semantics; the spoken tongue must always regard the reputation of both the individual and the clan.

When wielded carelessly, the spoken word has the potential to sever ties that have taken generations to forge. This illustrates how language, while a fundamental means of connection, also catalyzes estrangement and strife. Thus, the power of language manifests paradoxically: it unites people (amaan),[162] and when employed irresponsibly, it can unravel social relations and peace. This theme can be aptly illustrated through the dichotomy of caay and gubaab, two linguistic phenomena that encapsulate the nuances of verbal expression within Somali culture.

Caay[163] is a particularly virulent form of derogatory discourse within Somali culture, characterised by its excessive and scathing invective. This form of invective transcends mere insult; it constitutes a profound affront to the individual and collective honor of clan members, and it is wielded as a weapon within Somali society. To speak ill of one's honor, pride, or lineage is perceived as a calculated assault. A deliberate attempt to demean and belittle, often reducing the targeted individual to a mere object of ridicule.

The implications of such insults are far-reaching and can penetrate any society. As these barbs of insult are exchanged, they do not merely dissipate into the air; rather, they fester and proliferate, laying the groundwork for entrenched animosities and protracted conflicts. This category of insult often necessitates mediation through the invocation of xaal (compensation) to resolve grievances. Here, the aggrieved party may demand acknowledgment of the insult, an apology,[164] and financial reparation, typically less than what is available through diya.

The use of caay operates as a double-edged sword; while it may offer immediate satisfaction to the speaker through the act of belittling a rival, it simultaneously engenders a cycle of vengeance that can spiral into open hostility. In this environment, the words spoken become not mere utterances but rather incendiary devices that ignite latent tensions and precipitate violence. This illustrates the potent power of language as a source of conflict.

Gubaab conversely occupies a space within the realm of poetry. It represents a slightly less egregious form of poetic expression, albeit one that retains

162 Praise.

163 Insult or vituperation that causes humiliation. It can either be true or unfounded, it nevertheless has the effect of shaming the individual, the clan or whomever the receiver of the insult is.

164 Interview conducted with Boqor Abdullahi Geedi Shadoor.

its potential for inciting conflict as the medium of expressions is more sophisticated. This genre serves as a vehicle for criticism, social commentary, and reflection on communal grievances. It often employs satire, irony, and lamentation, allowing the poet to articulate concerns regarding social dynamics, familial relations, and broader societal issues without resorting to the excessive disparagement that defines caay. Though less overtly offensive than caay, gubaab can nonetheless provoke strong reactions, particularly if it delves into sensitive topics or critiques behaviors within a clan or community. The poet's ability to interlace elaborate narratives and allusions invites listeners to engage with the themes presented and a narrative that fracture relationships is advanced. Derision is still a constant theme. It has the effect of burning one on the inside. In instances where gubaab is perceived as an affront to clan honor or personal integrity, it may trigger a defensive reaction similar to that elicited by caay. There is potential for gubaab to serve as a source of discord, as the offended party may feel compelled to retaliate to preserve their honor and that of their kin. Thus, while gubaab lacks the direct malice of caay, its capacity to ignite conflict should not be underestimated.

So far there has been one constant theme in the causes of conflict, honour and shame for which the former is rigorously sought after, and the latter thoroughly avoided. A unique category of combatants and (secondary)[165] source of conflict emerges from a tale told by Professor Yaxya Caamir and it may be appropriate to mention it here. There is the concept of the *arr ma galo* which is distinguished from the of *bir ma geydo* (those spared from the spear)[166] the *arr ma galo* are those deemed incapable of being avenged. Their existence embodies a paradox: they may fall victim to violence, yet their very status renders them elusive which complicates the themes of vengeance and war.

There is first the poignant proverb, *nin aan aarsan waa ibtilooba* meaning a man who does not avenge is indeed a man who suffers, or he is a tormented man. The proverb eloquently encapsulates the significance of the following story.

In the Ceeldheer region, a member of the Waceysle clan was implicated in the death of a Mursade clansman and so a fierce desire for retribution had certainly awakened.[167] Driven by the imperative of *aar raadis*,[168] a contingent of

165 Meaning it is not an institutional or regular source of conflict but certainly still a relevant one.

166 As eloquently put together by the ICRC.

167 Note the Mursade and the Waceysle territories border each other in the region now known as Galmudug.

168 The quest for revenge.

Mursade warriors ventured into Waceysle territory with blood on their minds. In their quest, they identified a Waceysle man as their target and so he was taken ahold of. Yet after careful deliberation, they deemed the man as *mid aan aar galin* (a man who is not capable of being avenged). After expressing *kan aar ma galyo* (a man not subject to revenge), they chose to spare him.

Upon returning to Ceeldheer, the spared man was met with a 'significant sense of mortification' and humiliation among his clan and particularly from his wife, who reproached him for his perceived inadequacy. Her scathing question, *nin aan aar galin, ma nin baa?*, 'is a man who cannot be avenged truly a man?' absolutely pierces his honor and it leaves him in a state of deep mortification. In a desperate bid to reclaim his lost dignity and grandeur, he seized his spear and charges into Mursade territory, killing two of their clansmen. He does so without hesitation.

He proclaims boldly, 'I have slain these men, now, let them kill me,' as he seeks to demonstrate his capacity for revenge, fiercely determined to restore his honor. When urged to flee and especially in the name of peace, he defiantly refused, declaring that if they did not kill him, he would continue his vendetta against the Mursade. 'I will not return to my clan,' he insists, 'so that they may not be allowed to believe I am incapable of being avenged. I shall seek retribution not only for the one who fell at my clan's hands but also for these two lives taken by my own hand.' In the end, he met his own death, as he forced the Mursade hand. Here the Waceysle man was considered a martyr in the pursuit of his honor.

This tale captures the reflective complexities surrounding the concepts of dignity, honour, shame and vengeance within traditional Somali society. A man who possesses dignity is, by cultural decree, a man capable of seeking retribution.

This theme of personal and collective honour, and pride continues. Traditionally, clans prioritise seeking diya as a means of conflict resolution, recognising the inherent benefits of settling grievances amicably. This is what reinforces kinship ties and provides mechanisms which avert the escalation of violence. By accepting diya, clans not only acknowledge the loss suffered but also facilitate reconciliation, thereby preventing further bloodshed. However, there are occasions when the thirst for retribution overshadows the reconciliatory pursuit of diya. This desire for vengeance may arise either on the behalf of a deceased or as a collective clan reaction to the death of a clan member. In such instances, the urge for personal or collective vengeance becomes a catalyst for ongoing conflict, perpetuating cycles of violence and animosity between clans.

Professor Caamir points to another tale from the Warsangeli clan in which there is a potential for conflict to ensue in this dynamic between diya and vengeance. The story unfolds with a man from the Warsengeli clan who, in a moment of familial intimacy, is having his head shaved by his children. This tranquility is violently disrupted when a member of a rival clan approaches him with murderous intent. In a brutal attack, the man suffers grievous injuries, and as he teeters on the brink of death, he beseeches his children to avenge him, instructing them to kill his assailant, preferably in the same humiliating manner, while he is engaged in shaving his own children.

Upon their father's death, the children are weighed down by the promise of retribution, but they remain resolute in their quest for vengeance, disregarding the traditional pathway of seeking diya or reconciliation. As tensions simmer among the two clans,[169] the unresolved animosity festers and the atmosphere is ever so volatile. The children become fixated on finding their father's murderer, who is acutely aware of his actions and as such, has maintained a low profile. He is cloaked in secrecy and fear. He lives in constant dread, avoiding daylight and only returning home under the cover of darkness. This prolonged absence deepens adverse relations with both clans, as the desire for vengeance intensifies and the yearning for closure becomes increasingly palpable.

The children ultimately track down their father's murderer. In a decisive moment, they confront him while he is vulnerable, perched upon a tree. They confront him and, in fulfillment of their father's dying wish, they sever his head and execute him, fulfilling their father's dying wish. In their act of retribution, they proclaim, 'ha leygy aaro iidhow, oo yanaan iilka aali waynin'. This declaration captures the depth of their anguish, the ciil (anger) that has consumed them in their quest for vengeance.

They then bring the severed head to their father's grave, seeking a sense of closure. Standing before the tomb, they pose a poignant question to their deceased father, qabriga aa la weydiinaya (the grave is being asked), 'ontoro, aar mu ku galaa, mase wali eeh aa qabtaa?', "is the revenge sufficient or shall we add another person to your revenge?"

Thus, the story illustrates how the choice between seeking diya and pursuing vengeance can lead to further conflict especially at the times of acute tensions between the clans.

169 Both clans know there is a death waiting to be reconciled.

10 Kas iyo Kama, Premeditation and Unintentional Wrongful Murder

There is also the category of premeditated and unintentional murder, Kas iyo Kama in which conflict may ensue from. Each is steeped in its own moral gravity and each demanding a separately crafted remedy. These principles honor the weight of intention and proportionality as there is a delineation between deliberate affronts and inadvertent harm, with both paths shaping justice and the restoration of honor. Even when wrongful conduct disrupts relations, the first instinct is to return to the framework of *xeer* to repair the breach and restore harmony.

Kas are the deliberate transgressions (*ula kac*) which are usually described as premeditated and conscious murder. The calculated breach is treated as a violation of trust so deep that it not only causes damage to the individual, but it reverberates across the clan. As this category of transgressions are not a simple a personal affront, it's seen as a moral and social stain, a grievous lapse of *imaan* (faith) and *sharaf* (honor).[170] For such an offence, retribution is certainly required, and the response is relentless and there is no 'asxaan' (mercy) offered. After the payment of diya, the offender's assets, be they livestock, wealth, or land are systematically claimed to begin the process of reparation. Usually, this material compensation alone is insufficient as the severity of *Kas* requires that the offender himself, along with his clan, bear the weight of his transgression until the injured party is fully appeased. In particularly grave instances, the offender may be required to offer a woman from his family to the aggrieved clan. This gesture serves as an act of *ceeb reeb* (dishonor expiation), an attempt to erase the shame and restore relations to a state of mutual respect and peace. The woman offered becomes a *hijab*, a shield and a symbol of reconciliation between the clans. Through this union, the clans are bound as *xidhid*, family and kin, and a relationship of trust is forged and it is one that precludes future hostility.[171] This act establishes an enduring peace, transforming what was once a raw wound into a *nabar*, a healed scar. The animosity dissipates, *fitna* (discord) is extinguished, and there is no *deb daxdhood*, no lingering fire of animosity between the clans.[172] The ties formed through this

170 Odeyaal 135; Interview conducted with Haji Maroco; Interview conducted with Boqor Abdullahi Geedi Shadoor; Interview conducted with Imaam Daahir.

171 Odeyaal 135.

172 Odeyaal 135.

kinship prevent any future aggression as neither side would permit their own kin to rise in conflict against their mother's lineage.[173]

This is also considered a 'universally shared xeer … one [that] is static and does not change.'[174]

Conversely, *Kama* is positioned on the opposite end of the moral spectrum, and it acknowledges that some harms are committed without malice or forethought.[175] Unlike *Kas*, *Kama* occurs without intent or premeditation. This form of wrongful conduct emerges from misfortune or error, and it lacks the deliberate malice of *Kas* and as such commands a distinct approach under xeer.[176] Where *Kas* incites a call for comprehensive reparation, *Kama* is met with tempered justice, acknowledging the unintentional nature of the offence while still upholding accountability. It is viewed as less morally reprehensible and as it still disrupts the social order and still requires redress, the response it invokes within xeer is mitigated by compassion and proportionality. Remedies for *Kama* focus on balance rather than severe retribution. Restitution is offered (usually just the payment of the diya and acknowledgement of the harm caused), but the measures are less exacting, often limited to compensatory payments rather than overburdening the offender or his clan with any extensive retribution.

11 Jihaad

The concept of jihaad (a religiously sanctioned *struggle*) as a justification for warfare among Somalis totally emerges from the collective religious conscience Somalis possessed. It is an intersection between faith and the forms of martial engagement. The notion of jihaad for the Somali transcends typical clan skirmishes, instead invoking a sacred cause whereby warfare becomes a mode of fulfilling divine ordinance. A collective effort driven by the shared sense of identity, loyalty, and religious duty. *Jihasd fi sabeelillah* (Jihaad in the path of Allah) is the revered pursuit and sanctified struggle, where the purpose of combat no longer concerns personal or tribal grievances but instead in

173 Odeyaal 135.

174 Odeyaal 135.

175 Odeyaal 135; Interview conducted with Haji Maroco; Interview conducted with Boqor Abdullahi Geedi Shadoor; Interview conducted with Imaam Daahir.

176 Odeyaal 135; Interview conducted with Haji Maroco; Interview conducted with Boqor Abdullahi Geedi Shadoor; Interview conducted with Imaam Daahir.

defending and expanding the reach of Islam, fulfilling what is considered an immutable divine duty.

Sheikh Mohamed Da'uud articulates this motivation with remarkable clarity, '... absolutely, they will encourage their clan members to fight in the way of God. They will concoct certain warfare methods and campaigns that differ from how war is pursued against other Somalis and intra-clan warfare. Yesterday I was fighting a brother of mine, today I am fighting an enemy that fails to see any good in me, does not have any regard for me, and seeks to subdue me.' His declaration describes a heightened consciousness in which the stakes involved in jihaad far surpass those of internal conflicts. It emerges as an existential crusade wherein the enemy is not merely an opponent but rather an entity whose disbelief demands rectification through martial engagement.

The readiness for jihad is underpinned by the swift collective organisation and the communal commitment. As Sheikh Mohamed Da'uud continues to describe, 'tribes in orders of their relations will unite against external aggressors. They will meet at shir,[177] and decisions will be handed down that require specific contributions of men from Harti Abgaal, Waceysle, Wacbuudan, etc. It is a fight they will be ready for night and day.' This readiness is framed as a perpetual state, embodying both the fervor of immediate action and a broader, long-standing dedication to collective defense. The ulema (religious scholars) play a vital role in these preparations, reminding the men of the divine rewards of such a fight and the divine reward for emulating the Prophet Muhammad (PBUH), his caliphs, and the sahaba (companions) in the precision of their methods.

Similarly, Imaam Daahir, the current Abgaal clan head, confirms this unyielding commitment to divine warfare. He explains that jihaad for the Somali is always attempted 'as per the sharia [and that] we are driven and will always be ready to kill and to be killed in the path of Allah (SWT). The leadership with jihad usually comes about when a person seeks followers after witnessing a cause ... when the people believe [someone] is capable of leading the *jihad*, self-elected or elected.' This structure of leadership and consent indicates that *jihad* is not simply a chaotic rush into battle, but a calculated endeavour led by those deemed spiritually equipped to guide the clans in religiously sanctioned warfare.

The characteristics of jihad have also historically varied as it is contingent on the perceived nature of the adversary. Sheikh Wajis emphasises the nuanced nature of jihaad. 'Any single war is never the same as any other

177 Meetings, traditionally under the tree.

war … the circumstances are never the same and so the manner in which it is fought or responded to can never be the same.' His assertion highlights that jihad embodies a flexible approach to international warfare, with its structure, motives, and conduct tailored to the specific context of each conflict, especially when imbued with the solemn mandate of *fi sabeelillah*. Sheikh Wajis also contrasts the distinctly merciless nature of external wars against non-Muslims, especially with Ethiopians. He explains 'some wars are intentionally fought in a *cunsiri* (racist) and *xasuuqi* (genocidal) manner. This is particularly true of conflicts with the Ethiopians … they consistently attempted to enforce their faith on the Somali, a war of ideology (dagaal caqiidadodhi ku saabsan), devoid of any acts of *badhbaadis* (forgiveness or mercy).' This depiction illuminates how *jihad* differs when the adversary is seen as an existential threat to Islamic-Somali identity, intensifying the Somali combatants' resolve. This is where deviations from typical norms of restraint and mercy in warfare were justified and this is explained further below.

To example this category, there is Imam Axmed Gurey's response to the Incursion of Degalhan, then emperor Dawit II's military general as in the *Futuh Al-Habsehsa*. The Futuh Al-Habasha (The Conquest of Abyssinia) recounts the military campaigns of Imam Ahmad ibn Ibrahim al-Ghazi (known as Axmed Gurey in Somali) during the 16th century in the eastern most region of the Horn or Greater Somalia (encompassing regions from current day Ethiopia, Kenya and Djibouti). The Imam's campaigns are recorded as a struggle to expand Islamic rule and defend the Muslim Somali stronghold against encroachment by non-Muslim forces, particularly the Christian Ethiopian Empire. Many of his campaigns were imbued with religious purpose and fervour, which shaped the actions and motivations of the Imam and his followers.

Among the events recorded, is the response to the Incursion by Degalhan, a rival Ethiopian force that posed a challenge to Imam Axmed's campaign.

Yemeni[178] chronicler Shihab al-Dīn Aḥmad ibn 'Abd al-Qādir ibn Sālim ibn 'Uthmān writes,

> 'While he was preoccupied with this discussion on behalf of the Somalis, the imam heard about an important patrician, one of the tyrants by name Degalhan, a brother-in-law' of the [Abyssinian] king, with a vast number of patricians under him, who had readied the furthermost borders of the country of the Muslims, had plundered it, and taken by force their wealth, and made improper advances towards female members of

178 Some accounts describe him as a Harari. See Enrico Cerulli, *Islam Yesterday and Today*, Emran M. Waber ed (2013), 134.

their own families, amongst whom was the mother of one of the emirs of the imam, by name Abu Bakr Qatin. The infidels had more than six-hundred cavalry, while their army was like a plague of locusts. The imam made preparations for meeting them, arranging his army, its provisions and its number. The number of the Muslim horses and horsemen was two-hundred. They launched the attack, setting out at the time of the sunset prayer. They marched night and day until they readied a mighty river called Aqam at sunset on the second day where they encamped. The imam sent a band of the Muslims ahead, to try to ferret out some news of the infidels, but not one of them returned with news. So, after this he sent one of his emirs, by name Husain al-Gaturi, as his informant, with seven cavalrymen. These reached the proximity of the infidel army which was an immense force, and then doubled back, returning to the imam Ahmad, notifying him of their findings.

The imam and his army set out for the neighbourhood of the infidels, and arrived at a point where the only barrier between them and the infidels was a fortified mountain. They encamped there, and he climbed the mountain barrier separating the two armies, along with four of his knights ...

They overlooked the infidels who had made their camp in a place called Dir. Its lights were blazing. The imam and his companions then retraced their steps, returning to their army and settling down for the night, after they had made preparations for the battle.

The day after this, the infidels set out for their own country with the imam and his army on their heels. These had harnessed their horses and mounted them, after donning their armour and taking their weapons just as the poet says:

'How beautiful before the breaking of dawn is the voice of the herald "Come on the jihad to the races of men of noble rank who give their lives so highmindedly in order to please the magnanimous One.

On horseback, they arc like lions;

Dismounted they are the tent-pegs of the country.

While they were proceeding in this manner after them, some of the infidels turned around and saw the Muslims in their rear. They notified their companions, and all of them wheeled round and saw the Muslims behind them. Then they turned around, went back and drew up their battle lines, fixing the position of their forces – may the Most High God forsake them.

The imam likewise arrayed his forces – to the right, to the left, to the centre and with some on both flanks – and the advance proceeded.

The Muslims drew near, as compact as a construction whose pans were held together in such a way that there was no space between them; and the cavalry charged. The first of the Muslim knights to do so was one called Farasaham Sultan … of the tribe of Yamli. He was one of the most courageous heroes. After exclaiming 'God is Great' he attacked the infidels, breaking through their lines, scattering their massed forces and killing a group of them. He took prisoner one of the patricians … he grabbed him, pulled him from his saddle, and took him into the presence of the imam Ahmad who sent him to Arabia.

The emir … also attacked the infidels, killing many of them, and capturing [another] one of the patricians whom he presented to the imam. The Muslims appeared in battle like savage lions, galloping full tilt, with spears held high, army merging with army. The wretched infidels stood their ground before the attack of the noble Muslims as the tide of the battle rolled on relentlessly, with horses interlocked with horses, and infantry with infantry.

On that day, nothing was to be seen but cut-off heads, spirits in the throes of death, and palms of hands flying in the air. The Muslims cried out with a mighty cry: 'There is no God but Allah and 'God is the Greatest,' and prayed for the bringer of good news, and the herald; and all the tribes responded, and the earth trembled under them.'

On that day the battle-cry of the Muslims was 'Yahu. Yahu', and dismay fell upon the hearts of the infidels who began to desert. The imam showed himself to be a man steady of heart. No cavalryman came near him without being tossed to the ground; and he lunged with his spear at no one whom he did not slaughter. The infidels were as powerless before the Muslims as a Hock of sheep or goats before a lion.

How many thousands of infidels died only the Most High God can number. The Muslims took possession of horses, valuables and booty, and on that day, they took four-hundred-and-eighty-four prisoners, and livestock and mules too numerous to count. They also recaptured from the infidels the wealth that these had previously plundered from the Muslims. They returned the wealth of the Muslims, in its entirety, to its owners. Not one of the Muslims died; only a fewer suffered light wounds, from which they recovered.

The imam thereupon summoned the prisoners, who were brought into his presence. Some of them he sent to Zabid to the emir Suleiman the governor there. They were enslaved to the emir of Zabid. Some others of them he had killed. Others of them simply died.

How excellent are these Muslims and their imam! They waged the holy war for God whose due it was. They were patient and resolute in confronting the enemy. They made the sacrifice of their jihad in order to please God. They did not hold back until they had torn Faithlessness from its throne and plunged it into its grave. Islam was raised up, and manifested; and Faithlessness was humiliated, and forced to take flight.

Nor did they do any wrong, for the Most High God has said of the Muslims waging jihad in a passage of his well-known book: 'Do not consider those who are killed for the sake of God to be dead. Rather they live, and are provided sustenance by their Lord, rejoicing.' Know that God shows you mercy, that the martyr goes to his Gracious Lord and lives in a place whose dwellers never know death: and whose young never grow old. As He who is the most credible of speakers says, 'Hardship shall not afflict them [in heaven] nor can they ever be driven out from it.

The storyteller says: The imam Ahmad and his army went back, carrying with them vast booty', with the Most High God as his guide and companion on his journey towards his country of Harar: his status enhanced, triumphant, wearing the victor's crown, joyous. The imam at that time was twenty-one years old.'[179]

12 Hababka Dagaalka, Methods of Warfare

12.1 *Organisation*

In traditional Somali society, warfare between clans was a structured and purposeful activity, with each type of operation carrying its own designation and objectives. The nature of these war operations varied based on the desired outcomes, each with a particular purpose and tactical approach. The methods can first be understood in the context of external or international conflicts in which the Somalis united and internally in relation to inter-clan conflicts.

12.2 *Unification against External Threats*

In times of existential threat from foreign, non-Somali aggressors, the Somali clans, otherwise segmented by kinship affiliations and territorial disputes, would marshal a grand assembly of warriors. In these moments, inter-clan

179 Sihab ad-Din Ahmad bin Abd Al-Qader bin Salem bin Uthman, Futuh Al-Habasha: The Conquest of Abyssinia, tr Paul Lester Stenhouse and Richard Pankhurst (Tsehai Press, 2003) 22–25.

rivalries would be eclipsed by the necessity of defending Somali sovereignty. These armies transcended the boundaries of individual clans, combining the forces of numerous lineages under a singular purpose of safeguarding collective interests. Leaders of these alliances were figures of formidable reputation, like the caliber of the famed Imam Axmed Gurey. They embodied tactical genius but also an aura of providence believed to bring fortuitous outcomes. The force was organised meticulously, with each clan's fighters arranged to ensure cohesive action and unwavering commitment to the unified defense. This often-rare convergence was a symbol of fortification against external encroachments, allowing for the projection of might and for the protection of Somalinimo and land.

When an external aggressor was identified, or when a call for jihad came about the clan, a formidable assembly would take shape, extending beyond the standard ranks of warriors. While the primary military forces, trained and organised within each clan, comprised the main fighting strength, a second, auxiliary group often materialised alongside them *caawiyaal* (helpers or those shadowing pursuit).[180] This auxiliary group were particularly activated in cases involving non-Muslim adversaries.

These auxiliary fighters were typically men who did not ordinarily serve in the established military formations but were instead motivated by the spiritual and moral imperatives of jihad. They felt compelled to contribute to the conflict. Carrying their intense devotion, they rallied with a personal mission, to attain *shaheed* (martyrdom) or, in some cases, a share of the spoils, as prescribed under the rules of engagement.[181] Their contributions could take varied forms, some offered their strength in battle, reinforcing the primary forces, while others provided logistical support, supplies, or tactical assistance, each role instrumental to the overarching campaign.[182]

The *caawiyaal* (helpers or those shadowing pursuit), these men were bound by a collective drive that went beyond mere allegiance to clan and extended to a profound commitment to their faith.[183] Following the main force closely in their pursuit (*daba kacis*), they often displayed unparalleled zeal, a fervor driven by the hope of divine reward.[184]

180 Interview conducted with Sheikh Mohamed Dau'ud.
181 Interview conducted with Sheikh Mohamed Dau'ud.
182 Interview conducted with Sheikh Mohamed Dau'ud.
183 Interview conducted with Sheikh Mohamed Dau'ud.
184 Interview conducted with Sheikh Mohamed Dau'ud.

12.3 *Inter-clan Warfare and Raiding Traditions*

In contrast to the external unity against foreign threats, inter-clan warfare in Somalia was typically a matter of smaller, localised conflicts, often in the form of raids, or *duullaan*, conducted between clans or sub-clans with close or not so close historical, familial, or territorial ties.[185] Unlike the unified armies assembled for defending the Somali nation, these raids were generally limited in scope and targeted specific grievances or resources. Such internal conflicts were governed by traditional laws, or *xeer*, that aimed to contain the violence, prevent unnecessary bloodshed, and ensure a structured path to resolution. Inter-clan *duullaan* had specific objectives, each carefully considered within the objective for engaging in the raid.

12.4 *Objectives of the* Duullaan

The *duullaan*, or organised raid, held varied objectives within the structure of Somali clan society, each reflecting a particular motive built on the clan's honor, survival, or legacy and is easily understood within the dhiig-doon, dhaqan-dhoon and maal-doon categorisations.

12.5 *Diig-doon (Blood Vengeance)*

Diig-doon, or blood vengeance, was the path taken when a clan sought to avenge the death of one or more of its members, driven by the need to balance the scales after the loss of a clan member. Such an act was seen as an obligation of honor which restores dignity to the deceased and upholds the clan's reputation by not allowing the loss to go unchallenged. This retributive action served as a deterrent to future transgressions, signaling that any violent loss of life would be met with a deliberate and measured response. The act was not viewed as individual revenge but as a communal duty, where each member participates or supports the action as an extension of their role within the larger clan family. Diig-doon, therefore, reflects the clan's unity and the non-negotiable bond members share in maintaining both honor and justice.

The nature, style, and extent of a raid are carefully calibrated, depending on the depth of the grievance and the specific type of retribution sought. When a clan mobilises under the Diig-doon banner, they do so with an understanding that each raid must be proportionate to the offense, signaling both the seriousness of the transgression and the clan's unified resolve to restore their standing. The nature of the raid under Diig-doon particularly varies with the transgression. For example, if a high-ranking or respected clan member was

185 Interview conducted with Sheikh Mohamed Dau'ud.

killed, the retaliation often aims to make an equally significant impact on the offending party, targeting individuals of comparable social standing or symbolic importance within the adversary clan.

The style of the raid is equally determined by the offense's circumstances. If the killing was perceived as particularly dishonorable, the raid may carry with it an added intensity, exhibiting a more aggressive or unrestrained approach. Alternatively, if the death occurred in a more neutral confrontation, the raid might be conducted with greater restraint, signaling that the retribution sought is confined to a specific act of justice, rather than open-ended hostility.

12.6 *Dhaqan-doon* (*Pursuit of Tradition*)

The second common raiding method is in the dhaqan-doon category where the raid is conducted in the pursuit of tradition. Dhaqan-doon can be understood as a term that carries two meanings. The raid serves as a justification for the proper administration of traditional settlements, and it can be understood as the general cultural inclination toward traditional conflict resolution.[186]

In its role as a justification for the proper administration of traditional settlements, Dhaqan-doon is invoked when traditional agreements such as diya (blood compensation) or heshiis (peace treaties) have been breached or dishonored. When one party fails to respect or fulfill these collective judgments, the aggrieved clan is compelled to respond, often through a raid, to assert their own commitment to customary law and in order to demonstrate the clan's intolerance towards the disrespect of established laws. This use of Dhaqan-doon as a reason for duullaan underscores the concept of clan solidarity, where the offense against one individual or family member resonates across the entire clan, obligating them to seek rectification on behalf of the aggrieved.

This approach resonates strongly with Islamic principles, particularly those articulated in Surah Al-Hujurat (49:9), which calls on believers to seek peace and act with justice:[187]

---

186 The term *dhaqan-doon* reflects a broader cultural preference for traditional conflict resolution methods, even in the midst of conflict, as a way to ensure long-term peace and community stability. Rather than allowing violence to escalate, elders and clan leaders typically prioritise customary reconciliation as the first course of action. By facilitating discussions, initiating compensatory agreements, or formalising treaties, they aim to address grievances in a manner that respects the customary law while minimising bloodshed. When the conditions for such settlements are met and both parties agree to abide by the terms, conflicts are often resolved more sustainably, and inter-clan relations are restored. However, if traditional justice mechanisms are ignored or deliberately undermined by one side, it becomes the collective duty of the clan to uphold the integrity of these agreements, often through *duullaan*.

187 Interview conducted with Haji Maroco.

> And if two factions among the believers should fight, then make settlement between the two. But if one of them oppresses the other, then fight against the one that oppresses until it returns to the ordinance of Allah. And if it returns, then make settlement between them in justice and act justly. Indeed, Allah loves those who act justly.

The invocation of *Surah Al-Hujurat* (49:9) to some extent, can be read as reinforcing the legitimacy of a *duullaan* (raid) as a corrective action when an adverse clan refuses both Islamic and customary obligations. Here, the *duullaan* is seen not merely as a display of force but as a morally bound response to uphold justice and enforce accountability. The verse advocates for reconciliation among believers, urging the intervention of a just settlement when factions clash. However, it also commands the community to confront and correct any faction that persists in oppression, aligning with the Somali principle of *dhaqan-doon*, where traditional justice and reparations must be honored.

In this context, if a clan's traditional rulings or *diya* compensation has been ignored, then collective action becomes not only a customary duty but also an extension of Islamic justice. The verse's call to 'fight against the one that oppresses until it returns to the ordinance of Allah' parallels the cultural mandate for clans to seek enforcement when peaceful measures fail. Thus, the *duullaan* serves as both a culturally and religiously validated action, undertaken with the goal of re-establishing balance, ensuring compliance, and ultimately restoring peace.

12.7 *Maal-doon* (*Wealth Seeking*)

> *Nin xoolihiisi la qaaday 'ayaan daranoow' mooyee 'orod daranow' lama yidhaa*

Maal-doon further reflects this theme of collective obligation through the (customary) lawful recovery of lost or stolen property.[188] In a society where resources like livestock are essential to survival, maal-doon serves as a recognised and respected method for a clan to protect its economic wellbeing. This type of raid involves the participation of clan members who will seek to reclaim shared assets, and this reinforces the notion that the clan's property is collectively owned and collectively defended.

Sheikh Mohamed Dau'ud explains *maal-doon* as the Somali practice of reclaiming stolen or lost property, emphasising that it is at times, a collective

188 Interview conducted with Sheikh Mohamed Dau'ud.

responsibility of the clan. He notes that when a clan's wealth, often livestock has been stolen, it is the collective responsibility of the entire clan to ensure that it is reclaimed.[189] This practice is established on the belief that property is not solely an individual asset but a representation of the entire clan's well-being and survival.

The practice of *maal-doon* is also reflected through the actions of the early Muslims during the time of the Prophet Muhammad (PBUH), particularly in relation to the caravans of the Quraysh returning from Syria. Just before the Battle of Badr, the Prophet (saw) instructed the companions to raid and intercept the caravans returning in order to recover lost property.

The Quraysh, who had long been enemies of the Muslims in Mecca, had seized the properties and wealth of the early Muslims, many of whom had been forced to flee Mecca due to persecution. As the Muslims settled in Medina, their livelihood was certainly dependent on their collective efforts, and any loss of property or wealth especially through the unjust actions of the Quraysh was seen as a communal loss. The caravan raid was not an arbitrary act of aggression, but a necessary response to the economic and material injustices inflicted upon the Muslims

Just as the Prophet Muhammad (PBUH) and the Sahaba sought to retrieve what was rightfully theirs, Somali clans engage in *maal-doon* to restore lost property.

Conversely, *maal-doon* can also be in the form of a more individual or smaller raid and so the dynamics of such a raid will at times differ from the larger, more collective efforts seen in *diig-doon* (blood vengeance) or *dhaqan-doon* (seeking traditional justice). Unlike the larger, often more formalised campaigns of *diig-doon* and *dhaqan-doon*, *maal-doon* raids are more individualistic or operate on a smaller scale. They reflect a more direct pursuit of material wealth, typically livestock such as camels or cattle which are central to the Somali pastoral economy. These raids are not always driven by the need for collective justice or societal retribution but by the immediate need to recover property that is either lost or wrongfully taken.

While *diig-doon* and *dhaqan-doon* generally involve broader clan-level actions, often backed by larger forces due to their high stakes (avenging a clan member's death or enforcing customary law), *maal-doon* can, at times, take the form of a more limited and personal pursuit. In this regard, the raid might involve fewer warriors, potentially even just a handful of men, typically those with a direct stake in the reclamation, such as the rightful owner of the stolen

189 Interview conducted with Sheikh Mohamed Dau'ud.

property and a few other clan members. This smaller scale allows for more rapid and targeted action, driven by a focused objective to retrieve specific assets, rather than the broader goals of vengeance or legal enforcement.

The *maal-doon* raid also operates under different tactical principles compared to the larger raids. The targeting is often more stealthy, tactical, and swift as the involved warriors typically rely on their intimate knowledge of the terrain and the locations where stolen or lost goods are believed to be. The raid is thus less about prolonged conflict and more about strategically reclaiming what was taken or lost.

12.8 *Duullaan Jihaad ka tiirsan* (*A Jihaadist Raid*)

> *Bisin Alle nin bilaabay balaayo uma timaado – A man who begins with the invocation of God is not struck by calamity*

The duullaan also serves as both a tactical method and a strategic component within jihad campaigns. It is characterised by mobility, calculated surprise, and disciplined execution, often targeting key resources or undermining enemy morale. The duullaan represents a synthesis of military pragmatism and religious conviction, where preparation, execution, and the invocation of divine assistance coalesce into a mechanism for achieving strategic objectives.

A vivid example of this is recounted in the Futuh al-Habasha during the campaign led by Abu Bakr Qatin, under the command of Imam Ahmad ibn Ibrahim al-Ghazi.

In the passage titled 'Takla Haymanot is Oblivious of the Danger', the Imaam asks his cousins Abubakr and Zaharbou to capture leading Amhara General Takla Haymanot and it followed that,

> "Abu Bakr Qatin, meanwhile, marched by night, with the two guides with their hands tied leading them: he had appointed some men to stop them fleeing. They marched all that night, climbing down valleys and up mountains. When the moment came for dawn to break, the two guides stopped. He said to them, 'What are you looking at?' They answered. "We can see his camp, and we can see his fires."
>
> The emir Abu Bakr and his companions halted, and discussed what they should do. Some of them said, 'Let us attack them immediately, and catch them unawares.' But the emir Abu Bakr replied, 'As for me, I promised the imam to bring the patrician Takla Haymanot back as a prisoner. But if we pounce on him at this time, I am afraid that he will slip through our fingers, so rather let us be patient until morning and then we will

> attack him.' To which they replied, 'All right; you are our emir; do what seems best to you'. So they dismounted from their mules and waited. The emir Abu Bakr Qatin said, 'Recite the Surah* Yasin and call upon the Most High God in prayer.'
>
> Meanwhile, Takla Haymanot knew nothing of them. He had been drinking wine throughout the evening, and as night ended he went out of his dwelling, because he had spent most of it in conversation as a result of the wine. He saw lights on the road where the imam was, for they had set fire to houses along their route. When he noticed this, Takla Haymanot asked his soldiers who were with him, 'What do you think about this fire that I can see?' They answered, 'That is nothing but the fire of people robbing hives; or perhaps some of the robbers have set fire to houses.
>
> Takla Haymanot retorted, 'As for me. I say that all the signs point to its being the fire of a raiding party; in any case, harness your horses until morning comes. And if it turns out to be a raiding party, then we will go against it, and fight.' Even though he had no information concerning the emir Abu Bakr and the fact that he was close by him, they harnessed their horses and stationed themselves in front of his house, and then returned to their wine-bibbing until morning broke.
>
> The emir Abu Bakr then said to his two guides, 'One of you two will be set free, to accompany three of our foot-soldiers to see what Takla Haymanot is doing, whether he is lying down asleep, or sitting down with company; and then to return to us with the news. Your companion will remain with us, bound, and if you betray us we will kill him. And may God give us the victory.
>
> The guide set out with the three foot-soldiers, and by stealth arrived at the dwelling of Takla Haymanot. They saw the harnessed horses in the middle of the courtyard of the house. The guide, along with his companions, returned to the emir Abu Bakr and informed him of this. The Muslims then recited the Fatiha and prayed for victory.
>
> When day had dawned the emir Abu Bakr mounted his horse which was named Mubarak, put on his armour, and took his spear; and the thirty knights who were famous for their courage mounted their horses. They drew up their horses close to one another, and rode shoulder to shoulder as if they were a single, well-compacted building. As they drew near, they pointed their spears heavenwards, and slackened their horses reins, as the crier called out for the attack.

This account demonstrates the duullaan's reliance on careful reconnaissance, disciplined timing, and the invocation of divine aid. The spiritual dimensions, such as the recitation of Surah Yasin and Fatiha, and prayers for victory, infused the operation with a sense of higher purpose, blend tactical efficacy with the overarching jihad spirit.

12.9 *Abaabulka ama Qaab Dhismeedka Duulaanka, Organisation or Structure of the Duullaan*

The duullaan, or offensive raid, was a carefully planned and structured operation carried out by an organised force with the aim of launching an attack against another group. The endeavour required thorough preparation and strict adherence to traditional codes of conduct to ensure its success and for the preservation of the honour of those involved.

The process began with the selection of a leader, whose bravery, tactical expertise, and ability to command respect were of paramount importance. This individual's reputation was built on a history of victories and an unblemished record of honourable conduct.[190] His actions during the raid were bound by the dignity of his lineage, with any act of cowardice, such as abandoning the wounded or behaving disgracefully, resulted in profound dishonour for both himself and his family. This was also avoid any disrepute which would be considered *xeer kabax* (outside of acceptable conduct).

The assembly of a duullaan typically drew fighters from a single clan or several closely allied lineages, who shared common interests and lived in close proximity. Organising the force began with dividing men into units by clan or sub-clan, ensuring that no unit would forsake its wounded given they share lineage ties. Each clan was also led by their own appointed military leader. This is exampled in a passage in Futuh Al-Habesha where the storyteller explains in preparation and under the command of the Imaam Axmed Gurey,

> he assembled the Somali tribes: the tribe of Girri, the tribe of Marraihan, the tribe of Yibbri with the chieftain Ahmad Girri, the tribe of the Harti, people of Mait, the tribe of Jaran, the tribe of Mazzar. the tribe of Barsub: all of these were Somalis and they were ordered by the imam to hold the left. *Each tribe had its own emir.*[191]

190 The famed Ahmed Gurey is a prime example of this.

191 Sihab ad-Din Ahmad bin Abd Al-Qader bin Salem bin Uthman, Futuh Al-Habasa: The Conquest of Abyssinia, tr Paul Lester Stenhouse and Richard Pankhurst (Tsehai Press, 2003) 58. Importantly, this Emir or military commander is not the natural clan leader as they do not generally engage in battle. The military commander is responsible for organising and leading warriors in battle and the clan leader avoids direct involvement in battle to remain protected and ensure the clan's stability. See Imaam Daahir.

As the forces prepared to advance, the commander designated roles and the appointed poet was platformed to encourage and incite the warriors with stirring verses that celebrated bravery, honour, and the legacy of their ancestors. Through his poetry, he inspired unity, stoked courage, and reinforced the moral justification for the conflict, framing it as a defence of the clan's dignity and values.

Each unit was assigned a route, and a rendezvous point near the enemy's location. Upon nearing the target, scouts were dispatched to assess enemy movements, locate their resources, and confirm whether they were prepared for an offensive.

With this intelligence, final preparations commenced, animals were slaughtered for sustenance,[192] horses were watered,[193] and the warriors equipped themselves for the impending attack. The commander then convened with his lieutenants to finalise the strategy and addressed his men, instilling in them the focus and resolve needed for the mission. It was also very common to offer a prayer to Allah swt.[194] Before battle, a prayer was offered as a solemn invocation seeking divine guidance, protection, and success. This ritual often involved calling upon Allah to strengthen the warriors, purify their intentions, and grant them victory if their cause was just. The prayer served as a plea for divine support and here, in these moments, the role of the *ulema* (Islamic scholars) was particularly significant. They were called upon to address and inspire the warriors, grounding their efforts in religious purpose and elevating the struggle to one of faith and duty. The *ulema* would deliver powerful words, reminding the fighters of their higher calling as defenders of justice and faith. This reinforced the idea that their efforts were ultimately in service of Allah and in the administration of the rights and duties as decreed by Allah. They invoked verses from the Qur'an and sayings (ahdith) of the Prophet (peace be upon him). This platforming of the *ulema* also instilled a sense of accountability to their Creator.

---

192 Spared from the spear.

193 See Sihab ad-Din Ahmad bin Abd Al-Qader bin Salem bin Uthman, Futuh Al-Habasa: The Conquest of Abyssinia, tr Paul Lester Stenhouse and Richard Pankhurst (Tsehai Press, 2003).

194 In both the Battles of Badr and Uhud, the Prophet Muhammad (peace be upon him) demonstrated the integration of strategic preparation and spiritual reliance. Before engaging in combat, he led the Muslims in heartfelt prayers, seeking Allah's guidance, protection, and support. These supplications highlighted the importance of humility and trust in Allah, even with divine assurances of victory. At Badr, the Prophet made an intense *du'ah*, beseeching Allah for triumph despite the Muslims being outnumbered and under-resourced. Similarly, at Uhud, he turned to prolonged supplication, reinforcing reliance on Allah alongside military readiness.

As iterated in the Futuh,

> "The imam arranged his battle formation, and each group of Muslims prayed the two-fold prostrations, after two-fold prostrations, on account of the great things that had befallen them. The Quranic teacher 'Abd Allah, dismounted from his mule, took his shield and his sword and humbled himself before the Most High God: he was a Sufi, ascetic, pious, worshipful and learned."[195]

Present in the organisation of the duullaan was the rearguard formation or Ilaaliyaha Dhambe where the formation acted as a bulwark against surprise attacks or encirclement by adversaries. This structure complicated an enemy's ability to exploit perceived vulnerabilities in the rear.

As evidenced in the Futuh,[196] in the episode where Garad Kamal explains the tactics of the people of Bali,

> 'He said to the imam, I know some things about the people of Bali, and about their situation and their way of thinking.' The imam said, 'Tell us what you know.'
>
> He said, 'The people of Bali never fight in battle lines, and only fight by subterfuge. If you and your soldiers march at the front of your force, they will attack the stragglers at the rear of the army, and if you move against them, they will run away, but not far away. If you march in the rearguard, they will attack the vanguard of the army, and if you move against them they will run away, but not very far. That is their ruse, and their way of acting. So, you should understand how they behave. The imam Ahmad said, we will outwit them with a trick of our own.'
>
> When it was morning, the imam Ahmad spoke to the emir Abu Bakr, to the emir Mujahid, to Absama Nur and to Jamal ad-Din bin Garad Wadaj, and entrusted to them sixty knights and said to them, 'March in the van of the army, and only pay attention to whoever attacks you: fight them as

195 Sihab ad-Din Ahmad bin Abd Al-Qader bin Salem bin Uthman, Futuh Al-Habasa: The Conquest of Abyssinia, tr Paul Lester Stenhouse and Richard Pankhurst (Tsehai Press, 2003) 59. Although this passage is in the context of preparation for Jihaad, it was a common practice for any military engagement.

196 There are numerous records of the rearguard formation in the Futuh. See Sihab ad-Din Ahmad bin Abd Al-Qader bin Salem bin Uthman, Futuh Al-Habasa: The Conquest of Abyssinia, tr Paul Lester Stenhouse and Richard Pankhurst (Tsehai Press, 2003) 32, 87 and 100.

you march. Do not come to our aid, and we will not go to your aid.' Then he said to the rest of the army, 'You be with me in the rearguard'.

That same morning, the emir and his companions set out in the vanguard of the army. While the booty, the slaves, the pack animals and the baggage brought up the rear. The imam marched behind. The imam had no news of the infidels. They did not even know where they had spent the night, when suddenly they appeared like locusts, their forces split into four divisions.

Two of the patricians advanced with their two forces to where the emir Abu Bakr was and fought for an hour. The Muslims treated them as they deserved, with sword blows and spear thrusts, with the emir and his companions counterattacking with firm hearts. The infidels fled. Their patrician Salmun was killed by Ahmad Din, the brother of the emir Mujahid. Another patrician was killed by the emir Abu Bakr. Many of the infidels were killed. The others fled.'[197]

12.10 *The Bir Ma Geydo, Those Spared from the Spear*

The principle of Bir Ma Geydo, which translates to 'those spared from the spear,' is a cornerstone of Somali traditional law, xeer. This set of laws mandates that certain individuals or groups, specifically non-combatants, are to be entirely exempt from violence, regardless of the nature or circumstances of the conflict. This protection is never optional but is instead a fundamental moral, communal, and Islamic imperative that governs Somali warfare.

Bir Ma Geydo can further be characterised as an institutionalised legal framework that holds universal authority across Greater Somalia, transcending localised clan xeer. It is a law that cannot be questioned, a shield that must remain intact even in the most violent and turbulent of conflicts. The social aspect of Bir Ma Geydo is also deeply embedded in the Somali consciousness, where the sanctity of the protected classes is treated with the utmost reverence.

These individuals, women, children, the elderly, guests, and others are considered inviolable. To harm them under any circumstances is inconceivable and extraordinary. It constitutes a serious violation not just of the law, but of the Somali social and moral composition that sustains peace. A breach of this sacred code is considered *xeer kabax*, meaning it is unlawful, outside of accepted law, and a threat to social order. Such violations often lead to a

---

197 Sihab ad-Din Ahmad bin Abd Al-Qader bin Salem bin Uthman, Futuh Al-Habasa: The Conquest of Abyssinia, tr Paul Lester Stenhouse and Richard Pankhurst (Tsehai Press, 2003) 88–89.

prolongation of conflict, further military engagement, and a breakdown in relationships between the adverse parties involved.

The principles enshrined in Bir Ma Geydo also align closely with the core teachings of Sharia, which similarly emphasise the sanctity of life and the protection of vulnerable groups. As Sheikh Ali Wajis notes, 'traditionally and historically, women, children, elderly people, the sick, vulnerable, the people of religion whatever their status may be and even those sitting in Churches, [their religion is irrelevant], the nabaddoon, the men of tradition, clan leaders, the poets, and the like were absolutely exempt from the spear.'[198] His statement reflects the shared understanding within both Somali customary law and Sharia of the imperative to protect non-combatants, irrespective of their affiliation.

This convergence highlights how Bir Ma Geydo is also a spiritual and divine doctrine, shaped by Islamic principles. As Sheikh Ali further asserts, 'the xeer of Bir Ma Geydo is largely attributed to and inherited from the sharia. The sharia includes all of the exempt categories of people we just listed.'[199] Here, he underscores the connection between xeer and the Sharia. The Bir Ma Geydo exceeds a mere cultural practice but is instead aligned with the moral and ethical standards of Islam. Sheikh Ali links this practice to the teachings of the Prophet Muhammad (PBUH) and the early Caliph Abu Bakr (RA), both of whom reminded the Muslim community to uphold these laws: 'our beloved prophet (SAW) used to remind the ummah of these laws and so too did Abu Bakr (RAC).'[200] In doing so, he emphasises that these protections were not new or foreign with the advent of Islam but were already intrinsic to the Somali custom and laws.

13 The Immunity of Bir Ma Geydo and its Unconditional Nature

This principle of immunity applies to a variety of categories, such as women, children, the elderly, guests, and other vulnerable or neutral individuals, all of whom are categorically prohibited from harm.

The groups protected by Bir Ma Geydo are considered so sacred that they are not to be touched under any circumstances during war. This protection is *absolute*, and to harm any of these individuals is to violate the core ethical and legal principles of Somali society. The law is so deeply ingrained that any

198 Interview conducted with Sheikh Ali Waajiis.
199 Interview conducted with Sheikh Ali Waajiis.
200 Interview conducted with Sheikh Ali Waajiis.

breach is seen as a betrayal of one's own clan as the clan then takes responsibility for the actions. Further the consequences of such transgressions are not only legal but deeply social and moral.

14 Traditionally Immune Groups

14.1 *The Elderly, Sick and the Vulnerable*

This category includes individuals unable to defend themselves, such as those with disabilities or extreme frailty. The Somali tradition sees their protection as an essential marker of honour and integrity, ensuring that the powerless are shielded from the brutality of war.

Elderly individuals occupy a place of profound respect in Somali society, cherished as the guardians of ancestral knowledge and traditional continuity. As living repositories of wisdom and history, their roles as counsellors, mediators, and custodians of tradition demands their protection. To harm an elder is seen as an act of dishonour, severing a crucial link to the past and it induces a destabilisation where the act is regarded as a betrayal of traditional social values, with repercussions that tarnish not only the individual perpetrator but their entire clan.

Safeguarding the aged is thus integral to maintaining the continuity of knowledge and ensuring the community's ability to navigate (military and other social) challenges through their counsel. The protection of the elderly is a marker of collective dignity and a testament to the clan's commitment to honour.

Furthermore, the rationale for sparing the elderly (or the weak or vulnerable) in Somali society, as well as in broader Islamic teachings, stems from their inability to defend themselves due to age and frailty. In times of war, they are no longer combatants, they are physically incapable of participating in the conflict or defending themselves from harm. To target an such persons is a as a violation of moral decency and a profound injustice. It contradicts the very notion of honour and respect for human dignity, which dictates that those who can no longer fight, whether due to age, disability, or frailty, must be shielded from violence.

It is socially considered a cowardly act, and it demonstrates an abuse of power, as the vulnerable are the ones most deserving of protection, not aggression. Further, the strength of a warrior is not only measured by their physical prowess but also by their honour and integrity. To harm an elder, who has contributed to the community and family with wisdom and experience, is to violate this same value.

Such an act would invite social disgrace not only upon the individual who commits it but also upon their entire clan. It is considered an act that would be condemned in poetry, further escalating the dishonour and social alienation. The concept of protecting the elderly is therefore, a matter of maintaining social order.

14.2 *Women and Children*

> *Nin subag dilay su'aal ma leh – A man who has spilled the ghee needs no questioning*[201]

Women and children are historically spared due to their roles as nurturers and symbols of the community's future. Harming them is seen as a violation of Somali norms and a degradation of moral standing. IHL explicitly prohibits all forms of violence against civilians, and accords special protection to women and children in recognition of their particular vulnerabilities in armed conflict. Similarly, in traditional Somali society, women are exempt from direct participation in warfare, even though they may play an indirect role through poetic forms such as gubaab or buraanbur, which can heighten tensions and rouse warriors. This exemption reflects a long-standing cultural norm that shields women from physical harm on the battlefield, aligning in spirit with the protective principles enshrined in IHL.

Women especially hold a central role within the clan structure. They symbolise its continuity and honour. As bearers of lineage and custodians of the family unit, they are regarded as pivotal to the clan configuration. Harm inflicted upon women is beyond a personal violation and is instead received as a collective affront to the clan's dignity and reputation. Harming women is viewed as an unthinkable violation and utterly dishonourable. This action *xeer ka bax* destabilises clan relations and perpetuates violence and the cycle of vengeance continues, making their protection both a moral and strategic necessity.

Professor Yaxya Camir speaks on both legal and social repercussions as he aptly notes that 'women are not hurt as they are not a military target. If one attempts to make women a military target, he has engaged in the most shameful of acts. He or the clan will later on be insulted and shamed in the poetry spoken.'[202] When a woman is made a target, the repercussions extend far

201 It's often used to say: *When someone's wrongdoing (or mistake) is evident, there's no need to ask – the deed is plain.*

202 Interview conducted with Professor Yahya Amir.

beyond legal restitution through diya.[203] The offending individual, along with their clan, is subjected to public humiliation, ostracism,[204] and lasting condemnation in poetry. Poets immortalise the act in verses, ensuring that the shame endures wherever the perpetrators go. This social ostracisation is often more devastating than the material costs of diya. In every gathering, their violation of the Bir Ma Geydo is condemned, casting them as pariahs in the community.

Haaji Maroco further expands on the magnitude of this dishonour when he explains, 'there are some conflicts that have very excessive and deadly responses. For example, where women or girls are touched, killed, the response is extraordinary because they are completely off the table. It is the most shameful act combatants can engage in and they should be prepared for an extreme response. The one who kills a woman is shamed and asked, are you a woman when you are killing a woman?'[205] Maroco's words illustrate the societal outrage that accompanies the killing or harm of women in war. Such an act is viewed as an extraordinary violation, and the perpetrator is subjected to not just physical retaliation but also intense social and moral condemnation. The sense of shame then reverberates across the clan and it the unit that is then required to answer for the transgression.

14.3 *Shiekhs*[206] *– Men of the Book*

In Somali society, shiekhs hold a revered position as religious leaders, the men entrusted with guiding their communities in matters of faith and ethics. As outlined previously, their influence exceeds the religious realm, as they serve as arbiters of peace and mediators in times of conflict. The wisdom of the sheikh is often sought during moments of division or strife, as their moral authority carries significant weight. Given their central role in maintaining both religious and social harmony, attacking a sheikh is viewed as an extreme act of sacrilege. In Somali tradition, the sheikh's position is sacred, and any harm to them is considered a violation of the very principles that uphold the community's ethical and religious integrity.

14.4 *The Clan Leader (Imaam, Garad, Suldaan, Boqor, Ugaas), Odeyaal and the Nabaddoon*

Much like the protection offered to the Sheikhs, individuals such as the Imaam, Garad, Suldaan, Boqor, Ugaas, Odeyaal, and Nabaddoon hold positions of

203 Interview conducted with Professor Yahya Amir.

204 Interview conducted with Professor Yahya Amir.

205 Interview conducted with Haji Maroco.

206 Also known as Ulema.

social, political, and spiritual influence. These figures are entrusted with critical roles in managing the clan's affairs, politically, militarily, and economically but are not themselves combatants in times of war. They are the architects of the clan's governance, guiding it through interlocutions, negotiations, resolving disputes, and maintaining order. They orchestrate the clan's military efforts, ensuring that the warriors are mobilised strategically, but they are never on the front lines themselves.

The Garad, Suldaan, Boqor, and Ugaas are entrusted with political and military leadership but do not engage directly in battle. They are responsible for formulating strategies, organising the defence of the clan, and leading negotiations with other clans, all while maintaining the balance of power within their own group. Their primary role is to act as the guiding force that unites the clan, not as direct combatants.

The Odeyaal (elders) and Nabaddoon (peaceseekers) function as mediators and peacekeepers rather than warriors. The Odeyaal are revered for their wisdom and experience in conflict resolution, and they ensure that clan disputes are handled in accordance with tradition, xeer and the Sharia. The Nabaddoon, on the other hand, are tasked with mediating between rival clans, using their authority and respect to bring parties together and defuse tensions. Both groups focus on maintaining the social and political order, preventing violence, and negotiating peace, rather than engaging in armed conflict themselves.

Their absence from the battlefield is not a reflection of their impotence, but a sign of their distinctive role within the clan structure. These leaders are never expected to wield weapons, for their power lies in their ability to organise, influence, and mediate. They are the linchpins of the clan's political, economic, and military strategies, overseeing the operations of the warriors but never directly participating in the physical combat. They are protectors of the clan's cohesion, ensuring that its internal order is maintained and its future secured.

To harm these individuals is to risk the breakdown of the entire social and political structure of the clan. The leaders are spared from the spear because their existence ensures the clan's survival and their protection, therefore, is not only a matter of personal safety but a safeguard for the stability of the clan.

Every clan recognises and upholds this xeer, that their leaders whether they are Imaam, Garad, Suldaan, Boqor, Ugaas, Odeyaal, or Nabaddoon must be protected during times of conflict. This mutual understanding is a cornerstone of inter-clan relations. It is an unspoken, yet universally acknowledged, principle that the leaders of one clan must be spared from harm in the same way that a clan leader from another group would be granted sanctuary. Each clan knows that, in turn, their own leaders are entitled to the same protection and regard, and this creates a reciprocal system of protection. Just as the leaders of one clan are expected to remain unharmed, so too must this principle be reciprocated by other clans. The expectation is clear. The protection of a clan leader is a publicly recognised standard by which one clan shows deference and respect to another. When a clan leader is harmed or violated, the repercussions ripple outward, threatening not just the injured clan, but also the balance of inter-clan relationships.

14.5 *The Transient and the La Ilaaliye* (*Under Protection*)

The Bir Ma Geydo extends to those under the sanctuary and protection of clans both travellers or guests, and individuals regarded as la ilaaliye (those under protection). The La ilaaliye is a concept that emphasises and balances protection and honour. The category refers to an individual who for various reasons, finds themselves under the protection of another person, family, or clan. This could be someone residing among a clan that is not their own, such as a man living with his maternal clan, or someone who has sought refuge with a neutral party during times of conflict.

The term embodies the principle that any person seeking safety ought to be granted it, and their wellbeing becomes the responsibility of their host. The rationale behind the concept lies in the understanding that protection is a reciprocal and honour-bound responsibility. When someone seeks refuge or safety, the party offering protection does so not only out of compassion or moral obligation but also with the awareness that they might one day find themselves in need of similar assistance.

The role of the protector in ensuring the safety of the la ilaaliye is taken very seriously. Harm inflicted upon a la ilaaliye by an outsider is seen not just as an attack on the individual but as a direct affront to the honour of those who promised their protection. The host clan or individual would treat such an incident as if the attack were against themselves, demanding retribution or their hand may be forced to engage in further conflict in the restoration of their reputation.

The la ilaaliye tradition also extends to broader contexts. For instance, during inter-clan warfare, some individuals may seek refuge with a third, uninvolved clan to escape hostilities. Haji Maroco expands on this with the related concept of La Bixid (exemption or sparing during conflict). He explains "during conflict, if I notice someone, I have familial ties with, or even distant ties with, they are spared from the spear. You may not capture or kill them. If someone submits himself during the fight, waa laga qaleynaya – he is spared."[207] This act of sparing individuals is known as la bixid and it extends to those

207 Interview conducted with Haji Maroco.

connected through longstanding ties (xirir) or marital bonds, such as the family of a combatant's spouse.[208]

Maroco elaborates, "for example, the family of my wife or another clan where there have been longstanding ties. If there was a single or particular relation a combatant has with a person on the battlefield, there was a practice of carrying that person on their back,[209] and it is a signifier that this person is to be spared from the spear. He is saved by the relations I have", waa la bixiyay, he is spared or protected.[210]

This traditional obligation also applies to individuals who have performed notable favours for the combatant's family, and they are similarly exempt from harm.[211] Such gestures demonstrate the nature of reciprocation in the Bir Ma Geydo, where acts of kindness and respect are remembered and honoured even in the heat of battle.

Maroco further describes symbolic acts that communicate protection to others, "them standing behind you or on your back is a signifier everyone understands." These practices are not only about preserving relationships but also about maintaining the ethical boundaries of conflict. For instance, when a clan is defeated (marki laga adkaado), there is an explicit prohibition against an exacerbation of the situation by annihilating or excessively punishing the losing side. This restraint reflects a broader traditional (and legal) balance between justice and compassion, as Maroco notes, "where a clan has been beaten, an exacerbation of the conflict or finishing them off is disallowed. At the same time, this is reconciled with the need for revenge between clans. Revenge is a kind of Islamic development."[212] Here, revenge is understood not as unchecked violence but as a structured response informed by Islamic principles, ensuring that justice does not devolve into cruelty or destruction, and this is exemplified by the relationship between the two concepts of la ilaaliye and la bixid. The two reflect the broader code where the vulnerable are shielded, and the integrity of one's word and promise of sanctuary is paramount.

14.6 *The Wounded Warriors*

Under the Bir Ma Geydo, the treatment of wounded warriors is universally recognised. When a warrior from the enemy side is wounded after battle,

208 Interview conducted with Haji Maroco.
209 The person does not always have to be physically carried on the protector's back, the person can merely stand behind the combatant and it is the gestures given that signify protection.
210 Interview conducted with Haji Maroco.
211 Interview conducted with Haji Maroco.
212 Interview conducted with Haji Maroco.

the expectation under this code is to spare their life and, in some circumstances, provide them with care and medical attention. As Haji Maroco poignantly explains, 'when one is wounded, he was left in his state [to recover and was not finished off].'[213] This statement underscores a moral imperative to treat the wounded with the same compassion that is extended to those typically regarded as vulnerable, women, children, the elderly, and the sick. The wounded are considered, in their defenselessness, to share the same category of protection as these non-combatants.

The rationale for this practice stems from the understanding that a wounded individual, incapacitated by injury, becomes as helpless as those unable to engage in the conflict due to their inherent vulnerability. As such, the wounded enemy combatant deserves the same protections as other vulnerable members of society. Rather than being finished off, there is a nuanced decision-making process that might lead to their abandonment or, conversely, their care and protection.

The decision to spare or abandon a wounded enemy combatant is often contingent on several factors, including the individual's standing within the broader conflict and their relationship with the winning clan. For instance, if the wounded warrior is considered a significant military target, someone who is perceived as having been an instigator of the conflict or a leader of the opposing side, there may be a greater likelihood of his being left to die. However, if the warrior is viewed merely as a foot soldier or a member of the opposing clan who fought in defence of his own people, with no personal animus or larger strategic role, the expectation is that he should be treated with the same compassion as any vulnerable member of society.

This decision is influenced by the individual's perceived righteousness or status in the eyes of the victorious clan. If the wounded warrior is seen as having fought honorably for his clan, and not as an enemy inciting senseless violence, he may be afforded care and the opportunity to recover. Thus, the treatment of the wounded is not an automatic or absolute action but one shaped by the warrior's role in the conflict and his relationship, if any with the winning side.

This category of protection ensures that violence does not transcend the bounds of necessity. However, this tradition is not merely an act of benevolence, but also a strategic as acts of mercy, such as providing care for a wounded enemy, are integral to maintaining honour. By sparing a wounded adversary, the perpetuation of cycles of unyielding violence and vengeance is forestalled. It safeguards the conflict from descending into basic brutality.

213 Interview conducted with Haji Maroco.

There is also an inherent expectation that the combatant, knowing this universal understanding of mercy and protection, would similarly recognise the fate that could await him if wounded in battle. The warrior, fully aware of the xeer and the tradition of mercy, would expect the same treatment for himself as he would offer to his adversary. This shared understanding underpins the behaviour of combatants, who, knowing that their wounded form could place them at the mercy of their enemies, rely on the moral code to secure their own preservation should they find themselves incapacitated.

This code of mercy and respect for the wounded also carries weight beyond individual interactions, it sets a precedent for broader inter-clan relations, advancing ties of respect between clans. This adherence to a higher ethical standard helps to ensure that warfare does not devolve into an endless cycle of destruction but remains tempered.

In a complementary sense, the role of women in Somali conflict becomes relevant here, particularly when it comes to the treatment of the dead and wounded. As Prof. Yahya Amir notes, 'the dead bodies and the wounded are collected by women. They collect them in secret and hope to recover the wounded so that they may save those alive and then afford the dead proper burials.'[214] Women, in this context ensure that the wounded are cared for and the dead are given their rightful burial. In their role as caretakers and buriers, they remain protected from military harm. As Prof. Amir notes, 'if they are seen collecting bodies, they are not hurt as they are not a military target. If one attempts to make women a military target, he has engaged in the most shameful of acts. He or the clan will later on be insulted and shamed in the poetry spoken. There is also general ostracisation. Wherever they meet they will be condemned and shamed. Diya is also required. The insult and shame is worse.'[215] The sanctity of women in Somali tradition as non-combatants is evident in this understanding.

At the same time, as much as this code was universal, if some men were killed and others wounded, the wounded may in some instances be returned to and 'finished off,' a practice known as Diibitir. Diibitir, represents a significant deviation from the general rule of mercy towards the incapacitated. Although the traditional norm is that wounded warriors should be treated with compassion, there are circumstances where this rule may be disregarded. The act of Diibitir, as Professor Yahya Amir explains, "hebel waa la dibiitire," is a categorisation of post-battle executions of wounded warriors, and it highlights a

214 Interview conducted with Professor Yahya Amir.
215 Interview conducted with Professor Yahya Amir.

complex ethical dilemma where clan politics, military strategy, and personal vendettas are balanced.

The reasons behind the practice of Diibitir can be understood primarily through its link to the warrior's actions during the conflict. If the wounded combatant was considered to be a major instigator of violence or played a particularly nefarious role in the conflict, perhaps by leading or directing cruel or disproportionate acts of aggression, then the wounded man's life may be seen as forfeited. In such cases, the wounded warrior is not regarded as a victim of war, but rather as a hostile aggressor whose actions demand retribution, even in his incapacitated state. The logic behind Diibitir in this context is that the warrior, having caused suffering to others, may be deemed deserving of no mercy and will be finished off as a matter of necessity.

Secondly, Diibitir may be invoked when there is a sense that the warrior's survival would pose a future threat to the clan. If the individual is seen as having significant political, military, or symbolic value, perhaps as a leader or a strategic figure whose potential recovery could lead to further violence or revenge, then the clan may feel that the only way to ensure their own safety and prevent further conflict is to eliminate the threat. The survival of such a figure may be seen as an existential risk, compelling the victorious clan to make the difficult decision to finish off the wounded.

Additionally, the practice of Diibitir is a reflection of the fierce competition and the importance of maintaining strength within the clan system. If the wounded individual is seen as someone who has inflicted significant damage upon the clan or violated the norms of warfare, their death is framed not as a mercy killing but as a necessary act to reassert the clan's dominance and protect its future. In some cases, these acts of vengeance are seen as restorative justice, bringing balance to the conflict and satisfying the need for retribution.

However, it is crucial to note that Diibitir is generally viewed as dishonourable and taboo unless the circumstances are extreme. The Bir Ma Geydo is centered on mercy and the protection of the vulnerable, so executing a wounded enemy is often regarded as a violation (xeer ka bax).

There is also the similarly related concept of Bixis, which represents an act of mercy that transcends the brutality of warfare and one that produces long-term peace. As explained by Professor Yahya Amir, bixis occurs when a wanted individual, a key figure in the conflict, often sought for revenge (*aar gasho*), or in some circumstances, a general combatant, is granted protection in the midst of war.

During an ongoing conflict, such an individual, targeted for their significant role, would typically face death. The laws of Somali inter-clan warfare do not accommodate the taking of prisoners, leaving no alternative but execution.

However, bixis intervenes in this otherwise bleak scenario. A respected individual, often an elder or a person of standing, steps forward and declares, the exemption of this particular individual. It becomes a pledge that the target's life is now protected under their name and honour. This declaration not only spares the individual's life but also imposes an obligation on both parties as it is further declared that 'bixis aan kuugu leeyahay' (you are indebted to me by way of the exemption I granted you).[216]

In exchange for their life, the spared individual promises to abstain from harming the opposing clan ever again. The agreement is binding, upheld by the weight of clan honour. To cement this act of mercy, diya payments (blood money) are made as restitution, symbolising the resolution of the immediate grievance. A year later, to maintain good relations and honour the pact, the spared individual transfers ownership of a few camels to the person who brokered the bixis.[217] This gesture serves as a material acknowledgment of the mercy extended and a reinforcement of the bond between clans.

As time passes, the memory of this act is preserved through oral traditions and material exchanges. The children and grandchildren of the involved parties inherit the legacy of bixis, ensuring that the act of mercy is not forgotten. On special occasions, such as clan gatherings (*xus*), the family that facilitated the bixis may again be honoured with gifts, such as camels, as a reminder of their contribution to preserving life and avoiding the prolongation of war.[218]

14.7 *Prisoners of War – Maxaabiis*

The concept of prisoners of war (maxaabiis) in Somali warfare is regulated by both customary and religious laws, and its application varies significantly between external and internal conflicts. Historically, the practice of taking prisoners was primarily acceptable in the context of external or international conflicts, such as in the case of jihad, where warfare was conducted against non-Muslim entities.[219] This is well illustrated in the *Futuh al-Habesha*, an account of the 16th-century campaigns led by Imam Ahmad Gurey against Christian Abyssinia. In such instances, the capture of prisoners served strategic purposes, including negotiation, resource exchange and or demonstrating dominance.

In contrast, amongst the clans, it was traditionally deemed inappropriate to take prisoners of war during internal conflicts. Clan-based disputes operated

216 Interview conducted with Professor Yahya Amir.
217 Interview conducted with Professor Yahya Amir.
218 Interview conducted with Professor Yahya Amir.
219 Interview conducted with Haji Maroco; Interview conducted with Sheikh Ali Waajiis.

under different customs and laws, where kinship ties, xeer and the Sharia dictated the conduct of warfare. The tradition emphasised the resolution of disputes without resorting to practices that could deeply fracture inter-clan relations. As Haji Maroco explains, 'during conflict, if I notice someone, I have familial ties with, or even distant ties with, they are spared from the spear. You may not capture or kill them. If someone submits himself during the fight, *waa laga qaleynaya*, he is spared.'[220]

On the unusual occasion prisoners were taken, it was generally reserved for exceptional circumstances, often involving high-status individuals whose fate required deliberation by clan leaders and elders. 'There are limited occasions where a prisoner might be taken,' notes Haji Maroco.[221] 'A prisoner is generally only taken for high-status combatants and where their fate is yet to be decided. Where he must be taken back to the clan management for a decision regarding his fate.'[222]

The treatment of prisoners adhered strictly to traditional and religious laws, reflecting both the influence of sharia and the Prophet Muhammad's (PBUH) example. Sheikh Mohamed Dau'ud was held a similar position where 'Somalis are a Muslim people and their actions are led by the Sharia. At the same time, the level of knowledge on this area of the Sharia differs and that means as a corollary, their actions in this area of warfare and law differs.'[223]

Haji Maroco emphasises, the rule is that 'prisoners are never killed. They usually demand something that they require in order to return to peace. *Madax Furasho.*[224] If, for example, some of their own are prisoners, they request they be returned or if there is another *dhibaato* – issue, they are bartered with. The Prophet used to exchange prisoners with the Jews and the Quraysh. We try and emulate him and his practice as much as we can.'[225] Sheikh Mohamed Dau'ud's opinion was also consistent with this as there was 'either exchange prisoners, or … a monetary amount in exchange with them especially if an expensive member of our clan has been killed. It is contingent on the hunger of the day – the monetary amount.'[226]

However, certain individuals deemed exceptionally dangerous or guilty of grave crimes, such as murder, or dishonourable (war) crimes could face harsher treatment. 'There is also the permission to kill a category of people known as the

220 Interview conducted with Haji Maroco.
221 Interview conducted with Haji Maroco.
222 Interview conducted with Haji Maroco.
223 Interview conducted with Sheikh Mohamed Dau'ud.
224 Redemption.
225 Interview conducted with Haji Maroco.
226 Interview conducted with Sheikh Mohamed Dau'ud.

dhilaaga – the dangerous or the known killer,' explains Maroco.[227] 'We know of some instances where the Prophet (SAW) placed a bounty on some people's heads at the opening of Mecca and declared *waa madax banaantihiin* – you have permission to kill those dangerous people.'[228]

The intensity of the conflict and the nature of the offence influenced responses. Particularly heinous acts, such as harming women or girls, were met with extraordinary reprisals. 'There are some conflicts that have very excessive and deadly responses. For example, where women or girls are touched, killed, the response is extraordinary because they are completely off the table,' Maroco states. Such acts were considered profoundly shameful, and perpetrators were harshly condemned: 'The one who kills a woman is shamed and asked, are you a woman when you are killing a woman?'[229]

Conversely, disputes involving male combatants, whether over water rights, slander, or other issues, did not provoke the same degree of retaliation. Nevertheless, the restoration of honour remained paramount. As Maroco concludes, 'the importance is that there is a degradation of a person, a family's or a clan's honour and this must be restored. The infraction of honour is a serious unlawful act that has serious repercussions. No person will sit idle with a degradation of honour.'[230]

Sheikh Ali Wajis was of a similar view as he first situated the treatment of prisoners of war within a universal context, stating, 'before I answer you, there is a universal understanding of how a prisoner might be treated in these circumstances.'[231] He emphasised that many of the modern laws governing the treatment of prisoners of war emerged from European conflicts. However, he noted that [historically it did] not originate from Europe. 'In the Islamic world, we locate this as law, after the Prophet (saw) and his successors, [until] the Ottomans in the 13th century,' he explained.[232] He further credited the development of public international law to figures like Professor and Judge Dionisio Anzilotti, who urged practitioners of international law to recognise the interdependence of various civilisations' legal traditions. 'Each society or civilisation has its own law and tradition that are interdependent,' Sheikh Ali remarked. 'They function properly ... without imposition.'[233]

227 Interview conducted with Haji Maroco.
228 Interview conducted with Haji Maroco.
229 Interview conducted with Haji Maroco.
230 Interview conducted with Haji Maroco.
231 Interview conducted with Sheikh Ali Waajiis.
232 Interview conducted with Sheikh Ali Waajiis.
233 Here Sheikh Wajis was emphasising the commonality between Somali laws of war and the Sharia.

Shifting to Islamic principles, Sheikh Ali described the foundational role of Sharia in shaping the treatment of PoWs, presenting three key points of importance. 'First, when a prisoner of war is taken on, he may not be humiliated or tortured for any reason at all, under no circumstances'.[234] Second, he elaborated, 'they have rights to any requests made in the protection of their being, any normal human needs sought.'[235] He stressed that prisoners should be treated as members of the clan, or 'xerta',[236] with access to food, clothing, medical care, and other necessities, as their freedom has been temporarily curtailed. 'The practice and goal were also to exceed in the provision of their rights and duties, seeing as it is God who confers people their freedom,' Sheikh Ali explained.[237] He invoked the concept of accountability on the Day of Judgement: 'you will be held accountable on the day of deeds as well.'

The third point emphasised the safeguarding of a prisoner's future potential. 'No action should be taken against them that could reduce their capacity in the future,' he said.[238] This principle, he noted, becomes particularly relevant if the person is intended to be ransomed, as indicated by verses 4 and 5 of Chapter 47 of the Qur'an.

He continues to explain, the only lawful circumstance in which a prisoner of war might be killed arises when they have been given a chance to cease hostilities and refuse, persisting in their combatant status. 'This is a practice generally used in external aggressions and [is] not the starting point for prisoners of war,' he clarified. Referring to the Prophet's (saw) jurisprudence, Sheikh Ali cited the Battle of Badr, where the Prophet (saw), after consulting Abu Bakr (RA), opted for clemency over punitive measures.

Turning to Somali traditions, Sheikh Ali explained that, historically, the taking of prisoners was not a common practice in inter-Somali conflicts. 'On some occasions, prisoners were taken, but it was a strategic move targeting very valuable combatants.'[239] Both sides in such conflicts recognised the importance of these individuals and often negotiated exchanges, which served as a pathway to reconciliation. 'When the war reached a stage of reconciliation, the prisoners were returned with their rights and well-being intact,' he noted.[240] On occasion, prisoners were released as an act of kindness inspired by the Qur'an, which sometimes led to the cessation of hostilities. 'An unexpected return of a

234 Interview conducted with Sheikh Ali Waajiis.

235 Interview conducted with Sheikh Ali Waajiis.

236 The literal translation is a disciple but, in this context, could mean a follower of the clan or as part of the clan community.

237 Interview conducted with Sheikh Ali Waajiis.

238 Interview conducted with Sheikh Ali Waajiis.

239 Interview conducted with Sheikh Ali Waajiis.

240 Interview conducted with Sheikh Ali Waajiis.

prisoner meant the prisoner himself returned as a *nabaddoon*, not in the literal sense, but as an advocate for peace.'[241]

Sheikh Ali firmly denied the possibility of mistreatment toward prisoners in Somali tradition. 'It is not within the tradition to mistreat a prisoner. You will rarely find a case of a prisoner being mistreated,' he asserted. Instead, prisoners were often hosted by the eldest man of the tribe or the tribal leader, where they received the utmost care. 'A goat or some other animal is slaughtered in their name, and they are told stories, [*waa loo sheekeynjiray*]' he added and this makes 'Somalis and the tradition ... historically and always "[Gob]", noble.' It was also understood that Sadaqah (charity) 'arises in the circumstances. The captor has many obligations to discharge and sadaqah might be included. The even grander incentive is that the captor might enter into paradise for his conduct and treatment of the prisoner' and the following verses of the Quran were invoked:[242]

وَيُطْعِمُونَ ٱلطَّعَامَ عَلَىٰ حُبِّهِۦ مِسْكِينًا وَيَتِيمًا وَأَسِيرًا

And they give food in spite of love for it to the needy, the orphan, and the captive.

إِنَّمَا نُطْعِمُكُمْ لِوَجْهِ ٱللَّهِ لَا نُرِيدُ مِنكُمْ جَزَآءً وَلَا شُكُورًا

We feed you only for the sake of Allah, seeking neither reward nor thanks from you.

إِنَّا نَخَافُ مِن رَّبِّنَا يَوْمًا عَبُوسًا قَمْطَرِيرًا

We fear from our Lord a horribly distressful Day.

فَوَقَىٰهُمُ ٱللَّهُ شَرَّ ذَٰلِكَ ٱلْيَوْمِ وَلَقَّىٰهُمْ نَضْرَةً وَسُرُورًا

So Allah will deliver them from the horror of that Day, and grant them radiance and joy

وَجَزَىٰهُم بِمَا صَبَرُوا۟ جَنَّةً وَحَرِيرًا

and reward them for their perseverance with a Garden ⌜in Paradise⌝ and ⌜garments of⌝ silk.

241 Interview conducted with Sheikh Ali Waajiis.

242 At Chapter 76:8–24.

When asked about the possibility of mistreatment of prisoners of war, in the context of external conflicts, Sheikh Ali explained as follows:

> To be frank with you, societies are never exact. The tradition is longstanding and sometimes there are different practices present in different historical societies. Some wars are intentionally fought in a cunsuri (racist) and or a xasuuqi (genocidal) manner. And this is a theme particularly present with external or international conflicts. The best example would be distinguishing the fervour and the drive of combatants in their jihad and especially with the Ethiopians. The Ethiopians are the historically stark enemies with the Somalis. They were ruthless and did not have the same traditional restraints as we did. Dagal leysku caafiyo maba aheyn – war with them was merciless. Their conflicts with the Somalis were engulfed in cunsuri (racism) and they consistently attempted to enforce (compulsion) their faith on the Somali (dagaal caqiidadodhi ku saabsan). Even the weapons they used against the Somali was very unlike what the Somali would use. You would never find an Ethiopian engaging in badhbaadis (forgiveness or acts of mercy within war) and they would kill any and every person without thought. Any deviation from the Somali tradition or from the Akhlaaq Al-Harb (morals or manners of war) by the Somali is then understood as proportionate or relative to the kind of war being fought, especially against Ethiopians. Any single war is never the same as any other war. The circumstances are never the same and so the manner in which it is fought or responded to can never be the same.
>
> There are some circumstances where there are specific enemies who are detrimental and pose an existential threat and for which the only response is to have them killed even if they are in a prisoner of war status (qolo aan sii kale lugu badhbaadikarin). One can understand this rule emerging from Fatah Makkah.
>
> There is also the example of the people during the Fatah Makkah who had been sentenced to death by the Nabi saw for being utterly detrimental to the Muslims.
>
> The shar wadhoyaal (evil doers or villains) is a concept understood in many societies, it is not specific to the Somali. The actions of combatants are therefore a case-by-case basis contingent on the kind of enemy, the kind of war being fought (i.e. jihad), the area or geography of the war. It can never ever be universal or uniform.[243]

243 Interview conducted with Sheikh Ali Waajiis.

15 Xeer Ka Bax – That Which Is Unlawful

Much of the above is considered xeer and therefore, lawful. It may be appropriate to then mention, further to the Bir Ma Geydo, that which is considered xeer ka bax (unlawful or that which violates established norms and laws governing conduct during conflict). Any actions taken against the Bir Ma Geydo is of course, considered xeer ka bax. However, there are some further, somewhat unknown categories which enhance this explanation.

It is the principles of xeer that delineate the boundaries of acceptable conduct, ensuring that conflicts are governed by laws aimed at limiting harm and promoting resolution. Actions deemed xeer ka bax (unlawful or outside the bounds of xeer), violated these long-standing codes and often resulted in severe consequences. Prof. Aamir highlights the strict rules that defined these conflicts, 'the rules are known for example, a man or clan's well will not be dissolved (ciid in lagu duugo), trees and plantations are not burnt, property is not touched and there was no looting. [The focus was] only the man who is the military target.'[244] Such codes reflect a commitment to minimising collateral damage, safeguarding livelihoods, and ensuring that the focus remained on the combatant parties rather than the broader community.

The concept of xadgudbin (exceeding the limits or transgressing the agreed-upon customs) was central to the framework of xeer. As Xaji Maroco explains, xeer often took the form of treaties between clans, which outlined mutual rights and obligations. These treaties acted as peace agreements, with stipulations that 'explicitly lay out the rights and duties of one clan towards another. They usually agree not to kill one another at any cost, and there is a preference to resolve conflict through other traditional means [and ultimately] drink water together and for there to be no xadgudbin.'[245]

However, when a clan acted in contravention of these agreements, engaging in xeer ka bax, it was considered a grave violation. On the question of what occurs when there is xeer, a treaty or an agreement between two clans, and one decides to act outside of xeer making it xeer ka bax, Haji Maroco explained 'this is detrimental [and] a huge conflict ensues.'[246] Such violations – whether breaking a ceasefire, harming the Bir Ma Geydo (protected individuals like women, children, or elders), or damaging resources like fertile land or wells, shattered the fragile balance maintained by xeer. The repercussions were

244 Interview conducted with Professor Yahya Amir.
245 Interview conducted with Haji Maroco.
246 Interview conducted with Haji Maroco.

profound, triggering extraordinary remedies beyond the usual frameworks of compensation, such as diya (blood money) or maal (material restitution).

The response to xeer ka bax often involved neutral third-party clans mediating the resolution process, with judgments tailored to the severity of the transgression. In many cases, this went beyond material restitution, encompassing symbolic acts to restore relations and deter future violations. For instance, Xaji Maroco describes 'in some contexts, they might be ordered to present [or] offer some girls from their tribe to the other tribe and so clan relations are [fully] restored and … not be transgressed against again. They will also be ordered to present property of many kinds (animals, etc.) [and] raaligalin, an apology towards the other clan. This is in the punishment category as a (natural peace) treaty has been broken.'[247]

The punishment, or caqaab, is known as the gudhis process, a discharge of obligations owed as a direct consequence of the clan's actions. These extraordinary measures stress the gravity of transgressions against xeer and highlight the role of traditional justice in restoring equilibrium and ensuring enduring peace.

16 Metaphysical Social Deterrents

In Somali society, beyond the codified obligations of xeer, the structural reliance on clans, and the overarching authority of Sharia, metaphysical social deterrents have played a pivotal role in maintaining moral order and discouraging transgression. Among these, the concepts of Nabsi and Cuqobo stand out as deeply entrenched beliefs that regulate human behaviour and reinforce justice through divine and moral accountability.

17 Nabsi – the Levelling Force of Life

Nabsi might be understood as the mutable nature of one's providences in life. It is the recognition that material possessions, social standing, and personal success are transient, perpetually subject to change. This change is not random but is directly influenced by one's actions, creating a cause-and-effect dynamic sometimes akin to the concept of karma. Professor Abdi Ismail Samatar defines the concept as one 'closer to a curse' in that one has administered 'a wrong to

247 Interview conducted with Haji Maroco.

somebody else who cannot respond to it, waad kibirtay … so mother nature has its way of taking its revenge upon you for your arrogance and haughtiness and brutality.'[248] It is 'Allah (swt) and His Angels that with then deal with you.'[249] However, nabsi differs in its emphasis on the moral fabric of the universe, acting as an invisible yet pervasive force that rectifies inequalities and avenges arrogance. In the context of warfare, nabsi functions as a powerful deterrent. The belief is that any individual or clan that for instance, violates the principles of proportionality or indiscriminately inflicts harm is bound to experience the same fate. Their actions set into motion a metaphysical cycle of retribution, where the injustices they commit rebound upon them.

In this sense, nabsi embodies the principle of self-avenging fate, whoever's fate you transgress will avenge itself and find you. This belief is not isolated from Islamic teachings but rather resonates with Quranic principles. For instance, in Surah Yunus (10:23), Allah states, 'O humanity! Your transgression is only against your own souls.' The verse features the intrinsic harm one brings upon oneself through acts of oppression or aggression, aligning with the Somali understanding of nabsi.

Furthermore, the Quranic term 'baghy', frequently used to describe aggression and oppression, reflects a similar moral structure, illustrating the deep interconnection between Somali traditions and Islamic doctrines.

18 Cuqobo – the Fear of Divine Retribution

Cuqobo, on the other hand, represents the fear of divine punishment. It is the acknowledgment that Allah (swt) is the ultimate arbiter of justice, and every action, whether overt or hidden is subject to His scrutiny. This belief acts as a direct internal prohibition against unwarranted violence or disproportionate actions, particularly against the helpless, including women, children, the holy, animals, and even nature itself.

The concept of cuqobo asserts that transgression is not merely a physical or social act but a spiritual one with profound consequences. When one acts unjustly, they transgress against their own soul, causing mental and psychological turmoil. This is encapsulated in the understanding that Allah sees

248 Interview conducted with Dr Abdi Ismail Samatar, via telephone, on 3 December 2023 at Minnesota, USA and at Adelaide, South Australia; Dr Abdi Ismail Samatar is a scholar, writer, professor of Geography and a Senator in the Senate of the Federal Republic of Somalia.

249 Interview conducted with Dr Abdi Ismail Samatar.

all, hears all, and witnesses all. Furthermore, the two Angels on each shoulder meticulously record every deed, ensuring that no action, however small, escapes divine notice. This metaphysical accountability transcends human observation. Even if one's transgressions go unnoticed by their peers or society, they remain indelibly recorded by Allah and His Angels.

This belief nurtures a strong sense of moral restraint, particularly in circumstances where immediate repercussions are unlikely, as the ultimate judgment is believed to lie with Allah, either in this life or the next. Nabsi and cuqobo serve as critical alignments between Somali traditions and Islamic teachings. They instill a deep-seated awareness of accountability, not only to one's community but also to a higher divine order.

These metaphysical concepts bridge the temporal and the spiritual, reinforcing justice as a universal principle that governs both earthly and eternal realms. In essence, nabsi and cuqobo function as societal safeguards against transgression, ensuring that moral conduct prevails even in the absence of formal enforcement mechanisms. They embody the collective consciousness of Somali society, preserving harmony and justice through a balance of fear, reverence, and self-awareness.

19 Weapons

The spear, or *waran*, was perhaps the most iconic weapon in Somali combat, embodying both practicality and profound cultural symbolism. With a long, slender shaft typically crafted from sturdy wood, and a sharpened metal tip barbed for maximum impact, the spear was a versatile and indispensable tool in both warfare and daily life. Its design balanced durability, precision, and adaptability, making it effective for both throwing and close combat.

In battle, skilled warriors used the spear to devastating effect. From a distance, it could be hurled with remarkable accuracy, striking enemies before they had the chance to retaliate. In close quarters, the spear transformed into a formidable thrusting weapon, its length allowing the wielder to maintain a defensive advantage while delivering lethal strikes. The fluidity and precision required to wield a spear were hallmarks of Somali warriors.

As recorded in the Futuh, the impact of the spear was such that Somalis 'struck with their swords and stabbed with their spears until their spears shattered, and their forearms were numb from striking the necks and the heads of the infidels. Then one of the Muslim knights, by name the emir Mujahid bin Allbin AbdAllah Suha, charged. He was an illustrious horseman, and a voracious lion. He attacked the patrician ... striking him a blow that knocked him from his horse to the ground and God cast his soul quickly into Hell, an evil place to settle in.'[250]

On another occasion, the power of the spear to pierce and unhorse opponents is recorded where 'the Muslims met them with staunch hearts, and finely-honed swords, and penetrating spears. The first of the Muslims to attack one of the infidel cavalries was Muhammad bin Adruh who pierced him with his spear, throwing him from his horse to the ground: then God cast his soul into the fire, an evil place to settle in. Then, after him Kaled al-Waradi attacked one of the patricians, striking him a fatal blow with his spear, and he fell dead from his horse, may the Most High God not have mercy upon him. The infidels then turned tail and went back up the mountain, going down the other side. A detachment of them was utterly destroyed.'[251]

When Imam Axmed Gurey himself would strike with his spear, he struck with such precision that his spear would pierce the enemy, 'and its tip emerged [would] emerge from [the] back, glistening.'[252] Among the Imam's army was also Adam, 'commander of spearmen' who could kill the enemy with a single strike to eye.[253]

It was also not uncommon for the Ethiopians to employ poisoned spears and arrows which is a stark contrast from the Somali abstention. For instance, during the Imam's raid of Wasan Sagad'| s[254] Church in Andurah, 'the imam with his Muslim army arrived at the church, the custodians fled. There were custodians from Duba'ah there, one-thousand foot soldiers, carrying poisoned spears called jat.'[255]

250 Sihab ad-Din Ahmad bin Abd Al-Qader bin Salem bin Uthman, Futuh Al-Habasa: The Conquest of Abyssinia, tr Paul Lester Stenhouse and Richard Pankhurst (Tsehai Press, 2003) 27.

251 Sihab ad-Din Ahmad bin Abd Al-Qader bin Salem bin Uthman, Futuh Al-Habasa: The Conquest of Abyssinia, tr Paul Lester Stenhouse and Richard Pankhurst (Tsehai Press, 2003) 45–46.

252 Sihab ad-Din Ahmad bin Abd Al-Qader bin Salem bin Uthman, Futuh Al-Habasa: The Conquest of Abyssinia, tr Paul Lester Stenhouse and Richard Pankhurst (Tsehai Press, 2003) 63.

253 Sihab ad-Din Ahmad bin Abd Al-Qader bin Salem bin Uthman, Futuh Al-Habasa: The Conquest of Abyssinia, tr Paul Lester Stenhouse and Richard Pankhurst (Tsehai Press, 2003) 63, Patrician Maha Tenta was killed with this blow to the eye.

254 Advisor and General to the then Ethiopian Emperor Lebna Dengel.

245 Ibid page 63.

During the Battle of Sembra Kore, it was recorded that …

> The emir who was on the left, the wazir Addoli was accompanied by the Somali archers from the tribe of Marraihan who had their bows. Sometimes, when they fired their arrows, the infidels repelled them, and sometimes they repelled the arrows of the infidels. Among the infidels were the Maya, a people who used poisoned arrows, and they had archers with them.
>
> The imam had said that day to the Muslims, 'when they shoot arrows at you, collect them; don't leave them. For if you leave them on the ground, they will pick them up and they will shoot them at you a second time. Gather them all up and give them to me.' So it happened that when they shot arrows at them, the Muslims collected them, and at sunset, when the battle ceased, each emir came with his force, each of them carrying a sheaf of arrows that lie had picked up. They unfastened the sheaves in the presence of the imam who commanded that they be taken and given to one of his treasurers, the chief of them, whose name was Dakal. All of them were given to him. When night fell, a cow was butchered but there was no wood. Dakal said to his companions, 'Look at these arrows. Tomorrow, if we are captured, the infidels will take them. Why don't we bum them and use them to roast the meat?' They replied, 'What a good idea and did just that. They burnt them and roasted the meat of the whole cow above them. This was one of the most amazing things we saw in the battle of Sembera Kore in the year 935, less six months.[256]

The Maya[257] people were renowned for their expertise with poisoned arrows and demonstrated exceptional skill in the use of the bow and arrow. On one occasion, 'there came a huge force of infidels, and with them the Maya people who had long-bows and poisoned arrows. Whenever one of these latter struck someone, the hair on his head fell out from the strength of the poison.'[258] Further, anyone struck by these poisoned arrows loses all the hair on his head and dies instantly from the strength of the poison. They procure the poison from a tree that is well-known to them and to the Somalis. They collect its

256 Sihab ad-Din Ahmad bin Abd Al-Qader bin Salem bin Uthman, Futuh Al-Habasa: The Conquest of Abyssinia, tr Paul Lester Stenhouse and Richard Pankhurst (Tsehai Press, 2003) 51.

257 The Maya is an extinct ethnic group native to the previous Wej province in Ethiopia.

258 Sihab ad-Din Ahmad bin Abd Al-Qader bin Salem bin Uthman, Futuh Al-Habasa: The Conquest of Abyssinia, tr Paul Lester Stenhouse and Richard Pankhurst (Tsehai Press, 2003) 54.

branches and roots, light a fire over them to cook them, and then gather the sap and coat the tips of their arrows with it. It is mud-coloured, like tar.[259]

The use of poisoned weapons in warfare by Ethiopians, contrasted with the rejection of such tactics by Somali warriors, highlights a moral dichotomy fixed in differing ethical principles and approaches to combat. There is a contrast in martial strategies and cultural and philosophical values regarding the conduct of war.

The Ethiopian deployment of poisoned spears represents a calculated attempt to maximise harm and suffering. Poisoned weapons are inherently indiscriminate, designed not only to kill but to prolong agony, inflicting cruel and often irreversible damage on their targets. This approach demonstrates a willingness to prioritise tactical advantage over humane conduct, embodying a perspective on warfare that disregards principles of restraint or proportionality. The use of poison, which leaves victims to endure excruciating deaths, reflects an absence of ethical considerations about the dignity of combatants or the rules of engagement.

In contrast, Somali warriors, under the command of the Imam, exemplified a commitment to the moral frameworks articulated in Islamic principles of warfare. These principles, grounded in the Quran and the Sunnah,[260] emphasised mercy, proportionality, and the minimisation of unnecessary suffering, even amidst conflict. By choosing conventional weapons such as swords, spears, and shields, the Somali forces maintained the integrity of honourable combat, targeting opponents directly and avoiding tactics that would cause undue pain or violate the sanctity of human life.

The sword, known as *seef*, was a refined weapon, characterised by its lightness and curved blade. Somali swords were designed for swift, slashing movements, allowing the warrior to engage in quick, lethal strikes. The blade was often a work of art in itself, adorned with intricate designs that spoke to the blacksmith's craft and the warrior's status.

Alongside the sword, the dagger, or *toorrey*, played a crucial role, often serving as a secondary weapon for personal defense. Its compact design made it ideal for stabbing in close quarters, and it was frequently carried as a backup tool in case a warrior was disarmed. The dagger, much like the sword, was an heirloom of sorts, passed down through generations as a precious symbol of

---

259 Sihab ad-Din Ahmad bin Abd Al-Qader bin Salem bin Uthman, Futuh Al-Habasa: The Conquest of Abyssinia, tr Paul Lester Stenhouse and Richard Pankhurst (Tsehai Press, 2003) 101.

260 That is not to say that all of the Imam's campaigns were Sharia compliant.

family lineage and honor.[261] It was also common for the toorrey to be worn along the waist of Somali men. The dagger, typically housed in a decorative sheath, was fastened to a belt or tucked into a sash, ensuring it was readily accessible. Its presence at the waist was a visible reminder of the wearer's preparedness and vigilance, essential traits in a society where personal and clan security were paramount. The toorrey also signified maturity, responsibility, and readiness to protect oneself and one's community.

Lastly, the shield, or *gaashaan*, was indispensable in Somali warfare, serving as both a practical tool and a symbol of a warrior's preparedness and expertise. Typically crafted from toughened animal hide stretched over a robust wooden frame, the shield was both lightweight and durable. Its design allowed it to absorb and deflect the force of incoming attacks from spears, arrows, or swords, providing critical protection in the heat of combat. The shield's circular shape offered versatility, enabling the warrior to manoeuvre with agility, holding it in one hand while wielding a weapon in the other. This versatility allowed for a seamless balance between offence and defence.

---

261 Even today, the tradition of wearing the toorrey persists, particularly during cultural events, ceremonies, or as part of traditional attire.

CHAPTER 5

Changing the Narrative: a Reflection on the Impact of the Tool on African Traditions and the Preservation of Humanity during Warfare

Tamalin Bolus and Sarah Jean Mabeza

1 Introduction

"However universal its content, International Humanitarian Law is nonetheless, by design, an essentially Western institution".[1] A somewhat controversial declaration that requires consideration, but also a potentially dangerous assertion capable of diminishing the universality of this body of law. Indeed, the very value of International Humanitarian Law (IHL) lies in its global recognition and acceptance: IHL reflects a common heritage and encompasses rules governing warfare that transcend borders. Now, more than ever, when IHL is already under threat in the current geopolitical climate, it is imperative that the international community accept this common heritage. Globally, a number of voices are questioning its continued relevance, evidenced by a recent withdrawal of a "State Party" from a well-recognised IHL treaty[2] as well as a general reluctance to embark on negotiation of new IHL principles and rules. Now is the time to reassert the relevance and applicability of modern-day IHL to all people, cultures and religions. Now is the time to demonstrate the link between IHL and culture; to encourage all people groups to take ownership over IHL as well as its development.[3]

This chapter will consider the relevance and value of the Tool on African Traditions and the Preservation of Humanity during Warfare ("the Tool") as a means of highlighting the linkages between African traditions, customs and values pre-dating the 1949 Geneva Conventions with modern day principles of IHL. Such linkages highlight the manner in which pre-colonial Africa

1 Andrew Bartles-Smith, "Religion and International Humanitarian Law", *International Review of the Red Cross* (2022), 104 (920–921), 1731.

2 See Lithuania leaving Cluster Munition Ban undermines Agreement, threatens crucial norms, 2024, Lithuania Leaving Cluster Munition Ban Undermines Agreement, Threatens Crucial Norms | Human Rights Watch (hrw.org) (accessed 04.10.2024).

3 Focussing on the link between IHL and specific cultures is not an attempt to regionalize IHL, it is rather a means of highlighting the applicability of IHL to all peoples and cultures.

 | DOI:10.1163/9789004703094_007

approached limits in warfare, and remains a valid and valuable consideration in post-colonial Africa. It is not the purpose of this chapter to explore the origins of IHL; the focus will rather be on the added value of the Tool, both past and future, in changing the narrative on IHL in Africa.

As part of the introduction to volume 3 of this series on the Laws of Yesterday's Wars, the Tool has been described as follows:

> As a means of better explaining the relevance and authority of IHL, the ICRC undertook to examine the historical relationship between Africa and IHL, as reflected in traditional customs, with the objective that the resulting research could contribute to current debates on the relevance of IHL to Africa and thereby increase the understanding and acceptance of IHL rules on the African continent. From the research conducted it became evident that established norms that regulated the conduct of hostilities existed in many African tribes and cultures. As the research provided some clarity into the norms of traditional African customs in war, it became important to conceptualize a means of showing the link between culture and law that would effectively contribute to current debates on relevance of IHL to Africa and to and increase understanding and acceptance of IHL rules on the African continent. The outcome was the production of the "Tool on African Traditions and the Preservation of Humanity during War" (the Tool), a resource with which to engage various audiences on the relationship between Africa and IHL. The Tool consists of 11 cards, highlighting firstly the African traditional custom in question, secondly the African tribes or cultures who have a history of practicing that traditional custom, and thirdly the related rule under modern-day IHL. The cards are available in various formats, including as playing cards, which can easily be shared with armed actors manning check points, for example. They are also available as post cards, which are useful in a pedagogical context, and finally in a poster format, so they can be showcased as part of a photo exhibit. The tool has also been adapted into additional formats which it is hoped will be beneficial in operational settings – these include a short video that can be used on social media but also shown by humanitarian actors to armed actors on a mobile device, as well as the inclusion of the Tool in a recently produced ICRC notebook for armed actors in the field. Additionally, the Tool has been translated into French and Portuguese, with the intention to translate into further languages in the future.[4]

4 Mabeza, S and Bolus, T, 2024, Tool on African Traditions and the Preservation of Humanity during War in: The Laws of Yesterday's Wars 3, *International Humanitarian Law Series* (67).

The Tool by no means reflects a different set of IHL norms to be respected, neither is it an attempt to contextualise nor 'regionalise' IHL. Indeed, it is clear that contemporary IHL, both treaty and customary, is the definitive set of rules applicable today. Instead, the Tool's potential lies in its contribution as a collection of non-Western traditions to countering perceptions that IHL is comprised of "Western rules".[5] The hope is that by providing these examples and exploring the development of IHL on the African continent, the Tool will rather illustrate how IHL is relevant, and how it reflects a shared immunity. The ultimate hope is that the Tool may garner greater respect for the law, thereby contributing towards the reduction of suffering during times of armed conflict by encouraging and paving the way for enhanced compliance with IHL on the battlefield.

As a means of assessing the value of the Tool, this chapter aims to initiate an evaluation of the impact of the Tool. Such impact is difficult to measure, particularly at this early stage of the Tool's promotion, but the authors will attempt to assess the Tool's potential impact on the ground by considering its' use by ICRC Delegations across the African continent to date, the criticisms of the Tool received, and the extent to which it has begun to contribute towards or shape current debates on the relevance of IHL. This chapter will then turn to explore the potential impact of the Tool, particularly with regard to the contribution that the Tool can make to the future development of IHL.

2 Looking Back on the Development of the Tool and Its Operationalization: the Experience to Date

2.1 *Use of the Tool by ICRC Delegations*

The Tool was officially launched by the ICRC in 2021 and has been used in various ways to engage with audiences, both in Africa and beyond. Firstly, the Tool has been used as a pedagogical tool in IHL presentations by ICRC colleagues to African audiences in South Africa, Mozambique, Kenya, Nigeria, Ethiopia, Botswana, Zimbabwe and Malawi amongst others. Secondly, it has been used as a broader educational tool in ICRC training sessions with academics and students. Thirdly, it has been used as a promotional tool in the form of an exhibit and short video at various IHL-related events and at a number of different venues, including the reception area of the South African Department of International Relations and Cooperation, the University of Pretoria Law Faculty, the welcome reception of the 6th Commonwealth Conference on IHL,

5 Andrew Bartles-Smith, "Religion and International Humanitarian Law", above note 1, p. 1731.

the Dar es Salaam Art Museum as well as the ICRC headquarters in Geneva, Switzerland. And finally, its use in a more operational context has begun, where the Tool has been shared by the ICRC with armed actors in Mozambique and during dissemination sessions with armed actors in the Democratic Republic of the Congo.

2.2 *Criticisms of the Tool and Questions to Be Addressed*

A number of the criticisms of the Tool received by the authors have been related to the methodology of the research conducted for the Tool. The research, initially conducted by the authors and in recent years augmented by African post-graduate students and academics, was guided by a purpose-driven approach. As such, the researchers identified a relevant custom or tradition and then highlighted its correlation to contemporary IHL. This approach suited the objective of the research, which was simply to illustrate the universality of the fundamental principles of IHL. However, utilizing a purpose-driven approach has also resulted in a fair critique of the Tool. For example, where the tradition or custom does not directly correlate to a strict application of IHL, particularly in relation to the classification of a conflict, is not always clear as to whether the tradition applied in a non-international or international armed conflict. Another example is where tribes that are featured in the Tool for respecting limits in warfare as part of their traditions, customs and values are also synonymous with and renowned for quite severe violations of contemporary principles of IHL. How can the Tool balance the protection offered by some traditions with the truth that the same tribes also violated the principles of modern-day IHL through other customs? Does the fact that a tribe violated one principle of contemporary IHL take away from the fact that the same tribe respected a different principle of contemporary IHL? For the authors, in the context of the objectives of the Tool the answer is no, although there is certainly merit in asking the question.

An additional challenge regarding the methodology of the research conducted relates to the collection of the relevant traditions, customs and values. Many of the traditions that the researchers were seeking are purely oral in nature. This led to difficulties in terms of accessing those traditions, as the research was no longer purely desk research in nature, and some of the interviews conducted with elders required translation into English. When the oral traditions were received, could the researchers guarantee the reliability of the source and objectivity of the information collected? Although the authors of this chapter are lawyers by training, this research required researchers to look above and beyond typical legal sources, and, for example, consider poems and songs as possible avenues for discovering new traditions to add to the Tool.

This raises the question as to whether anthropologists or sociologists would be better suited than the authors to conducting further updates of the Tool!

Turning aside from the methodology, another challenge encountered has been the request for the authors to effectively manipulate a round peg into a square hole. In some instances the authors have been asked to 'find' traditions, customs and values that would help in discussions with African audiences on a particular aspect of IHL. Unfortunately, researchers cannot create something that doesn't exist, or perhaps it is merely that one cannot find something that has not yet been researched and published. In addition, given the multi-cultural and multi-dimensional environment in Africa, there are often requests made to the authors to incorporate into the Tool traditions, customs and values from other parts of Africa and other tribes. While the limited geographical reach of the Tool is a valid observation, the authors have certainly attempted to be as inclusive as possible,[6] limited by the information available and the resources of the ICRC. It would be beyond the capacity of the ICRC to embark on a study of relevant traditions, customs and values in each and every one of Africa's 55 States, although the authors are excited by the keen interest from IHL practitioners and students across the continent to start researching their own particular tribes' traditions, customs and values on the regulation of warfare. This can only but enhance the mainstreaming of IHL in Africa.

A future challenge to be aware of is the growing use of the Tool outside of the hands of the ICRC. While this is a positive development, the Tool was initially designed as an ICRC tool, and its use by academics in their IHL curricula or by African diplomats abroad was not necessarily foreseen. The Tool may need to be adapted in some ways to accommodate this growing use, for example by adding clearer instructions on its use or by creating a stand-alone website or webpage on the ICRC website providing all necessary resources for its proper use.

And finally, a more overarching critique relates to the relevance of traditions, customs and values in today's landscape. Are they still relevant? Do they warrant consideration during contemporary discussions on IHL? For those who think not, they would view the Tool and its inspirational impact as passé. While this potentially warrants further discussion, the authors would highlight that the Tool forms part of a wider toolbox of ICRC dissemination tools on IHL, and its use may not be appropriate in each and every context. It is at the discretion of the ICRC Delegation, or the academic, or the diplomat, using the Tool to

6 The ICRC will be releasing version 2.0 of the Tool before the end of 2024, and this version will incorporate new traditions, values and customs from 4 additional contexts in Africa, namely South Africa, Zimbabwe, Ethiopia and Mozambique.

assess whether its use in each particular scenario will contribute to stimulating reflection and debate around IHL in Africa. This is, after all, one of the main objectives of the Tool.

2.3 *Assessment of Its Use to Date*

Perhaps the most important point to highlight at the start of an assessment of the Tool is that when the Tool was initially envisaged, it was quite innovative in nature. There were not many resources available on African traditions, customs and values related to restraint in warfare. Indeed, only few relevant publications existed, and of those, many of the written resources were very dated. In addition, the value of the authors' research into African traditions was not immediately evident for all. Indeed, the authors of the Tool faced many questions as to the potential value of the Tool and how it would contribute to, and not diminish, the universality of IHL. The authors even faced the criticism that the Tool was a form of neo-colonialism.

Today, however, there are a plethora of activities taking place to research, analyse and promote African values in war. Indeed, the Tool has become part of a much wider movement to reflect on our shared humanity and the role that traditions, customs and values related to the regulation of warfare may play in generating greater respect for the contemporary rules of IHL. As an illustration of this broader engagement on the links between law and culture, the authors can point to additional ICRC Delegations that have chosen to embark on research studies at the national level, including for South Sudan and Ethiopia. In addition, academics and civil society actors have started to conduct their own research into African traditions (Somalia, Ethiopia[7] and East Africa), and some academics have even begun to incorporate the Tool into their teaching. On this point it has been encouraging for the authors to learn that African academics have started to integrate the Tool into their existing IHL curricula in order to highlight the synergies between indigenous knowledge and IHL. According to Mathibedi and Bradley, "in the drive to disseminate IHL the ICRC has not restricted its activities to paying attention to treaty law and customary IHL. It has embraced the contribution of religious teaching and of traditional values that align with IHL to achieve greater compliance and to facilitate a better comprehension of the norms that underpin IHL among

7 See Looking back to old laws and customs of war in Ethiopia: establishing groundwork for further research, 2021, Looking Back to Old Laws and Customs of War in Ethiopia: Establishing Groundwork for Further Research (aauihl-clinic.org) (accessed 5 September 2024).

the target audience."[8] The University of Johannesburg Law Faculty's IHL curriculum "relies on the ICRC's interrogation of religious norms and traditional values underpinning the rules of IHL aimed at, amongst other objectives, promoting an understanding of IHL to wider audiences and overcoming biases that IHL is exclusively western".[9]

Whether or not the Tool can take credit for this broader engagement on African traditions and IHL is not clear. What is clear is that in its use by the ICRC at least, it has added a valuable dimension to its presentations and discussions with African audiences. It has provided substantial food for thought and opened up avenues for discussion on the fundamental principles of IHL that might not have existed otherwise. The authors and many of their ICRC colleagues have noticed that when presented in the context of existing African traditions, customs and values, African audiences engage with IHL in a much more intimate way.

To date the Tool has mostly been used in peaceful contexts, but more recently its use has been tested in more operational contexts, notably in Mozambique and the DRC, where it has been well-received. The presentation of the traditions, customs and values was particularly positive where the Tool was used to introduce the notion of IHL principles before leading to a more in-depth discussion on modern-day IHL. It was also noted to be relevant in that it provided armed actors with a hook to connect with the IHL dissemination, whereas more traditional disseminations on pure modern-day IHL were sometimes seen as not tangible or too far removed from the context in question. The results of the use of the Tool in operational contexts remains to be fully seen, however, once there is more data as to its use, reception and impact, the authors will be in a better position to begin to answer fundamental questions about the impact of the Tool. These include the following:

1. Is it sufficiently convincing that by merely demonstrating the links between culture and law there is an effective means of generating increased respect for the law?
2. Does respect and implementation of IHL rules depend on such a clear correlation between the applicable rule and local customs?

---

8 Faith Mathibedi and Martha Bradley, "Integrative law as a lens: correlating International Humanitarian Law with Indigenous Knowledge Systems using Integrative Learning approach", 11.

9 Faith Mathibedi and Martha Bradley, "Integrative law as a lens: correlating International Humanitarian Law with Indigenous Knowledge Systems using Integrative Learning approach", above note 8, p. 7.

Essentially, by being in a position to answer these questions, the authors will begin to better understand the value of the Tool, as the importance of this project rests on its impact, and ultimately in a reduction of suffering in times of armed conflict.

3 Looking Forward: the Contribution of the Tool to the Advancement of International Humanitarian Law

"The potential of the Tool has not yet been reached; the full value of the Tool is still to be realized".[10] These words, spoken by the Deputy Head of the Pretoria Delegation of the ICRC, highlight the importance of the Tool, but they are also a clarion call to the ICRC to ensure that the Tool is properly promoted on the African continent and that the appropriate resources are set aside for its regular update. After all, the Tool is a living project that should aim to expand regularly, both in terms of the traditions, customs and values it encompasses, as well the geographical reach that it has.

In developing the Tool, the authors of this chapter aimed for it to have pedagogical value, but they also saw the potential of the Tool to make a concrete, tangible and marked impact on the African continent. The authors hoped that the impact would be reflected in how African actors view IHL, in the level of ownership they take over it, in how they value compliance with IHL as well as in how actively they participate in the law's development. While the first section of this chapter focused on looking back, highlighting how the Tool has been viewed and used to date, this next section will focus on looking forward, sharing the authors' aspirations of the difference the Tool may make in the future implementation and development of the principles of IHL on the African continent.

3.1 *Development of International Humanitarian Law in the Current Geopolitical Climate*

While the provisions of the Geneva Conventions and their Additional Protocols provide the international community with the bedrock of IHL, it is clear that due to the changing nature of warfare, the law does need to be developed in order to reflect current and future realities of armed conflict. Indeed, Janssens and Wouters assert that "the 'hard law' regulating today's armed conflicts, especially concerning non-international armed conflicts … is outdated

10 Mutsa Mugangavari, Deputy Head of Pretoria ICRC Delegation, interview on 18 July 2024.

and inadequate in many respects".[11] Droege and Giorgou agree and highlight that "the development of the law can and will never stop … old lacunae have never been filled … and new ones will arise".[12] In terms of new lacunae that have arisen, the ICRC's most recent Challenges Report[13] highlights a number of areas of the law requiring clarification, and points specifically to issues such as hybrid warfare, proxy warfare, urbanization of armed conflict and the application of IHL to new technologies of warfare. Considering old gaps that need to be addressed, Stephan suggests that some of the current challenges for IHL extend to the legal status of people taking part on behalf of non-State actors through extraterritorial attacks as well as proliferation of weapons of mass destruction.[14] Droege and Giorgou add to the list by highlighting "Non-International Armed Conflict law, obligations of Non-State Armed Groups, the protection of women, the protection of children, the protection of the environment [and] weapons issues" as areas of IHL requiring clarification.[15]

And yet despite this clear need for development and/or clarification of certain aspects of IHL, there is a growing fear that the setting is not ripe for the international community to adopt new hard or soft law to enhance existing IHL principles, given how polarized the international community is currently. Indeed, according to Stephan, "across the board and around the world, projects to build international law and international institutions have become stuck. The liberal international consensus that seemed to emerge in the 1990s has unraveled. The present moment of crisis has many causes – geopolitical, economic and cultural. What it means as a practical matter is that the formal adoption of new international rules through international agreements faces roadblocks that seem likely to persist for some time".[16] He highlights factors that have contributed to this current impasse as geopolitical and economic in nature, and cautions that "the present moment finds the world as dangerously

11 Pauline Charlotte Janssens and Jan Wouters, "Informal international law-making: a way around the deadlock of international humanitarian law?", *International Review of the Red Cross* (2022), 104 (920–921), 2112.

12 Cordula Droege and Eirini Giorgou, "How international humanitarian law develops", *International Review of the Red Cross* (2022), 104 (920–921), 1835.

13 See 2024 ICRC Report on IHL and the Challenges of Contemporary Armed Conflicts, 2024, 2024 ICRC IHL Challenges Report | ICRC (accessed 07.10.2024).

14 Paul B. Stephan, "The crisis in international law and the path forward for international humanitarian law", *International Review of the Red Cross* (2022), 104 (920–921), 2079–2083.

15 Cordula Droege and Eirini Giorgou, "How international humanitarian law develops", above note 12, p. 1834.

16 Paul B. Stephan, "The crisis in international law and the path forward for international humanitarian law", above note 14, pp. 2079–2096.

divided and on the edge of international violence as any in the last thirty years".[17] Janssens and Wouters agree, noting a hesitation in the last 20 years on the part of States to adopt IHL instruments or even "to be formally involved in the development of IHL".[18]

Not only may the current setting be unripe for negotiation and adoption of new IHL treaty law, but it may be foolish even to try. Droege and Giorgou issue a caution, noting that "embarking in a norm-creating exercise in the face of strong reluctance or even downright opposition by influential States is not always a wise course of action".[19] In the current global setting, little can be taken for granted. In order to navigate the uncertainty that exists, the authors propose the need for champion States who are willing to take a stand both for the implementation of existing IHL as well as for the development of IHL in a way that enhances and strengthens the law. The authors assert that a number of African States could fulfill that champion role, and would place their hope in the Tool as a means of encouraging and supporting those States as they do so.

3.2 *Potential Options for the Development of International Humanitarian Law*

African governments are no strangers to the process of development of IHL. Indeed, they have played a crucial role in the negotiation and adoption of a number of IHL instruments, including the 2002 Rome Statute on the Establishment of an International Criminal Court, the 2008 Cluster Munitions Convention, the 2013 Arms Trade Treaty and the 2017 Treaty Prohibiting Nuclear Weapons. Through the African Union, African States have also taken groundbreaking steps in the development of specific IHL thematics, including the adoption of the world's first binding legal instrument on the protection of internally displaced persons,[20] as well as the more recent adoption of a Common African Position on Cyber Warfare.[21] An important aspect to interrogate is what has facilitated the active involvement of African States in processes to develop and

17 Paul B. Stephan, "The crisis in international law and the path forward for international humanitarian law", above note 14, p. 2079.

18 Pauline Charlotte Janssens and Jan Wouters, "Informal international law-making: a way around the deadlock of international humanitarian law?", above note 11, p. 2111.

19 Cordula Droege and Eirini Giorgou, "How international humanitarian law develops", above note 12, p. 1836.

20 African Union Convention for the Protection and Assistance of Internally Displaced Persons in Africa, adopted 23 October 2009.

21 African Union Common African Position on the application of international law to the use of information and communication technologies in Cyberspace, adopted 29 January 2024.

clarify IHL? Has it been where the States in question have suffered from the very issue the treaty they helped negotiate exists to address or where they are acting in solidarity with African countries who have suffered from the issue in question? Has it been where the issue in question is one that corelates with specific values of the people of the State in question?[22] Or is it simply where the issue to be addressed in the treaty negotiations is relatively straight forward area of IHL to which the State is comfortable contributing?

In the experience of the authors in collaborating with and supporting States in Southern Africa over the past 15 years, in many instances it is a combination of a number of factors that have played a key role in setting the scene for governments to actively participate in negotiation and adoption of IHL instruments. Firstly, the support from the African Union for the thematic, whether through formal common positions, informal common positions, existing regional instruments on the topic (for example, the existence of the nuclear weapon-free zone in Africa created by the Pelindaba Treaty paved the way for African involvement in the negotiation of an international instrument prohibiting nuclear weapons), work of Special Rapporteurs on the thematic or engagement by the African Union Office of the Legal Council or the African Union Commission on International Law on the thematic. Secondly, where the thematic in question is a low-hanging fruit for African States, either due to its relative non-sensitivity in the region or a general consensus from the region that it is a topic that needs to be addressed. A third factor to be considered is the existence of competent and passionate individuals within African governments who are willing to take the topic forward. This was particularly evident in how the negotiation of the Treaty Prohibiting Nuclear Weapons progressed, with individual government representatives from South Africa, Nigeria, Kenya and others carrying the beacon for nuclear disarmament and non-proliferation. And finally, a sense of ownership over the thematic is crucial to the involvement of an African government in the development of the law on that topic. This sense of ownership can be engendered due to first-hand experience with the issue (this was clear with Africa's engagement on the negotiation of the Arms Trade Treaty), to a sense of solidarity for African brothers and sisters who have suffered due to the issue at hand (this was evident from the negotiation of the Cluster Munitions Convention), or to an identification with the aims, objectives and values of the treaty being negotiated. What has certainly been

22 Indeed, Droege and Giorgou highlight "the strength of strong and coherent arguments based on a premise of widely shared principles and values" as a contributing factor to the development of IHL. See Cordula Droege and Eirini Giorgou, "How international humanitarian law develops", above note 12, p. 1838.

clear in the experience of the authors is that over the last two decades at least, African States have valued a consensus-based approach to development of the law. Common African Positions, adopted by the African Union, are an important step for African States in the development of hard law. Few African governments would 'stick their necks out' on an issue that they don't suspect most of the continent would support and follow.

Does this approach to law-making still make sense in today's current geopolitical climate? A number of academics have written on the topic of different approaches to the development of IHL, highlighting various motivations for States to engage in such development of the law. According to Stephan, the inspirational approach to developing IHL, which the authors would argue has been favoured to date by African governments, is the more traditional approach that the authors generally witness, where the international community proposes an idealized legal system where new law is adopted with the hope that it will inspire and lead other stakeholders to follow the same path. While this has worked well in many instances, including for example with the adoption of the TPNW, Stephan argues that "during periods of political and technological upheaval and growing uncertainty about and alienation from group norms, socialization may do less work than is supposed."[23] He opines that in the world we live in today, the inspirational approach to development of IHL will face challenges in that what is built will not come to pass for a long time. The danger in this is that "the longer a proposal goes unadopted, the easier it is for people to conclude that the community regards it as lacking social value".[24]

As such, Stephan proposes an alternative approach to development of IHL, which he calls the entrepreneurial approach. This approach entails leading by example, where a State insists on a norm that it knows is not necessarily well-accepted worldwide but that the State believes in and is willing to defend. Such an approach relies on narratives related to State behaviour and values of importance to those States, and highlights issues where a State feels a sense of ownership over the issue. "To succeed, the programme requires a significant national actor ... to announce and comply with rules that constrain its behaviour".[25]

---

23 Paul B. Stephan, "The crisis in international law and the path forward for international humanitarian law", above note 14, p. 2092.

24 Paul B. Stephan, "The crisis in international law and the path forward for international humanitarian law", above note 14, p. 2092.

25 Paul B. Stephan, "The crisis in international law and the path forward for international humanitarian law", above note 14, p. 2094.

Are African States ready to pivot to this alternative approach to law-making when it comes to development of IHL? And if so, could the Tool possibly encourage African States to do so? Could the Tool inspire African States by assisting them in their recollection of their cultural values and obligations and how those obligations match modern day principles of IHL? In the opinion of the authors – yes, yes and yes.

3.3 *The Potential Contribution of the Tool to the Development of International Humanitarian Law in the Current Geopolitical Climate*

The authors propose that the entrepreneurial approach to development of IHL requires courageous States to take a stand on issues they believe in – issues that reflect a strong link to a cultural norm, value or practice. It requires champion States, or champion individuals within those States, to play a prominent and significant role in the development of the law. It requires States who are willing to lead by example. Given Africa's past experience in the development of international law, the authors are in little doubt that many African governments would be ready and willing to embrace this alternative approach to law-making. What may be needed is a 'little nudge' in the right direction. It is this last element where the authors are convinced that the Tool could make a small but vital contribution.

One way in which the Tool could help nudge African States to take steps towards the development of IHL is through the exhibit of the posters of the Tool. Through these exhibits, the Tool has captured the attention of government representatives, diplomats, civil society actors, academics, students and the general public. It is the authors' aim to facilitate the display of the Tool exhibit in the headquarters of the African Union, the various Regional Economic Communities on the continent, and even at the level of the United Nations headquarters. The images displayed on the posters have also been posted on social media, along with specific messaging about certain provisions of IHL that are relevant to ongoing armed conflicts at the time.[26]

Another way to nudge African States in the right direction is through the use of specific traditions collected in the Tool, where those traditions are particularly relevant for the development of a certain thematic of IHL. Indeed, the ICRC legal advisors overseeing the update of the Commentaries to the 1949 Geneva Conventions are considering utilising the tradition on treatment of prisoners of war collected from Somalia in the update of the Third Geneva Convention on Prisoners of War. Colleagues from the ICRC's forensics

26 See for example https://www.instagram.com/p/C-SdM4js1uv/ and https://www.instagram.com/p/C-cDXXERIa8/ (accessed 05.09.2024).

department have used the tradition on management of dead bodies also collected from Somalia in their engagement with stakeholders in a number of African countries. As the body of customs collected in the Tool expands, it is hoped that the operational value of specific traditions, customs and values will increase. Overall, the ambition for the Tool is that it's use in operational settings will contribute to a process towards the reduction of suffering during times of armed conflict.

Finally, it is proposed that simply starting African regional experts' meetings on topics related to IHL with a viewing of the ICRC's short video on the Tool will help set the tone of the meeting, roundtable or negotiation. It will remind African experts of the relevance of IHL to Africa as well as the of the responsibility that Africans have to continue to respect, promote and develop IHL.

4 The Potential Benefit of the Tool for the Work of the Humanitarian Actors

While the above section has focused on the benefit the Tool can have in terms of development of IHL, this final section will briefly highlight how the Tool may also benefit humanitarian workers, including ICRC colleagues, in their work on the continent. This aspect of the Tool being used by other organisations was not necessarily foreseen by the authors, as the Tool was conceptualized within the ICRC, for the ICRC.

And for the ICRC, the value of the Tool is clear. The ICRC aims to build bridges between cultures, religions and IHL in order to enrich its narratives on IHL, anchoring them more effectively in diverse settings and customs. It aims to do so both by furthering ownership of IHL principles by African States but also by fostering the perception of IHL as a universal set of norms. The Tool fits squarely within this objective. It is also important to note that for the ICRC, the idea behind the Tool is not new. Already in 2004 the ICRC embarked on research into the Roots of Behaviour in War, with the objective of identifying those factors crucial to influencing the behaviour of armed actors during conflicts.[27] In 2018 the ICRC published an update to this research, entitled "Roots of Restraint in War", which identifies "the sources of influence on various types of armed forces and armed groups, ranging from those with a highly

27 The Roots of Behaviour in War, 2004, The roots of behaviour in war – Understanding and Preventing IHL Violations (icrc.org) (accessed 08.10.2024), 2.

decentralized structure to those embedded within their communities".[28] One of the major findings described in the report is as follows:

> An exclusive focus on the law is not as effective at influencing behaviour as a combination of the law and the values underpinning it. Linking the law to local norms and values gives it greater traction. The role of law is vital in setting standards, but encouraging individuals to internalize the values it represents through socialization is a more durable way of promoting restraint.[29]

Indeed, this recognition of linking law to the values underpinning it is also now reflected in the ICRC's current Institutional Strategy 2024–2027,[30] which represents the ultimate acceptance of the Tool for the ICRC as an institution.

However, it has become very clear that not only is the Tool of interest to other organisations, but it could be of value to those organisations too. It is therefore sincerely hoped that a number of humanitarian organisations working to promote IHL on the African continent will engage with the Tool and find a way of using it within their own work as a useful resource. One element the ICRC will need to reflect on is how to facilitate such use, including ensuring all aspects of the Tool (posters, playing cards, postcards, instructions for their use) are available publicly. Another element to consider will be where the ICRC will continue to have added value in terms of the Tool. The authors would propose two avenues in this regard. Firstly, the ICRC should remain responsible for the regular updates of the Tool. Secondly, the ICRC may be one of the only international organisations with mandate, presence and acceptance in ongoing armed conflicts to ensure that the Tool is disseminated to armed actors. This operational aspect may be the element that distinguishes the ICRC from other actors – the ICRC's access to armed actors on the ground.

5 Conclusion

While some criticism of the Tool is valid and does need to be addressed, the authors would contend that this Tool has contributed something unique and

28 The Roots of Restraint in War, 2018, The Roots of Restraint in War | International Committee of the Red Cross (icrc.org) (accessed 08.10.2024).

29 The Roots of Restraint in War, ICRC publication, 2018, shop.icrc.org/the-roots-of-restraint-in-war-print-fr.html (accessed 08.10.2024), 9.

30 ICRC Strategy 2024–2027, 2024, ICRC launches 2024–2027 institutional strategy | ICRC (accessed 08.10.2024).

relevant to regional discussions on IHL. Although its full value is still to be realized, particularly when it comes to the 'operationalisation' of the Tool, the authors are of the opinion that the Tool has already achieved a great deal, particularly with regard to changing the narrative on IHL in the African context. For the ICRC, the Tool has certainly opened a door to deeper engagement on IHL with governments and academics bringing us closer to one another in a sense. In addition, the Tool has been, to some extent at least, a catalyst for further interest and research into the idea of linking culture and IHL on the African continent, and has contributed to mainstreaming the value of researching contextualized proof of the relevance of IHL.

Turning from the past and looking to the future, the authors are convinced that the Tool may play a small role in ensuring the continued and proper development of IHL. As Stephan argues, "in a period of conflict in and transformation of international relations, States need to find new ways of discovering points of common interest and signalling willingness to conform to particular norms."[31] The authors propose that the Tool can help encourage African States to discover these points of common interest based on their own customs and practices dating back centuries. Indeed, Bartles-Smith opines that "morals are more powerful than law in influencing behaviour, and ... people are more motivated to adhere to the law if it resonates with their identities and moral values".[32] He suggests that "given that law, religion and culture still interpenetrate in all but the most secular contexts, IHL frequently requires some degree of religious or cultural validation if it is to gain real traction in societies at large, and across religious and cultural divides."[33] Highlighting the correlation between cultural values and modern-day principles of IHL is the very essence of the Tool.

Continuing to measure the impact of the Tool will be vital, as will the continued and regular update of this living project. After all, as commented by a South Sudanese student after joining a session on the Tool at an ICRC event in Kenya, "I now see that IHL was not cooked up by the West, it is embedded in all our cultures".

31 Paul B. Stephan, "The crisis in international law and the path forward for international humanitarian law", above note 14, p. 2096.

32 Andrew Bartles-Smith, "Religion and International Humanitarian Law", above note 1, p. 1733.

33 Andrew Bartles-Smith, "Religion and International Humanitarian Law", above note 1, p. 1731.

CHAPTER 6

West African Laws of War – Adopting the Marxist Stages of Historical Development

Godfree Matthew

1 Introduction

This research seeks to establish the existence of certain customs and traditions of warfare among the ancient kingdoms of West Africa that are similar to the rules of modern international humanitarian law (subsequently referred to as IHL). It also seeks to discover the existence of such customary practices regulating warfare among ancient kingdoms of West Africa before the advent of modern IHL promoted by Henry Dunant. Adopting the Marxist typology of historical development of human society, this research deploys the hybrid of periodization techniques[1] in order to show the evolution of these customs and traditions of warfare overtime. For this reason, the Marxist concept of historical materialism[2] is the theoretical yardstick upon which this research is based. However, the research also resorted to similar historical, archeological, theological, sociological and anthropological concepts, in order to enrich the work. This approach is also relevant because it gives this research a multi-disciplinary posture.[3]

---

1 Some of these periodisation techniques in history include hunter-gatherer Period, Craft-Agrarian Period, Industrial Period, and information-scientific period. See Leornid Grinin, "Periodisation of History", Proceedings of the Xxii World Congress of Philosophy, p. 1. These techniques are found to be useful in analyzing state formations and political transformations of states from one stage to another. See Svetlana Osipova, "Political history Periodisation and its Methodological Possibilities As a Tool to Study the Process of State Formation" (T.G., Shevchenko Pridnestrovian State University, Tiraspol, 2015), pp. 193–194.

2 Michael Haralambos, "*Sociology: Themes and Perspective*" (Oxford University Press, 1980), pp. 13–14.

3 The Multi-Disciplinary Approach refers to use of different views from other disciplines to address a common issue or problem. It helps to provide an understanding of a particular issue to people from different views from the lens of their disciplines. Thus, it has the advantage of reaching and attracting wider audience. It could further include interdisciplinary research and cross-disciplinary research. Interdisciplinary research seeks to integrate theoretical frameworks from different disciplines in order to establish the existence of a particular position. It uses study design and methodology that is not limited to any field.

 | DOI:10.1163/9789004703094_008

Flowing from the above, this research is structured into ten sections. The first section discuses the theoretical frameworks relating to the research. Thus, concepts such as the background to this study, motivation for this research, and factors that causes wars among the kingdoms of West Africa, were examined.

In the second section, the research analyses the theoretical discourse of historical materialism propounded by Karl Marx. It examines each stage of the historical development expounded by Karl Marxist. Additionally, this section discussed the reflection of Marxist stages of development within the historical context of West African Kingdoms. It also attempts to introduce and link the study to the central theme of this work. It situates each of these historical stages, within the context of laws and customs of warfare in the ancient Kingdoms of West Africa.

In section 3, this research highlights the Marxist's historical stages of development and the historical evolution of ancient kingdoms of West Africa. Section four examines the laws and customs of war among the West African kingdoms during the primitive stage expounded by Karl Marx. This part of the study brings out factual instances of warfare in ancient kingdoms of West Africa, where rules were set and violated. It discusses the permissible actions in warfare as well as the prohibited and forbidden acts during bellicose. Punishments and sanctions for the violation of such laws and customs have been examined.

Further discourse on the slavery stage, feudal stage and capitalist stage are analysed in sections 5, 6 and 7 of this study. The yardstick for analysis is the same as those highlighted in the primitive stage. That is, there was an existence of factual rules and regulations governing warfare as well as sanctions for the violation of such rules (in some instances) against offenders. Section 8 of this study deals with the main findings of this research. It examined the findings of laws and customs of warfare that predated modern IHL. It also examines some of these laws and customs of warfare changed overtime as a result of interface between ancient West Africa and Islam as well as colonial masters.

Section 9 is like a postscript of this research. Having examined the historicity of laws and customs of warfare in Ancient West Africa, this study further interrogates how contemporary is IHL in West Africa today? Thus, the work

---

Thus, it requires the use of the analytical and empirical skills and methods of the disciplines involved in various stages of development. Trans-disciplinary approach deals with research carried out by joint – team of investigators from different disciplines in order to create or invent novel concepts, theories or translational innovations that integrate and move beyond disciplines – based approaches to address common problems. See Ohio State University, "Why Cross-Disciplinary Research Matters".

has established that many West African States are committed to the Geneva Conventions and their Additional Protocols by being signatories to these laws. Equally, the weaknesses of their commitments in the areas of implementing and complying with such laws are equally examined.

Section 10 concludes this work. It highlights the summary of the findings of the research. It also examines the areas of dilemma associated with the research. The work makes recommendations on how to address some of the challenges experienced in the course of this research. Finally, this research concludes by recommending suggested areas for further studies so as to enrich the knowledge of laws of armed conflicts from ancient to present, and also expand the spheres of African military jurisprudence.

1.1 *Background to the Study*

The origin of IHL was mostly ascribed to Western civilization due to the works of Henry Dunant in "Memory of Solferino", 1863[4] and Francis Lieber's "Code of Lieber" of 1861 which was written to reflect the war situations during the American Civil War.[5] Other laws that subsequently developed the principles are the Hague Rules, the Geneva laws and their protocols. These *corpus juris* are believed to be the bedrock of modern IHL.

The development of modern IHL inspired by the works of Henry Dunant and Francis Lieber, created an impression that the idea of modern warfare is solely of Western origin.[6] Because of this perception, there was an assumption that other parts of the world did not have the rules governing armed conflict. These assumptions extend to Africa.[7] There were several reasons which led to the spread of these assumptions in intellectual circles. Some of these reasons include the enlightenment in Europe, the emergence of books and printing press in Europe, industrial revolution as well as the development in science and technology in Europe. These advancements were able to give Europe and other Western countries, an edge over some parts of the World in the areas of intellectualism and sciences. Thus, Africa was less developed in advanced sciences and technological developments as well as political organisation and military warfare. However, as rebuttal to this hasty generalisation, ancient West

4 Sam McFarland, 'A Brief History of an Unsung Hero and Leader-Jean Henry Dunant and the Founding Of the Red Cross at the Geneva's Convention', *Journal of Leadership and Change*, Vol. 5. Iss. 2, pp. 41, 42.

5 International Committee of Red Cross, "*Development of Modern International Humanitarian Law*", ICRC, 2010.

6 Aksamitowska Karolina, 'Traditional Approaches to the Law of Armed Conflict', *Journal of International Legal Studies*, 11 (2020), p. 13.

7 Ibid.

Africa once had an established kingdom that lasted over 1000 years.[8] Also, West Africa was known to have discovered iron ore earlier than other parts of the globe.[9] These Kingdoms were built by military might which required conquest and warfare to protect, expand, defend and consolidate their territorial sovereignty.

Therefore, the discovery of iron in West Africa further helped those political kingdoms in four ways: (a) warfare (b) commerce, (c) industrialization and (d) agriculture. These indices are very instrumental to the political, military, commercial and diplomatic status of a nation. Once a nation is capable of having these indices, it can be said to be a strong political and military nation.

Flowing from the above exposition, it is not in doubt that West African kingdoms had rules of warfare as one of the spheres of their civilization and inter-group relations. A further interrogation is, how were these wars prosecuted? What traditional norms and values were operational among the ancient West-African kingdoms? Were there ways that these customs and traditions of warfare among West African States confluence/converged with modern IHL? Were the rules and customs governing war in ancient West Africa static overtime? Or did these customs and traditions changed overtime? Lastly, were these rules and customs on warfare the same in all kingdoms of West Africa? It is in attempt to respond to these questions that give birth to the title of this research, "West African Laws of War: Adopting the Marxist Stages of Historical Development."

1.2 *Areas of Research*

The geographical entity known as West Africa today was made up of various tribal kingdoms, chiefdoms and empires.[10] These geographical entities started their transmogrification due to certain geographical and political developments that later made them what they are today. For example, the Old Ghana Empire later declined and balkanised into Songhai Empire.[11] Then out of Songhai Empire came the Mali Empire.[12] Those kingdoms were formed in mili-

8 Bruce Lenman P. and Boyd Katharine, "*Chambers Dictionary of World History*" (Chambers Harrap Publishers, Ltd, 1993), p. 487.

9 Connah Graham, "*African Civilizations: An Archaelogical Perspective*" (Cambridge University Press, 3d Edn. 2015), pp. 1–4. See also Smithsonian National Museum of Art, "Africa's Iron Origins: Archaeological Evidence".

10 Boston University, 'Kingdoms of Ancient and Medieval West Africa and Trade across the Sahara', *Pardee School of Global Studies*.

11 Ibid.

12 Ibid.

tary campaigns which implied the likelihood of either abuse or ethical compliance with customs of warfare.

Some of the prominent kingdoms that were militarily developed and organised, were the Asante Kingdom, the Akan Kingdom, and the Kanem-Bornu Empire. The Dahomey Kingdom, the Fon Kingdom, the Kwararrafa Kingdom and the Madinka Empire could also be categorised. Others were the Old Oyo Empire, Benin Empire and the Hausa-Fulani City States. These were some of the Ancient West African Kingdoms that were militarily organized.

With the coming of colonialism and post-colonial independence, these Kingdoms, Chiefdoms and Emirates, assumed a new political identity of nation-states; especially, with the attainment of political independence from their colonial masters. It is from these angles that these states assumed a different political identity with new names such as Benin Republic, Burkina Faso, Cape-Verde, Ghana, Gambia, Guinea, Guinea-Bissau, Ivory Coast, Liberia, Mali, Niger, Nigeria, Senegal, Sierra-Leone and Togo.[13] Today, as of 2023, West Africa is an African sub-region with the population of 444, 705,552.[14] The nations of West Africa today are independent political entities enjoying sovereignty, which qualifies them to freely enter into international relations with other members of international community. It is from this perspective that all the West African States are members of the major instruments of IHL such as the Geneva laws and its protocols.[15]

2 Section 2: Marxist's Stages of Development

Karl Marx analyses the stages of human development into the following, primitive communism, slavery stage, feudal stage, capitalism, socialists and stateless communism.[16] These stages show how human society developed from one level of civilization to another. This stage shows the evolution of human society from simple/rural society to complex/modern society.[17] The stages are examined below.

---

13 ECOWAS, 'ECOWAS Member States'.

14 Worldometer, 'Population of West Africa (2023)', December 8, 2023.

15 ICRC, "*Implementing IHL In West Africa: 2018 Report*", p. 913. Also, see United Nations Treaty Collection,' Geneva Conventions'.

16 The Hindu, 'Karl Marx in Core Five Ideas', May 5, 2018.

17 'Unit 14 Approaches To Stages of Development'.

2.1 *Primitive Communism*

This stage deals with the organization of human society in its simplest nature. It was nature-based and less complex. In this stage humanity was closer to nature in a simple way of living. The main features of this society were hunting, nomadic pastoralism and stationery agriculture.[18] The social units were organized along tribal lines. Modes of production were actualized via communal efforts and thus all properties were communally owned. There was no private ownership of properties in this stage. The main traditional technologies at that stage included stones, woods and sticks. In this stage, there was no class division.

2.2 *Ancient Slavery*

This stage was characterized by improved means of production and technology. Due to the progress human beings made in the areas of technology, production also increased. The increase in surplus of goods produced further led to the notion of private ownership of property. Thus, in order to acquire forces of production and own property, that stage deployed the use of force to acquire human labour. The human beings acquired by force were slaves.

This stage society further divided the society into owners of properties and those that did not, and between the slave owners and the non-slave owners. Those who owned slaves became the aristocrats of the society and were able to wield power and made decisions on behalf of the society. They could deploy their slaves to defend their territories such as lands and water ways and to attack others.

2.3 *Feudalist Stage*

This stage was characterized by class divisions between landlords and the serfs. The Landlord was the employer of the Serfs. The Serfs were tied to the lands owned by the landlord.[19] They cultivated the lands and paid by the landlords for the land used. The feudal stage showed that productions of goods and the domination of the serfs by their landlords led to upheavals, which in turn leads to revolution that evolved into capitalism.

2.4 *Capitalist Stage*

This was the advanced stage of human development that ushered in mass productions of goods. Technology was so advanced that it led to mass productions

18 Ibid.

19 Ibid.

of goods and services. In this stage, the class was further divided into owners of factors of production known as bourgeoisie, and the workers known as the proletariat. In this stage, labour is the power which the proletariat would use for exchange in order to survive, while the bourgeoisie was the purchaser of that labour to produce surplus value characterized by mass production of goods.[20] Thus, capitalist stage was characterized by private ownership of forces of production and profit maximization.

According to Karl Marx, capitalist stage is characterized by unequal relationship between the bourgeoisie and the proletariat. That unholy relationship characterized by exploitation of the working class will lead to revolution that will overthrow the capitalist structure. It was after that revolution that the proletariat will be free from the shackles of capitalism.

2.5 *Socialism/Communism*

This stage, Karl Marx postulated, was characterized by collective ownership of means of production. It was a state that envisages human beings to be free from exploitation and other hostile means of production experienced under the capitalist stage.

In communism, this stage envisages an egalitarian society where people are free from domination. It is a classless society. Further exposition on communism by Marx and Friedrich Engels reveal that there is a distinction between a lower and a higher form of communism. In the lower form of communism, workers are paid for their services according to their inputs. The ownerships of the means of production are controlled by the state. In the higher communism, the motion of state is withered away. Thus, it is a stateless society where every distribution of resources will not be regulated by the state; rather, distribution will take place based on the principles of 'ability' and 'needs'. Thus, "each will take according to his abilities and each according to his needs".[21]

3 Section 3: Interfacing Marxist Stage of Development within The Periodisation of West African Historical Evolution

This section of the research is aimed at situating how the historical stages of Karl Marx could interface with the historical periodisation of African States. It seeks to further examine certain historical periods that are relevant in the

20 Michael Haralambos, Op. Cit. p. 14.
21 The Hindu, Loc. Cit.

organic development of Africa (including West Africa) and to align each of these periods of African history within the Marxist stages of historical development. However, before situating the Marxist stages of development within the West African context, it is important to note that, the development of human society is not strictly tied to this notion of Karl Marx. It is not accurate to conclude that all states serially developed along the same line in a progressive manner as outlined by Karl Marx. Thus, some states may likely experience historical developments by skipping one stage.[22] They are some states that may experience primitive stage, slavery stage, feudal stage and capitalist stage; but not socialism/communism. Nevertheless, there are nations like Russia who experienced feudalism-capitalist stage and socialism, but never experienced the primitive and slavery stages.[23] Similarly, countries like China and others only witnessed feudalism and communism, and never experienced slavery and capitalism.[24]

The stages of historical developments that will be examined here include African state formation, encounters with Europe, state of legitimate commerce, colonial period, decolonization period and post-colonial period.[25] These stages are examined in the subsequent part of this study.

3.1 *African State Formation*

This is the age when many African States started developing into political units. During this stage many African states started developing into mighty political kingdoms.[26] These political and economic growths were due to long distant trade with the outside world such as Trans-Saharan trade with the Arabs and

---

22 Botchwey Kwesi, 'Marxism and the Analysis of the African Reality', *Africa Development: A Quarterly Journal of* CODESRIA (1977) 2(1), pp. 9–16, https://www.jstor.org, accessed 28 October 2023.

23 Economic Institute of the Academy of Sciences of the U.S.S.R, *Political Economy: A Textbook issued by the Economics Institute of the Academy of Sciences of the U.S.S.R*, 1st edn. (Moscow 1954), Part I: Pre-capitalist Modes of Production, Chapter 1, https://www.marxists.org/subject/economy/authors/pe/pe-ch01.htm, accessed 28 October 2023.

24 Wei Liu, 'Combining Marxism and China's Practices for the Development of a Socialist Political Economy with Chinese Characteristics', *China Political Economy* (2018) 1(1), pp. 30–44, DOI: 10.1108/CPE-09-2018-001, https://www.emerald.com/insight/content/doi/10.1108/CPE-09-2018-001/full/html, accessed 28 October 2023.

25 The Saylor Foundation, *Major Periods in African History*, HIST252 Subunit 1.2 (Saylor Academy, n.d.), 1–4, https://resources.saylor.org/wwwresources/archived/site/wp-content/uploads/2012/05/hist252-1.2-Major-Periods-in-African-History.pdf, accessed 2 October 2023.

26 Ibid.

the Muslim worlds. Kingdoms that thrived under this historical age include Old Ghana Empire, Songhay, Mali and the Swahili City States.[27]

The stage of African State formation as an historical period in the development of Africa aligns with some stages of developments expounded by Karl Marx. The existence of distant trade (Tran-Saharan slave trade) aligns with the feature of slave trade propounded by Karl Marx. It also reflects the features of feudal stage espoused by Marx. This is evident in the fact that most of the Kingdoms such as Old Ghana Empire, Songhai Empire and Mali Empire were kingdoms that were built via military conquest where slavery and feudalism played a major role.[28]

3.2 *Encounters with Europeans*

This period established that while Africa was in contact with other parts of the world, it only come into contact with Europe from 1450 to 1815.[29] That period characterized trade with Europeans in slave trade. The peculiar feature of that age was the advent of the Trans-Atlantic Trade where many Africans were shipped across Europe and America. This stage led to the emergence of class of persons known as slave masters or slave owners.

This period aptly fits into the slavery stage expounded by Karl Marx. The difference between the slavery stage expounded by Karl Marx in encounters with Europe and that of the African State formation stage is that, in the latter, it was Africans that were mostly slave owners.[30] In the African State Formation Stage, the slave trade is between Africans and Arabs. However, under the stages of encounter with Europe, Europeans were the slave dealers. The slave dealers in turn supplied guns to the Africans to continue the war of aggression to hunt for more slaves. This development birthed the phenomenon known as gun-slave-circle.[31]

3.3 *Stage of Legitimate Commerce*

This stage started in the Middle of 19th Century when slave trade was abolished. The abolition of slave trade gave rise to the emergence of industrial

27 Joseph Bradshaw M., "The Bandiagara Emirates: Warfare, Slavery and Colonisation in The Middle-Niger, 1863–1903" (a Dissertation submitted to Michigan State University in Partial Fulfillment for the Degree of History-Doctor of Philosophy, 2021), p. 4.

28 Ibid.

29 Saylor Academy, Loc. Cit.

30 Gregory Slack, "Did Marx Defend Black Slavery?".

31 Ibid.

revolution. That trend, in turn, gave rise for demands for more raw materials to sustain the industrial revolutions in Europe and America. Consequently, commercial activities in raw materials boomed between Africa and Europeans. It was these developments that ushered the emergence of European commercial companies such as the Royal Niger Company that was later used as an instrument for colonial political infiltration into African Kingdoms. This development further created a class of wealthy merchants among Africans.

This stage of legitimate commerce aptly fit into what Karl Marx termed as capitalist stage. Here, reference to commercial activities and industrialization are key capitalist terms that Karl Marx propounded as elements of capitalism. The trading on African commodities is termed as an unequal transaction between them. Equally, the existence of the wealthy class that owns the factors of production (who are supported by the state), fall under what Karl Marx term as the Bourgeoisie. The bourgeoisie then exploit the working class called the Proletariat. Thus, capitalism established class distinction between two classes i.e. the bourgeoisie and the proletariat.

3.4 *Colonial Period*

This period started with the Berlin Conference of 1884 when Europeans shared the African continent among themselves. In this period, the Europeans conquered and subjugated the African Kingdoms. This was actualised through violent and conquest of African kingdoms by Europeans.[32] This stage agrees with Marxist historical stage of capitalism. This is because contradictions that arise as a result of exploitations of the weaker class by the stronger class. The brutality of colonialists like King Leopold II and others found reification in the prediction of Karl Marx about the exploitation of Capitalism. Conflicts during the capitalist stage (including colonial stage) are evident in the Even Years' Samoury Wars with the French colonialist as well as other African Kingdoms that tried to defend themselves against colonial invasion.[33]

With respect to West Africa, historical developments with reference to laws and customs of warfare, this research restricts itself to the stages of primitive communism, slavery, feudalism and capitalism. This is because Africa has constructively passed through these historical stages in a very confrontational manner; first, with itself, and second, with the wider world.[34]

32 Toyin Folala, "*Colonialism and Violence In Nigeria*" (Indiana Press Ltd, 2009), p. 8.

33 Michael Crowder, "*West Under Colonial Rule*" (Hutchinson & CO. Publishers Ltd, 1968), p. 8.

34 Ibid.

3.5 *Decolonisation Period*

This stage is when African leaders started asserting political independence from their colonial masters.[35] This assertion sometimes takes a peaceful approach through series of constitutional conferences. Countries like Ghana, Nigeria, Democratic Republic of Congo, Cameroun, and others got their political independence through constitutional conferences.[36] However, there were other states that got their independence through violent approach known as liberation movement. This approach entailed physical confrontations with colonial powers giving rise to abuse of human rights and violations of laws of wars. This is seen in the Italian and French uses of gases against the Algerians and Somaliland.[37]

The decolonization process aligns with the Marxist notion of capitalist stage that is characterized with conflict of interest due to exploitation and desire for domination. The decolonization period that is characterized by armed conflicts between Africans and their colonial masters, amounted to exploitation envisaged by Karl Marx.

3.6 *Post Colonial Stage*

This is the stage where many African States achieved political independence. Many of them are now states that enjoy the status of separate political entity in the committee of nations. They are now subjects of international law, which can enter into a diplomatic relations with others nations and international organisation.

Post colonial stage could still be situated between the capitalist and the socialist stage of historical development postulated by Karl Marx. This is because immediately after their independence most African States adopted the capitalist economic ideology as a pattern of development, only few African States, who were considered radicals, adopted the Socialist economic policies.[38] Some of these states included the socialist government of Tanzania under Julius Nyerere, through the *Ujaama* principle. Similarly, Ethiopia, under Halle Mengitsu, adopted the socialist political ideology where his reign was tagged with a lot of crime against humanity.[39]

One of the reasons why the Post-colonial stage of African history aligned with Marxist historical stages of development is because of the prevalence of

35 Meredith Martin, "*The State of Africa*" (UK, Simon&Sucher, 2011), p. 218.

36 Ibid.

37 Kwesi Botchwey, Loc. Cit.

38 Meredith Martin. Loc. Cit.

39 Ibid.

cold war in the early 1950s to early 1990s. The cold war provides competitive choices to the newly independent states. The competition is so gross that it led to coups and counter-coups as well as civil wars among African Nations.[40]

4 Section 4: Primitive Communism

This section of the study discusses the laws and customs of warfare that existed during primitive stage in ancient West Africa. It examines the periodisation of primitive stage in West Africa. After that laws and customs of warfare available during the primitive stage in the various kingdoms of West Africa are also evaluated. The permissible and prohibited practices as well as the sanctions, regulating warfare will also be examined.

4.1 *Periodisation of Primitive Communism in West Africa (5000 BC–600 BC)*

The Marxist's notion of primitive stage could be categorized in history as Pre-classical (primitive) period which spanned from 5000 BC–600 BC.[41] As such the developments in West Africa on laws and customs of warfare at the primitive stage are examined under this time frame, where possible.[42] Also, the periodization of Marxist Primitive stage aligned with the work of Freeman-Greenvice on chronology of world history.[43] He was able to relay how some principal events in West Africa (including wars), where he made references to certain dates and events relating to warfare in West Africa.[44] It is from this prism that the laws and customs of warfare in West Africa will be examined in this work.

---

40 Meredith Martin, Op. Cit., pp. 218–220.

41 Robert W. Boyle refers to Primitive Stage as pre-Classical Age relating spanning from 5000 BC–600 BC. To him the civilization that thrive around that time include the Sumerian, Babylonian, Egyptian and ancient Greece. It appears that archeology refers to the primitive state as a stage in which tribal society developed through Paleolithic, Mesolithic, and Neolithic ages. See Barnes & Noble, "Gold: History and Genesis of Deposits/Edition 1 by Boyle".

42 Ibid.

43 G.S. Freeman-Greenvice, "*Chronology of World History: A Calendar of Principal Events From 3000 BC–1976 AD*" (2nd Edn., Rex Collins, London, 1978), pp. 170, 286, 290, 292, 376, 442, 448, 454, 480 and 490.

44 Ibid.

4.2 *Laws and Customs of West Africa during the Primitive Stage (5000 BC–600 BC)*

In this stage, most wars were fought using simple tools like stones, arrows, bows, knives, and other less traditional weapons. Most wars at primitive stage could be termed as endemic war, a sort of war that is often characterized by a number of taboos and rituals that restricted the number of casualties and the duration of warfare.[45] It is also known as ritual warfare. For purpose of clarity, this work will use the word ancient in describing the laws and customs of war governing some West African kingdoms during primitive stage.

4.2.1 Ancient Nigeria

Among the Mwaghavul tribes of Nigeria there are two types of warfare; intra-tribal warfare and the inter-tribal warfare.[46] The inter-tribal war is not lethal. This is because it is forbidden for members of the same tribe to kill one another. Thus, lethal weapons were prohibited in intra-tribal wars. The weapons used are mostly sticks in hurting and debilitating fellow tribesmen. However, in the inter-tribal war, the Mwaghavul killed their enemies. This war is lethal because it involves other members of tribe. The weapons of warfare used here are arrows and cannibalism.[47]

Also, the Ngas were warriors who were known for using spears, bows, knives and poisonous arrows as weapon warfare.[48] They also used cannibalism on the defeated enemy.[49] They similarly deployed the use of their rocky enclaves for military purpose, especially in guerilla warfare and the use of stones as military weapons.[50] Thus, one of the means and methods of warfare used by them is their natural environment.

Again, among the people of Bassa–Nge arrows, bows and spear are used as means and methods of warfare.[51] Once enemies surrendered and sued

---

45 Freeman-Greenvice made references to wars in ancient West African Kingdoms such as the as The Old Ghana Empire, The Yoruba Kingdom of Oyo, Kanem Bornu Empire, Hausa-City States, the Dahomean Wars as well as those of the Ashanti Kingdom of Ghana. See pages 260 to 460 of Freeman-Greenvice's work, referred to at footnotes 64 of this Study.

46 Jos Oral History And Literature Texts, "*Mwaghavul, Ngas, Njak and Mupun Oral History Texts*" (One Harmattan, 1981), pp. 24–29.

47 Ibid.

48 O. Temple and C.L. Temple, "*Notes on Tribes, Provinces, Emirates and States of Northern Provinces of Nigeria*" (Cape Town, 1919), pp. 10–11.

49 Ibid., p. 11.

50 Gofwen Rotgak, "*The History and Socio-Political Organisation of The Ngas: An Anecdotal Compendium of Anthropological Notes*" (St. Stephen INC. Books House, 2007), p. 97.

51 Joel P. Dada, 'Pre-Colonial Military Organisation in Bassa-Nge' 2001, p. 53.

for peace, the victor would acknowledge that.[52] The rules of wars applied separately. For example in an inter-tribal wars, daughters of Bassa–Nge who were married to the enemies were not attacked, neither will they be taken as captives. However, those who are not from their tribes could be objects of attacks and capture.[53] Perhaps, it was for this purpose that the use of tribal marks was necessary for identification.[54]

Another means and methods of warfare used by them at that stage was the use of charms and amulets. The charms and amulets were believed to prevent the enemies' weapons from coming towards them.[55] Of peculiar interest to this people was that, the timing for fighting wars was decided by the belligerents. Thus, most wars were fought in day time, and wars were not fought at night.[56]

Further, customs and traditions governing armed conflict abound in the various Kingdoms and societies in Nigeria. It is noted that wars were fought under rigid conventions among the people of central Nigeria. For example, among the Goemai, Montol, Ngas and Kofyar of Central Nigeria war drums, war horns and smokes were deployed to indicate certain means of communication in warfare.[57] Drums and war horns were used to indicate the beginning and continuation of wars, while smokes were used to indicate surrender by the vanquished or triumphs by the victors.[58]

Even during colonialism, war among the central peoples of Nigeria was governed in such a way that related communities were not killed. Thus, where a war occurred between two or more communities that are related to each other, it was forbidden for people to kill each other.[59] Doing so constitute fratricide, and where such acts occurred, they could be termed sacrilege, and propitiation was needed to atone for the acts. Under this type of war, the only military object that were permitted, was to debilitate the enemy. Killing among this people was only allowed when the war was between communities that were not related.

Moreover, the Goemai, Montol and Kofyar people were said to have deployed the use of spears, daggers, bows and arrows in warfare.[60] Among these people

52 Ibid., p. 53.
53 Ibid.
54 Ibid.
55 Elizabeth Isichie, 'Study in the history of Plateau State of Nigeria', in "*Colonialism Resisted*" (MacMillan Press Ltd., 1982), pp. 204–206.
56 Ibid.
57 Ibid.
58 Ibid.
59 Jos Oral History And Literature Texts, Loc. Cit.
60 Elizabeth Isichie, Loc. Cit., p. 206.

war was governed by a number of rigid conventions.[61] One of such conventions that were made available was that, communities had to deploy non-lethal weapons in warfare. Thus, when tribal wars ensued among communities related by blood, they fought with clubs, but do not kill each other.[62]

4.2.2 Ancient Songhai Empire

Warfare in Songhai Empire was harsh and full of cruelty. This is probably due to the roles of the various leaders that governed the empire. That was coupled with the fact that the empire was characterized by series of internal political upheaval relating to succession.[63] It was under these circumstances that a king like Sunni Ali became a ruler of Songhai Empire. He deployed the use of terror in warfare. He killed his foes mercilessly. He believed that by terrorizing his opponents the other ones would easily lay their arms and surrender, thus, economizing resources and time.[64] It was based on this belief that Sunni Ali ordered the genocide of the Fulbe in Songhai Empire. He also recruited the prisoners of wars into his regular army.[65]

Sunni Ali had special hatred for intellectualism and learning and thus, targeted scholars as his objects of military attacks.[66] Sunni Ali was aggressive and hostile towards scholars and was alleged to have set the famous Timbuktu library on fire in 1468.[67] King Sunni Ali was described by the Timbuktu Chronicle as "The Shedder of Blood", "Notorious evil Doer", and "the Killer of so many people that only God the Most High Knows the number".[68] A lot of negatives remarks on terror were attributed to Sunni Ali that keeps one to doubt the authenticity of such reports.

One account has it that Sunni Ali asked a mother to pound her baby in a mortar, and used its flesh to feed his horses.[69] Accounts like this could be termed as propaganda or exaggerations by historians, considering the fact that

61 Ibid.

62 Ibid.

63 Mammoudou Seyni, "Economic and Political Factor of Songhay Empire The Emergence of Kebbi Kingdom Nigeria, C.1500s" Scientific Research Publishing.

64 School History, "Songhai Empire Facts & Worksheets".

65 Lumen Leraning, "Songhai| Early Civilisations".

66 World History Vol. 2., "The Songhai Empire".

67 Valacy Rasmussen, "The Manuscript of Timbuktu: Armed Conflict and The Preservation of Memory", A Thesis Submitted to the Graduate Division of the University of Hawa'i at Manoa In Partial Fulfillment of the Requirements For The Degree of Master of Library and Information Science, May 2014.

68 Joel Wilson, 'In Search of Askia Mohammed: The Epic of Askia Mohammed as Cultural History and Songhay Foundational Myth', *Jason Madison University*, 2016, p. 23.

69 Valacy Rasmussen, Loc. Cit.

Sunni Ali was reputed to hate scholars.[70] It is also possible that Ali's successors might have blackmailed him in order to get the loyalty of their subjects.

Askia Mohammed was Ali's successor whose rule of war was humane. Under his reign, civilians were protected and were never attacked during armed conflict. However, Askia Muhammed was adjudged to be the first initiator of Trans-Atlantic Slave trade. This is because those he captured as prisoners of war were sold as slaves to Arabs and Europeans in exchange for guns and horses.

The Empire of Mali was one of the powerful kingdoms during the primitive age. The weapons used included bows and poisoned arrows and knives.[71] The armies were also organized along two army formations; professional armies and *levee en masse*.[72] Under Askia the Great, women were carried as war booties. Women of the conquered enemies were taken as captives and sometimes married to the royal families and the soldiers.[73]

Similarly, during armed conflicts, attacks on in-laws were prohibited. So, whenever there was a war between communities, if those communities are bound by marriage, there would be no attack.[74] Attacks would be carried out against those who were not related by marriage. This follows the African proverb that "one does not war against ones in-laws."[75]

4.2.3 Ancient Senegal

In Senegal, there was respect for environment, sacred and religious centres. Thus, tree like baobab trees and wood were prohibited from destruction during wars. Similarly, huts that were meant for fetishes objects, tombs of ancestors and places of cultural initiations were not objects of attacks. Such places were considered sacred and thus, prohibited from attacks.[76]

Equally, asylum in warfare was recognised in ancient Senegal. As such, any warrior who ran to hide inside fetish shrine or huts of an enemies' chief will not be killed, he would be granted asylum.[77] Such acts might be considered an

70 Joel Wilson, Loc. Cit.

71 Saylor.org, 'Ancient Civilization World/Empire of Mali'.

72 E.W. Bovil, "Caravans of The Old Sahara: An Introduction To History of The Western Sudan" (Oxford University Press, 1933), p. 94.

73 Ibid.

74 Okorie Haggler, 'Contemporary International humanitarian and Traditional African Warfare', *Joseph Ayo Babalola University*, Vol. 3. NO. 2, 2016, pp. 66–67.

75 Ibid.

76 Ibid.

77 Ibid.

act of submission to the chief and the gods of the enemy; as such, the person doing so was immune from attack.

4.2.4 Burkina Faso

The ancient Burkinabes also observed rules of engagement in warfare. They abided by certain ethical practices in armed conflict. One of these rules was that a disarmed enemy could not be struck. He would only be captured.[78] It was forbidden to strike an enemy from behind while fighting at a Sahelin Zone.[79] This was adjudged to be unfair practices in warfare. They believed that fighting had always to be face to face.[80]

4.2.5 Benin Republic (Ancient Dahomey)

In ancient Dahomey, prisoners of war were taken as slaves.[81] Children were offered as a sacrifice to appease the gods before a community would embark on warfare.[82] In other words, women and children were used as weapons of warfare against an impending enemy as a pre-emptive attack. It was a sort of a class suicide for the benefit of the community.

5 Section 5: Slavery Stage (1700–1850 AD)

This section examines the laws and custom of warfare that was prevailing in Ancient West Africa during the slavery stage. The periodisation of the slavery stage also forms part of discourse under this section. Reflections of the laws and customs of warfare among the African Kingdoms are also examined.

78 Diallo Yolande, "*African Traditions and Humanitarian Law*" P. 394, International Review of Red Cross (ICRC), Geneva, 1976.

79 Ibid.

80 Bello, E., 'African Customary Humanitarian Law', p. 14, Geneva, ICRC, in Okorie Hagler, Lo. Cit.

81 Archibald Dalzel, Governor at CAPE – COAST CASTLE, "The History of Dahomey, An Inland Kingdom Of Africa, Compiled From Authentic Memoirs With An Introduction And Notes" (T.SpillsBury And Sons., Snowhill (M.DCC.XCII., 1793), p. 27.

82 Ibid. pp. 171–173.

5.1 *Periodisation of Slavery Stage in West Africa*

The periodisation stage of slavery in West Africa could be tagged as starting from 1700 to 1850.[83] The slavery stage in West Africa, according to Marxist stages of historical development can be classified into (a) domestic slavery and (b) external slavery. The domestic slavery is a situation where people engage in enslaving their natives as form of punishments or indenture.[84] Such practice is mostly applied as punitive measures against deviants and social misfits such as thieves and troublemakers. The external slavery was where foreign powers participate in enslaving the native of particular community. This is done by either exporting the natives to the land of the foreign powers. It is from this perspective that the Tran-Saharan slave trade and the Trans-Atlantic Slave Trade flourished.

5.2 *Nigeria*

Some of the customary practices that governed warfare in Nigeria include those of the ancient Kingdom of Kwararrafa. That art of warfare recognised peace treaty during armed conflict.[85] Therefore, whenever an enemy surrendered, such surrender was accompanied by peace treaty. Such treaty was actualized by symbolic gesture such as giving of royal or military emblem of the vanquished to the victor.[86] It could also be done via oath taking among the warring parties. The essence of the surrender is to ensure that such an enemy would never revolt, and that it was willing to pay war indemnities. Again, after the surrender of the enemies, those taken as the detainees were treated humanely.[87] This is done in based on the ethics the victor is expected to be magnanimous in victory towards the vanquished.

Among the Bassa-Nge, war followed a systematic procedure. In the first place, before war commenced there is espionage to appraise the strength and

83 Steven Mintz, 'Historical Context: Facts About The Slave Trade and Slavery', History Resources, Gilder Lerhman Institute of American History. This periodisation is for the purpose of the analysis of Marxist historical development. other sources attributed to periodisation as 1450–1900 which ended slavery with anti-Abolition Movement. See Patrick Manning, "Slavery and Slave Trade in West Africa, 1400–1930." The History of African Development, and, Britannica, "Western Africa: The Slave-Trade Era".

84 Patrick Manning, Ibid.

85 Think Africa, "Federation of Kwararafa (13th–18th Century)", 2019.

86 Ibid.

87 Ibid.

weakness of the enemy.[88] This was mostly carried out by spies known as *Atuchi*, who then presented to the Council of Chiefs reports of their espionage.[89] After the spies presented their reports, the Council of Elders together with the military commanders would then deliberate at the house of *Nda Etrugutzian* and there, made a war proclamation/declaration against an enemy.[90]

The Jere people also used animals in warfare. They would command animal like bees to help them against an opponent. Tradition has it that there was a time when the Jere people were about to be defeated in a war, a heroine emerged as a *Deus ex machina*. This lady pressed the nipple of her breast, and chanted the following native words: '*Tenkeme ven ven: Tenkeme ven ven: Tenkeme ven ven: Tenkeme ven ven*'. These words were an incantation, charging the bees to stink the enemies. Fortunately, the bees stung the enemies who fled and the Jere people were victorious in that war.[91]

Moreover, the wounded soldiers were treated among the Hausa-city states during wars. This was the sole responsibility of *Wambai*, who was the medical doctor responsible for treating the wounded and sick in the battlefield. He was expected to have the knowledge of different types of wounds associated with battlefields.[92]

Further, among the Hausa Kingdom of Gobir vengeance or reprisal was forbidden. Rather, absence of vengeance is used to sue for peace in warfare. One of these instances was when the King of Gobir took many of his enemies' cows.[93] He returned to seize their cow again, for the second time. The *Phulas* said, 'Is it right on us to take vengeance?' But the King of Gober took some of their cows and returned to them, saying, 'Let there be peace between us.'[94]

The use of biological warfare was another feature of the pre-colonial Hausa state. Waters and food could be poisoned in order to achieve military objectives.[95] This was usually deployed to weaken and debilitate the mobility and military might of the enemy.

---

88 Joel P. Dada, "Pre-Colonial Military Organisation in Bassa-Nge", p. 53, in, *Mangdyen Journal of Central Nigerian Studies* (Early Rains, 2001), p. 53.

89 Ibid. p. 54.

90 Ibid.

91 Ibid. pp. 219–220.

92 Balla Aetti, "Arms and Armour in the Pre-Colonial Hausaland" (African Study Monographs, 1998), p. 154.

93 E.D. Moreell, "Affairs of West Africa" (Frank Cassas And Company Ltd., 1902), p. 125.

94 Yusuf Turaki, "Tainted Legacy: Islam Colonialism and Slavery In Northern Nigeria" (Isaac Publishing, 2010), pp. 57–58.

95 E.D. Moreell, Loc. Cit.

The Sokoto Jihad further enriched the laws and customs of warfare in Nigeria and some parts of West Africa.[96] The jihadist imbibed the Islamic tenets of warfare. Such tenets that they deployed in Northern Nigeria included not launching attacks on certain times considered as sacred hours, and not to attack people in mosque. However, this customary practice applied only to Muslims belligerents; those consider as pagans were not beneficiaries of these customs.

Again, the principle of humanness was highly observed during warfare in ancient West Africa. This is seen in the fact that the choice and timing of warfare had humane consideration. Fighting was agreed by the belligerents to commence in the evening so that whoever was exhausted can take rest in the night and resume the next day.[97] In a similar manner, during warfare belligerents are prohibited from completely encircling an enemy.[98] They were bound by tradition to allow some space that would serve as an escape route for the enemy whenever he was defeated.[99] Allowing escape route for an enemy was an ethics in ancient West Africa.

One of the aims of war is to establish one's might. It is meant to show who is stronger and not who is the most villainous. For this reason, Basil noted that:

> As Oral records show that battles were demonstrations of force rather than bloody massacres. Victory went to the strongest side by weight of numbers in the field. Or selected champions might fight it out in front of the assembled multitudes, and the winner would decide the day. Few were killed, the wounded were exchanged, and there would be compensation for the side that had lost the more.[100]

From the above remarks, it is clear that warfare was characterized by humane consideration. The exchange for the wounded and sick as well as the compensation for the most wounded side was a recognized practice among Africans. Instances of compensation could include given of foodstuffs and some animals

---

96 Ibid.

97 Basil D., "African Kingdom," Life-Time International, (Netherlands, 1967), p. 64. Culled from, Samgena Galega & Bidou Nguimasa, "Law of Ware: Non-International Armed Conflicts And Respect For The Law", *Ahmadu Bello University, Zaria, Journal of Private and Comparative Law*, p. 100.

98 Ibid.

99 Basil D., "The people's Cause: A History of Guerrillas in Africa" (Longman, 1981), p. 27 culled from Samgena Galega & Bidou Nguimasa, Loc. Cit.

100 Ibid.

to the offended as well as offering sacrifices to the gods for propitiation.[101] Equally, in order to ensure this that blood shedding was not the aim of the warfare, but establishing military might, even weapons were designed in such a way that they could minimise bloodshed.[102] Thus, Blacksmiths are prohibited from making that are too lethal such as being poisoned swords, heavy double-edged swords or poisoned arrows.[103]

In the Kingdom of Kano, warfare involved the tactics of surprise attacks and ambushes as well as direct attacks. There were constant attacks on civilian residents. To protect the society from such attacks during wars, fortifications were built. Fortification of cities with walls protects the society from conflagration and siege by enemies.[104] In the cause of warfare, prisoners were not spared, they were made slaves, and looting was a common practice among the Hausa-city states.[105]

Among the Ibos, certain customary practices were deployed in warfare. Certain weapons were not used when fighting fellow kinsmen from similar village-group.[106] Thus, weapons such as spears, bows and arrows were used.[107] However, when dealing with enemies and outsiders from the village groups, guns could be used.[108] Thus, when fighting an outsider it was permissible to use guns.

Another customary practice was that when a person was killed in war; his kinsmen were given the opportunity to come and pick his body for burial. Failure to do so on time would give the other enemy the reason to come and cannibalize the corpses.[109] Two reasons could be advanced for cannibalism among the Agbalaja people. The first was to boast to the enemy that they were not men enough to protect their corpse. The second reason was to promote one's ego of been macho and stone-hearted; thereby, intimidating the opponent.

---

101 Haggler Okorie. Loc. Cit.

102 Bala Achi, "Arms and Armour in the Warfare of Pre-Colonial Hausaland", *African Study Monographs*, 1988, 8(3), p. 148.

103 Ibid.

104 B.A. Ogot, "UNESCO International Scientific Committee For The Drafting of A General History Of Africa: General History of Africa from the Sixteenth to Eighteenth Century" (University of California Press, Berkeley Press, 1992), pp. 274.

105 Ibid. pp. 471 and 473.

106 Ibid.

107 M.M. Green, "Ibo Village Affairs Chiefly with Reference To The Village Umueke Agbaja" (Brown & Sons Limited, OH, Hull, 1947), p. 7.

108 B.A. Ogot, Loc. Cit.

109 M.M. Green, Loc. Cit.

The Ibos also used to choose times and seasons to battles.[110] Times of festivities were regarded as sacred. As such people did not go to war at that time because of fear of sanctions by the gods. The Council of Elders and the Gods of the land made rules governing warfare. Warfare could be intercepted by truce and the parties who were affected by loss of lives were compensated. Any warrior that breached the rules established by elders and the gods is sanctioned by the gods. However, certain civilians were protected during war among the Ibos. Women and priests were not assaulted and the village shrines were not attacked, especially, where they share the same deity. Rather, women and priests were instrumental in peace making. For these reasons they enjoy special protection in warfare.[111] The warfare among the Agbalaja People of Nigeria during slavery stage has shown that West African nations had detailed information regulating laws and customs of warfare.

The existence of laws and customs of warfare among Southern Peoples of Nigeria, during slavery stage, is made available in this work.[112] This study was able to discover detailed information about laws and customs of war among the peoples of southern Nigeria. It stated the laws and customs of warfare that were prohibited as well as the sanctions for their violations. This information is available in a document attached to this study as *Appendix 1*.

5.3 *Dahomey*

The Dahomean warriors were very harsh on the enemies during the stage of slavery.[113] They were harsh on their enemies including women and children. In their warfare, women and children were not spared. One would assume that since the Dahomean Amazons were women, they should have humane treatment; but the reverse was the case. The Amazons were known to have unleashed mayhem on women and children.[114]

In warfare among the Dahomeans, prisoners of war were not treated kindly.[115] Some of them could be used for sacrifice to celebrate victory in a battle. Others could be sold as slaves. Dahomeans were known to launch

110 Zartman William I, "Traditional Cures For Modern Conflicts", African Conflict 'Medicine' (Lynne Rienner Publishers, London), p. 58.

111 Ibid.

112 Talbott Amouri P., "*Peolples of Southern Nigeria; A Sketch of their History, Ethnology and Languages with an Abstract of 1921 Census*" (Frank Cass & Co. Ltd, 1969), p. 850.

113 Daryl Forde and P.M. Kaberry, "West African Kingdoms in The 19th Century (ed) With Introduction" (Oxford University Press, 1967), p. 80.

114 See, "The Legendary Battles of Amazons" on YouTube.

115 Archibald, Loc. Cit.

indiscriminate attacks on civilian environments such as farmlands, residences and shrines.[116]

5.4 *Ghana*

5.4.1 Mende

The customs of warfare among the Mende during the stage of slavery showed that there was some respect and protection accorded to women and children. However, prisoners of war were dreadfully treated. Among the Mende, women and children of the conquered enemies were shared among the Mende warriors and the chief.

Where the enemy wanted to make peace among the Mende people, the chief of the enemy who wanted to avoid war or attack would send a woman of light-coloured skin as his ambassador.[117] This woman could either be his wife or concubines. She would carry with her white clothes,[118] a gun and some salt and submit it to the conqueror chief. By doing these gestures, she had become the wife of the conqueror, and that could be termed as surrender which brought the war to an end.[119]

5.4.2 Ashanti and Akan

The war between Ashanti and Akan provided us with ancient norms of warfare that was bound by agreement among the belligerents. In the war that ensued between Ashanti and Akan in 1741, after the both belligerents exhausted their guerrilla strategies (because they were in forest zones), they agreed that they should engage in open battle. But they had problem with their geography, as such they have to deploy 20,000, people to cut down the forests so as to have clear battle field for 'transparency' and visibility in warfare.[120] During the

116 Daryl Forde and P.M. Kaberry, Op. Cit. p. 82.

117 Ibid.

118 It is important to note that before the official use of white flag to signify surrender Africans have been using White clothes; just as in Ancient China and Medevial Europes. See Evan Andrews, "When did White Flag Became Associated with Surrender?", History, Channel, May 28, 2018. Thus, the IHL got it perfectly to adopt the use of white flag to signify surrender and cessation of war. Thus, IHL prohibits the use of white flag and sanctions the violators of this rule. See Article 23 (2) of the Additional Protocol II of the 4th Geneva Convention and Article 8(2) (b) (vii) of the Rome Statute.

119 Daryl Forde and P.M. Kaberry, Op. Cit. pp. 245–246.

120 "Pre-Colonial Warfare in Africa: Forest Kingdom Kingdom" on YouTube.

cutting down of trees, there was a cessation of hostilities.[121] Thus, they were able to create a clear battlefield where they would fight.

5.4.3 Sierra Leone

The Kamajories were ancient hunters of Sierra Leone. The Kamajories were prohibited from engaging in looting and rape during wars.[122] This was because it is probably believe that sleeping with women could weaken the potency of one's charms during wars. It was believed that, as warriors, the Kamajories were expected to be spiritually fortified by abstaining from sexual intercourse during wars.

5.4.4 Senegambia

Armed conflicts among the people of Senegambia regulated attacks on civilian centers. Similarly environment was protected during armed conflict. Thus, during warfare, the sacred baobab tree and wood were not objects of attacks. This is due to the fact that these objects also served as objects of worship.[123] For this reason, during armed conflict, protective fetishes were kept in the chief's hut and they served as protective shelter to all those that entered into it. Huts harbouring fetishes (inanimate objects of worship), places of initiations and tombs of ancestors were places of asylum in the ancient Senegambia region.

5.4.5 Mali

In Mali, apart from cemeteries, there were other traditional places considered to be places of asylum. At *Koulikoro*, the twin hills called *Ninakoulou* (Nianan Hill) served as a safe haven for any person within its vicinity or inside it. Accordingly, a person could not be touched and any prisoner who escaped from his master to *Nianan* was a free man.[124]

Moreover, it is factual that slaves were used for military consolidation and expansion of Malian Empires. Thus, it was reported that the *Funtakes*, when fighting the *Fulbe* warriors incorporated the enslaved enemies.[125] These slaves are mostly prisoners of war from previous campaigns. Once they pledged their loyalty to the Malian Kingdom after surrender, they could be incorporated into

121 Loc. Cit.

122 Karolina Aksamitowska, "Traditional Approaches to Laws of Armed Conflicts: Disseminating IHL through the Receptor Approach", *Journal of International Humanitarian Legal Studies*, 11, (2020), pp. 6–7.

123 Ibid.

124 Ibid.

125 Joseph Bradshaw M., Op. Cit. p. 4.

the army for further military campaigns. During that military campaign, starvation was deployed as military strategy, where *Fulbes* were starved to make them surrender.[126]

Under the ancient Mali, men who were captured during warfare could be taken to forced labour camps. They were taken to work as labourers in places known as "cultivation villages."[127] Children and women were also captured. Children were sold into slavery, while women were married to soldiers. In Mali, slavery was also adopted as means of depopulating bellicose regions. This practice was believed to have weakened them.

6 Section 6: Feudal Stage (1700–1810 AD)

This section focuses on the law and customs of warfare applicable to West African kingdoms during the feudal stage envisaged by Karl Marx. This section also examines the periodisation of the feudal stage in West African history. The communities in ancient West African kingdoms that observed some customs in warfare were also discussed.

6.1 *Periodisation of Feudal Stage in West Africa*

Under the feudal stage, Marx posits that society is divided into serfdom and feudal. The Serfs are under the control of the feudal lords who served as their masters. The Serfs as servants are subjects of the feudal lords. In West Africa, certain practices exhibiting norms and customs of warfare existed.

6.1.1 Nigeria

The modern day Nigeria, had some pre-colonial states where feudal lords thrived via warfare. The role of military warfare in feudalism is an established principle recognized by Marxist scholars. This is aptly captured in these words, "military leaders, relying on the clan aristocracy and the members of their retinues, began to concentrate power in their hands and became kings – monarchical rulers."[128]

---

126 Ibid. p. 50.

127 Ibid. p. 65.

128 Economic Institute of Academy of Sciences of the U.S.S.R., "Part 1: Pre-capitalist Modes of Production, Chapter III: The Feudal Modes Of Production", Marxist Internet Archive.

The above principle of Marxism found its historical reflection among the Kanuris, Niger Delta people[129] and the Yorubas of Nigeria.[130] Among the Kanuris, feudal stage was characterized by deployment of military commanders by the *Mais*. The *Mais* sent their military commanders on conquest of distant land. The *Mais* paid the military lords for their loyalty by giving them some part of the territory of the conquered lands.[131] Under the Kanuri Empire, there are two types of military commanders; those from royal family and those not from royal family. Those not from Royal Family are known as *Kogena*.

In pre-colonial Bornu, deceit was allowed as a method of warfare.[132] Deceit as military strategy that was adopted by the Old Bornu, was inspired by *Mune*; an Islamic literature which permits deceit as warfare. The position of *Mune* on deceit was aptly captured by Wrya Tijani when he remarked that, "*Mune*; an Islamic (quasi) document allows for deceit in warfare. One of the commandments of Mune is: not to cheat except in war, for war is deceit."[133]

The Fulanis do not kill fellow Fulanis in intra-tribal war.[134] Defeated enemies from other tribes were enslaved and conscripted into the Fulani military teams. These captives both men and women were later integrated into the Fulani society as part of it. This was done through marriage (in case of women as concubine) and conscripted soldiers in case of men captured during warfare.[135]

Among the Ijaws, a certain class of military professionals emerged, at the end of slave during slave trade. They are known as the members of the "Canoe House system".[136] The members of the Canoe House system were both military and trading class. They could embarked on naval warfare for the protection of their commercial interests as well as provide escorts for their commercial articles. They observed military rules such as prohibition of dumping the body of an enemy or fallen soldiers inside water; for doing so might be a dishonor to the sanctity of *Egbetsu* the Ijaw water and military god. Women, especially pregnant women, and children were not customary objects of attack during

129 Eluwa G.I.C., et al. "A History of Nigeria For Schools and Colleges" (Africana – First Publishers Ltd, 19998), pp. 22–23, and p. 70.

130 Ibid.

131 Ibid.

132 Wrya Tijani, 'The Mune in Pre-Colonial Borno' (Berichte Des Sendefrischung Sbereichs 268, BD.2, Frankfurt, a.M., 1993), pp. 227–254.

133 Ibid.

134 Zartman William I., Op. Cit. p. 59.

135 Ibid.

136 Ibid. p. 70.

warfare.[137] The Ijaw warriors were governed by the *Egbetsu* ethics in warfare.[138] Under this ethics Ijaw warriors do not usually attack for the first time. They attacked after the enemy attacked them. This was premised on the belief that the *Egbetsu* ethics only allowed for warfare in self-defence, and not aggression. As such, when an Ijaw warrior was first attacked, either by gun or spear, and he was invincible to these weapons, this was a sign that he had the protection and approval of *Egbetsu*, to retaliate. A Senior Ijaw warrior remarked that before an Ijaw warrior could attack an opponent, it must be shown that he must have received at least three shots from the enemy.[139] To Ijaws, war is only fought as self-defence.

The Ijaws under the *Egbetsu* ethics were enjoined to avoid pillage, looting and attacks on civilians. The Ijaws also had what was called principles of transparency in warfare. This principle deals with acts of confessions for every unlawful or sinful act to the priest of *Egbetsu*. These confessions were for atonements of sins and errors committed during warfare. Despite this, under the *Egbetsu* war ethics, victory could be denied to the Ijaw soldiers, where such victories were achieved by killing women, pregnant women or children. This was usually done by renunciation of such victory by the *Egbetsu* priest-who was the mouthpiece of *Egbetsu*. It was for this reasons that warriors adopted the principle of transparency to atone for their sins.

Wealthy titled men in the Niger states maintained their own war and trading canoes which were called *Ugbo Ekele*. It was reported by Trotter that among the Abo people, many of them were manned by their slaves and poorer agnates.[140] Trotter described the naval fleet of Abo people having fair capacity to combat an enemy effectively. The first-grade war canoe could carry about twenty people. There were naval military alliances between the chiefs and vassal states under them. The vassal states were enjoined to contribute their own quarters of naval fleet to support their overlord in their military campaign, according to their military strength. It is reported that:

137 Omolere Monday E., "The Scourge of Lagoon Warfare In The Coast of Niger Delta: the Ilaje-Ijo War of 1998–1999" in *Historical Exploration.*

138 Elias Courson and Michael Odijie, "Egbetsu: An African Just War Philosophy and Practice", *Journal of African Cultural Studies*, 2020.

139 Ibid.

140 Ikenna Nzimiro, "Studies in Ibo Political Systems: Chieftaincy and Politics in Four in Niger States" (Frank Cass, London, 1972), pp. 134–135.

> On an extraordinary occasion, it is said that the King can muster about three hundred, many of them armed with muskets and canon in the bows, these last especially, are not however very formidable, as they re lashed to the bow, rendering the aim uncertain. A chief is sent from Abòh to command the expedition.[141]

Naval warfare was also concluded with peace. Parties could after fighting resolve to conclude by signing peace among them. The armistice was arranged on a neutral ground where the belligerent parties had to negotiate. The parties will now choose who will mediate for them in their armistice. Two historical instances showing these facts abound. The first instance was the appeal to the Obi of Oguta to meditate between Abo and Igala during one of their long drawn out naval encounters. The second instance was the invitation of Odumegwu of Ihiala by the Osomari people to mediate between them. After years of protracted warfare between the States of Osomari and Ogwu, the parties agreed for armistice and wanted the Odumegwu of Ihiala to broker peace between them. Thus, the Odumegwu summoned both parties to a neutral ground. He came with his own warriors well armed, and asked both fighting communities to lay down their arms and accept his peace offer. Then he ordered his men to shoot in the air and they did so, covering the whole spot with smoke. After the smoke had cleared, he made the leaders both of Osomari and Ogwu swear an oath together and sent them back as friends.[142]

The Yorubas in Nigeria were advanced militarily during the feudal stage. Their military organization was governed by strict rule of command and discipline. This age led to the rise of Warlords and Soldier Boys in Yorubaland.[143] The reasons for the emergence of military feudal or warlords in Yoruba land included:

(a) The struggle for self-independence of weaker states from imperial nations.
(b) The quest for stronger states to incorporate a weak state in order to spread its political influence for specific interests.
(c) Military federalism paved way for prominent warriors who controlled the activities of the military group of the state to reckon with in the Egba politics, till the eve of colonial administration in 1854.[144]

141 Ibid. p. 134.

142 Ibid. p. 135.

143 G.N. Uzoigwe, C.N. Oko-Otu, G.C. Aro, O.C. Eze, I.N. Enwo-Irem and F.M. Nwankwo, "Warfrae in Pre-colonial Africa: An Examination of The Role of African Blacksmiths", *Journal of Asians and African Studies* XII, 1–4, University of Michigan.

144 Zartman William I., Op. Cit. p. 69.

Despite its military prowess, warfare among the Yorubas was controlled by limited ways. The Yorubas believe that war should not be about total destruction, but that it should have limitations in terms of loss of resources and human lives. This principle is reflected in a Yoruba proverb that says "the fact that we are quarrelling [fighting] does not mean that we want our enemies to die."[145] Thus, to them, traditions require that loss of life should be minimal. However, this trend changed from the fifteen century.[146] This was due to the outbreak of the civil war that brought a lot of hostilities among the Yoruba chiefdoms in the 19th century.

Among the Ikwere people of Nigeria, before commencement of war, parties were at liberty to choose their means and methods of warfare. This was usually actualized by sending the Ikwere people a notice of war to their enemies. This notice was symbolized by two sticks; one dry stick and another green stick.[147] The enemies had to choose between the two sticks. If they chose the dry stick; it meant the enemy wanted war, for dry stick symbolized death, which also meant the enemy wanted to die.[148] But with the emergence of cannonball, the Ikwere sent cannonball and Yam. Thus, if the enemy chose cannonball, it was obvious that they wanted war.[149]

Moreover, the feudalist stage in Nigeria witnessed instances of Islamic jihadist in central Nigeria. During the Sokoto Jihads which started from 1804 to 1808, under usman Dan Fodio, Northern Nigeria was a theatre of war.[150] In their confrontations with the natives, the Jihadists' killed their enemies only on military necessity.[151] However, they preferred capturing them alive for two reasons. The first reason is for manumission, i.e. to make them convert to Islam, while the second reason was to enslave their captives on large scale for domestic servitude and imposition of taxation.[152]

Again, the wars between the Islamic communities among the Nupe People of Nigeria show some application of rules and customs governing them. When starvation was adopted by Masaba, as military strategy against Usman Zaiki, Masaba incited the Nupes, who surrounded the town of Raba for one year, without letting anybody coming in and going out. This in turn led to starvation where a lot of people are died of hunger. Masaba was remonstrated by

145 Ibid.

146 Dike 1956, 18 culled from Zartman William, Ibid.

147 Zartman Williams, Loc. Cit.

148 Ibid.

149 Ibid.

150 Arnett E.J., Op. Cit. p. 25.

151 Turaki Yusuf, Op. Cit. p. 56.

152 Ibid. pp. 40–41.

Abdulkadir, a Fulani jihadist, who maintained that it was not good to adopt starvation against men of the same race and religion.[153]

6.1.2 Togo

In Togo, a group known as notables among the two groups would meet and reason with the chiefs of both camps. Any attack must be with warning. Similarly, there is restriction on the choice of means and methods of combat.[154] Religious centre were not object of attacks certain animals or periods were not conducive for war.[155] Also, during feudal stages, Togolese had an established customs of warning an enemy before attacking.

6.1.3 Ancient Songhai Empire

Under this empire, slaves were deployed to fight as soldiers for their masters. Slavery was more of military advantages than economic consideration in feudal Songhai Empire. Thus, non-Muslim prisoners of war would be taken as captives and redeployed as soldiers by their detaining power.[156] However, it was illegal to capture a fellow Muslim army of belligerent party and sell him as slave.[157]

It is important to note that it was the military activities of the feudal Lords in the ancient Songhai Empire that gave birth to the Trans-Atlantic Slave Trade.[158] This is because in the Songhai Empire, defeated armies of the enemies were sold to Europeans and Arabs for guns.[159] The concept of conscription of crown slave was a permissible practice.[160] Thus, slaves who were tagged as mere slaves could move up to the social ladder by assuming similar status to Serf. These slaves, who became serfs, could enjoy special status upon conscription as crown slaves.

153 Elephinstone K.V., A.G. Res Ilorin, "Gazzeteer of Ilorin Province" (WaterLow & Sons Ltd., 1921), p. 34.

154 Nurudeen Olatoye Aro'Gunde, 'War and Diplomacy', in *Culture and Customs of the Yoruba* Toyin Falola and Akintunde Akinyemi (Eds.) (Austin Texas, Pan-African University Press, 2017), p. 654.

155 Zartman Williams Loc. Cit. See also Haggler Okorie, Loc. Cit.

156 Joseph Bradshaw M., Op. Cit. p. 46.

157 Ibid.

158 Ibid. pp. 46–50.

159 Ibid.

160 Nurudeen Olatoye Aro'Gunde, Loc. Cit.

7 Section 7: Capitalist Stage (1880–1945)

In this section, the study examines the laws and customs among the ancient Kingdoms of West Africa that regulate warfare. Periodisation of colonial era by this study is also captured in this section. The permissive and the prohibitive acts of warfare among African Kingdoms as well as their sanctions were also examined.

7.1 *Periodisation of Capitalist Stage in West Africa*

The end of capitalist stage is estimated by historians to start from 1884 to 1945, the end of the Second World War. This is because after the Second World War, the enactments of Universal Declaration of Human Rights 1948, and the United Nation Charter 1945, served as legal instruments that gave birth to the end of colonialism.[161] Thus, while Abolition Charter marked an end to slave trade, the Universal Declarations of Human Rights, initiated the move towards ending colonialism, when it provides for rights to self-determinations of people

For better analysis, this research adopts the typology of colonialism into Proto-colonial, Colonial era, Period of Conquest and Occupation, Period of Colonial Pacification and Administration, Period of Colonial Rule Proper, and Period of Decolonization.[162] This periodisation is relevant for analysis of the events that transpired during the different phases of colonial periods in West Africa. This periodisation is outlined as follows:

NOs	Periodisation	Appellations
1	1880 to 1885	Proto colonial period
2	1885 to 1900	Era of conquest and occupation
3	1900 to 1919	Era of pacification and expansion
4	1919 to 1939	Period of colonial rule proper
5	1939 to 1960	Decolonization

161 See Resolution 1514 (XV) Declaration on The Granting of Independence to Colonial Countries and Peoples.

162 Crowther Michael, "West Africa under Colonial Rule" (Hutchinson & Co. Publishers LTD, 1968), p. 19.

It is from the periods in the above table that this research will examine the principles of warfare that African states and Kingdoms adopted during armed conflicts with the colonialists.

7.2 *Available Customs of Warfare in West Africa during the Capitalist Stage*

7.2.1 Mali

During the early days of colonialism, prisoners of war were sold as slaves in Mali. Thus, selling of prisoners of war was an acceptable practice among the people of ancient Mali. The interaction between French colonialists and Malians showed that some of these prisoners of war could be commodities of transactions on slave trade. A table reflecting slave prices in Bandiagara Emirates of Mali is reflected below:[163]

NOs	Age of the enslaved persons	Prices estimated in francs
1	A 12-year old boy	200–250
2	An 8-year old boy	200–300
3	A man	250–230
4	A young woman Bambarabe	300–400
5	A young woman Samo or Bobo	80–100

7.2.2 Nigeria

Among the Calabar people of Southern Nigeria, getting a spirit of strong enemy after his death was permissible. It is a means of military fortification.[164] Thus, the best way to get a spirit of a strong enemy is to cut his head.[165] This belief is common among some African communities.[166] It was based on this belief that the Ashantis have treasured the head of brave general McCarthy.[167]

163 These details are culled from Joseph Bradshaw M., Op. Cit. p. 80.

164 Mary Kingsley, "Travels in West Africa" (Charles Knight & CO. LTD London, 197[illegible]), p. 9[illegible].

165 Ibid.

166 Ibid.

167 Ibid.

7.2.3 Ghana

In the present day Ghana, customs and rules of war were observed by the Ashanti and the Mende people.

7.2.3.1 *Ashanti*

The Ashanti people regarded warfare as a very sacred and serious affair. Rumours pertaining to war were prohibited.[168] This was a military discipline amidst soldiers to ensure the success of surprise attacks on the enemy. Among the Ashanti people, killing an enemy and keeping his skull was a glorious act and a caution to an impending enemy.[169] The Ashantis were hard on their enemies. When they captured their enemies they used them as domestic slaves.[170] The Ashantis adopted peaceful settlement in the course of wars. Whenever there was war between them and others, if they perceived that the enemy was stronger than them the Ashantis would negotiate for peace.[171]

The Ashanti warriors and chiefs were bound by War Oaths.[172] These oaths were held with sacredness and secrecy; breaching them was equal to disobeying the gods.[173] These oaths of secrecy include certain war rituals and military strategies which soldiers were forbidden to disclose to others.[174] It also includes the manner in which the war charms and some rituals will be handled during warfare.[175] Violating these oaths was sanctioned by misfortune, diseases and death. Cowardice among the Ashanti warriors was punishable by death.[176] Thus any soldier who exhibits fear during war or spread fear once war is about to commence, such as stating that the enemy is stronger than, the Ashantis, such act could amount to cowardice.

The Ashantis protected women and children during war. This was partly because; Ashanti women played a vital role during warfare. Whenever Ashanti

---

168 Darryll Forde and P.M. Kabbery, "West African Kingdoms in the Nineteenth Century" (Oxford University Press, 1967), p. 23.

169 Ibid.

170 Henry Brackenberry, "The Ashanti War: A Narrative", VOL. 1. (Frank Cass & Co Ltd, 1968), p. 19.

171 Ibid. pp. 81–82.

172 Manuel Manoe J., "'The Days of Their Heedless Power Were Over and Done': Dynamics of Power in the Military Structures of the Pre-Colonial Asante' 1874–1900", *Journal of African History*, (2021), 62(2), 254–270.

173 Ibid.

174 Ibid.

175 Henry Brackenberry, Op. Cit. pp. 20–22.

176 Ibid.

women were on war, the women engaged on *mmomomme*, a sort of spiritual warfare. The word, *mmomomme* is a spiritual warfare, where the Ashanti women engaged in performing rituals for the protection, victory and safe return of their warriors. That ritual would continue everyday of the war till their men returned from the war.[177]

7.2.3.2 *Mende*

The Mende people were warriors who imbibed certain laws and customs of warfare. Women and children were prohibited from being harmed. Thus, whenever women and children were captured they were kept in safe and protective custody of the Mende warriors.[178]

Among the Mendes combat, was hand to hand which involved the use of swords, spears and shields, made from hard wood.[179] Guns were rarely used among the Mendes at that time. Most of the guns used were Dane guns and muskets, which were slow in battlefield because of the tendencies of reloading them after the first shot.[180] In order to protect themselves against guns and spears of their enemies, the Mendes used charms.

The Mendes had a special way of treating prisoners of war. They grouped their captives into three. The first prisoners of war were those who resisted the Mende warriors fiercely. Persons in that group were put to death. The second were those who did not give the Mende warriors tough times during, such groups of warriors were kept as domestic slaves. The third group comprised of women and children. That category of captives was shared to the head warriors, the army who made the capture and the Chief of the Mende.[181]

Moreover, among the Mendes, truce was deploy in warfare. Thus, where a Mende Chief decided to truce with an enemy during war, he would send a light skinned woman as his ambassador.[182] This woman was usually a daughter of the chief or one of his favourite wives. This female emissary would then carry a white clothe, a gun and some salt.[183] She would then present those items as offer of peace, and once the enemy accepted them, it meant that he had accepted the truce, and the emissary would become the wife of that enemy chief.[184]

177 Ibid.
178 Darryll Forde and P.M. Kabbery, Op. Cit. p. 245.
179 Ibid.
180 Ibid.
181 Ibid. p. 246.
182 Ibid.
183 Ibid.
184 Ibid. p. 246.

7.2.4 Present-Day Senegal

7.2.4.1 *Samouri Toure of Madinka Empire*

One of the interesting military encounters between colonial powers and African Kingdom was the in war the between French and Samourie Toure. That war availed us with some of the customs and wars adopted by Samouri Toure. That war showed that military alliance is a strategy among the West Africa Kingdoms. This is captured in Samourie message to Seiko Ahmaodu when he said:[185]

> If you continue to make war on your own, the whites will have no trouble in defeating you. I have already undergone the experience in trying my strength against them. Let us therefore unite. You will hit the French from the North, I will harass them in the South, and we will certainly manage to get rid of them.

Under Samouri, treaty was established between Samouri and the French known as Treaty of Bissandougu. It was the breach of that treaty that led to war between them and the French.[186] Samouri deployed high intelligence to ensure military targets were the objects of attacks. Thus, through his guerrilla warfare, he would attack the military units of the French and later retreated into his hidings.[187]

7.2.4.2 *Dahomey (Present-Day Benin Republic)*

The concept of *levee en masse* was deployed in the kingdom of Dahomey in order to adapt with emergency situations. These *levee en masse*, numbering about 1,200, could be deployed to compliment regular soldiers to fight the against external foes.[188] Again, in order to ensure precise military targets, the Dahomeans embarked on intelligence gathering. This enabled the Dahomeans to achieve surprise attacks on their enemies, especially the French who always lived in fear of surprised attacks by Dahomeans.[189]

---

185 Crowther Michael, Op. Cit. p. 87.

186 Ibid.

187 Ibid. p. 187.

188 Obichere I. Boniface, "West African States and European Expansion: The Dahomey-Niger Hinterland, 1885–1898" (New Haven and London, Yale University Press, 1971), p. 196.

189 Ibid. p. 104. See also, "Legendary Battles of Amazon" on YouTube.

8 Section 8: Findings on Customs of Warfare in West Africa

In the course of this study, it was established that ancient West African kingdoms had established norms and customs of warfare. These customs and traditions predated modern IHL. While it is factual that those laws and customs of warfare were not the same throughout West Africa, because of cultural and sociological variations, there were certain traits that cut across all of them. This view is supported by Nigerian Legal scholar, Okorie, when he remarks thus:

> Although no common yardstick can be used to measure the attitude or legal approach of traditional African treatment of non-combatants in war, there is what can be called "a single thread" that ran through the majority of exercises conducted or belief held by these tribal societies. This is that women, children, the aged were to be spared during military expeditions. These women who are daughters of enemy clans took water to the warriors on the battle field, dragging away casualties from the battle zone or by encouraging the fighters with their shrilling and trilling cries. These women on the battle field played the role of ICRC by taking care of the wounded, the dead and the unarmed, albeit of only one side of the battlefield.[190]

It is also important to note that some of these laws and customs of warfare changed overtime in the course of history.[191] They also changed due to contacts between Africa and Islamic world as well as contacts between Africa and Europe. From this study some of the norms and customs of warfare that were established to have been in existence include peace offer before commencement of war, neutrality in warfare, choice of means and methods of warfare, permissible (military necessity, proportionality, humane treatments, distinction), prohibited (indiscriminate attack, starvation), armistice, and sanctions.

8.1 *Peace Offer*

In ancient West Africa, war was not usually commenced without notice. The notice was meant to give the offer of peace for the other opponent. This period for offer of peace was meant to remind the other parties to reconsider their stands before embarking on war. By this practice, the belligerents have to be

190 Culled from Haggler Okorie, Op. Cit. p. 67.
191 Darryll Forde and P.M. Kabbery, Loc. Cit.

put on notice so as to give them the option of continuing with the war or suing for peace.[192]

8.2 *Neutrality*

The principle of neutrality was a common practice among the ancient West African Kingdoms. Kingdoms that were not part of war did not participate rather; they acted as peacemakers and truce brokers among the warring parties. The neutral parties also helped in some instances and ensure to treat the wounded and sick and provide safety for women and children.[193]

8.3 *Armistice*

In ancient West Africa, parties engaged in war could reach a truce for armistice. During armistice, parties observed the terms with utmost good faith and breach of which was termed as an abominations.[194] Armistice as a custom and tradition of war was highly recognized as legitimate practice in warfare.

8.4 *Established Means and Methods of Warfare*

Another interesting discovery by this study was the deployment of means and methods of warfare by ancient West African kingdoms. Those kingdoms were able to agree on the means and methods of warfare with respect to the types of weapons to be used as well as the time for the conduct of warfare.[195] They were also able to determine which rules of engagement for the conduct of warfare. They had to agree to cut down forests in order to enhance visibility for parties to have free and open access to each other.[196] They also deployed the methods of resting to allow belligerent parties that were weak to rest and get refreshed to resume the fighting.[197]

8.5 *Permissible Acts*

This study found that the ancient West African kingdoms had established practices that were permissible during armed conflicts. These permissible practices include military necessity, humane treatment, proportionality and distinction in warfare.

---

192 B.A. Ogot. Loc. Cit.

193 Nzimiro Ikenna, "Studies in Ibo Political Systems: Chieftaincy and Politics in Four Niger States" (Frank Cass London, 1972), p. 135.

194 Ibid.

195 Jos Oral History And Literature Texts, Loc. Cit.

196 Darryll Forde and P.M. Kabbery, Loc. Cit. See also, "Pre-Colonial African Kingdom: Forest Kingdom" on YouTube.

197 Ibid.

Military necessity was prevalent in ancient West African kingdoms. Parties were allowed to kill others for the purpose of achieving military objectives. In some African kingdoms, warfare was meant to showcase military prowess, thus, once the military superiority was established by the winning party, the war would be brought to an end via surrender.[198] Since wars were fought to showcase military superiority, military necessity was, no doubt, a recognized practice among the African kingdoms.

This study further established that the practice of humane treatment was recognized as an age-long practice among the West African Kingdoms; from primitive stage to the capitalist stage. In some kingdoms, women and children were not attacked, the aged and sick were also spared, prisoners of war were treated with respect and dignity. In some instances, enemies from royal families were treated with royal respect by their hosts.[199]

The ancient West African kingdoms ensured that warfare was conducted based on the principle of proportionality. Force and weapons used should be commensurate. Thus, in intra-tribal or inter-community wars, must ensure that the weapons were of equal strength and impact. In order to ensure fairness, sometimes, the parties inspected these weapons before fighting, especially sticks, so as to ensure that they were not poisonous.[200]

In ancient West Africa, conduct of warfare was not entirely a haphazard act. The military objectives were targeted. Military targets such as belligerents were attacked, and civilians were exempted. Those wounded and surrendered were taken as captives, and not killed. Sacred civilian centres like shrines, houses, worship centres, ritual sites and other related centres were not attacked during the armed conflicts. Animals were not attacked; rather, they were taken as war booties.[201]

8.6 *Prohibited Practices*

This study has shown that the ancient West African kingdoms had certain customs prohibiting certain practices during warfare. Practices that were against established norms and customs of warfare were not allowed to be violated. Doing so would be a deviation from the norm. For that reason, attacks on women of whatever status and children were prohibited in some kingdoms. Equally, practices that degraded humanity were prohibited; such as rape, starvation, dumping corpse of an enemy inside water or refusing to release the

198 Okorie Haggler, Loc. Cit.

199 Bradshaw Joseph Op. Cit. p. 11.

200 Jos Oral History and Literature, Loc. Cit.

201 UNESCO, Op. Cit. p. 473.

corpse of an enemy to his family members. In some customs, certain measures with regard to means and methods of warfare were prohibited. Thus, using poisonous and lethal weapons on members of the same tribes/communities during intra-tribal wars were prohibited. Similarly, attacking daughters of the assailants who were married to the enemies or the children of such daughters was prohibited during warfare.

Equally, attacks on the enemies in the night were a prohibited practice. In the same vein, attacking an escaping enemy, or refusing to allow an escape space during warfare was prohibited. Attacking those *hors de combat* and pillaging were prohibited acts.

8.7 *Sanctions for Prohibited Acts*

This study has established that there were sanctions for the violations of customs of warfare in ancient West Africa. Some of these sanctions include incurring the wraths of gods. This study has shown that where a community violated laws of warfare, it was likely to incur the wrath of the gods.[202] That community would experience outbreak of diseases, famine and meager harvest. Thus, for that community to get itself off the hook of that judgment there must be sacrifice and propitiation to appease the gods.[203]

This propitiation was done through confessions by the warriors who committed the 'war crime'. In some instances where offences were grievous, such as killing pregnant women or children, the offender would be sanctioned with death.[204] Reprimanding violators of customs and laws of warfare was another sanction regime in ancient West Africa.[205] The elders of the community and the war council often reprimand persons involved in such acts. This reprimand would then serve as deterrent to potential offenders.

Another sanction was to deny the warring party their status of victory; where such victory was obtained as a result of the violations of customs of warfare.[206] Thus, if a community won a war by killing women and children, in violation of the community's custom of warfare, such victory would be renounced.

Fines and ostracism were adopted as sanctions against warriors who breached customs of warfare. That was mostly in intra-tribal wars where killing of members of the same family was seen as fratricide.[207] As such, the offender

202 Elias Courson and Michael Odijie, Loc. Cit.
203 Ibid.
204 Omolere Monday E. Loc. Cit.
205 Elias Courson and Michael Odijie, Loc. Cit.
206 Ibid.
207 Jos Oral History Text and Literature, Loc. Cit.

must be ostracized to purge himself and escape the wraths of the gods and to prevent bringing collective catastrophe on his community. In addition to fines, compensation was another method of sanctions during armed conflicts. It was imposed to assuage the harm suffered by victims of the war or any prohibited acts of warfare.

9 Section 9: Conclusion

West Africa is one of the regional blocs that are committed to the development of IHL. As at the year, 2023, all the 15 West African countries were signatories to major treaties relating to IHL.[208] The nations of West Africa have agreed to be implementing the principle of IHL in their municipal jurisdictions. They are committed in promoting the enforcement of principles of IHL in their respective jurisdictions. Thus, violators of the principles of IHL are sanctioned by their municipal jurisdictions. Today, the implementation of IHL in West Africa has become a serious endeavour in which West African States cooperate with the International Committee for Red Cross (ICRC) by producing a periodic report for the implementation of IHL in West Africa.[209]

West Africa as a regional bloc has contributed to the development of the jurisprudence of IHL. One of such example is the case of *Charles Taylor v Prosecutor*, where the Special Court for Sierra Leone (SCSL) for the first time classified rape as offence against offence of terrorism committed by state actors.[210] Another example is the situation in Côte d'Ivoire. Here, while not being a party to the ICC Statute, Cote d'Ivoire, accepted the exercise of jurisdiction by the ICC regarding crimes committed on its territory since the events of 19 September, 2002.[211]

208 ECOWAS CEDEAO, "ECOWAS Member States Experts Commit to enhancing the International Humanitarian Law (IHL) in the Region", September 12–14, 2023. See also ICRC, "Treaties and State Parties".

209 ECOWAS CEDEAO, Loc. Cit.

210 Godfree Matthew, "The Trial and Sentencing of Charles Taylor: A Critical Examination of the Principles of International Law And New Development", *The Arbiter*, Vol. 4. NO.1, 2012, p. 36.

211 See Press Release of February 15, 2005, Declaration under Article 12(3) of the Rome Statute, 18 April 2003, and Situation in the Republic of Cote d'Ivoire, ICC PT Ch.III. This decision was pursuant to article 15 of the Rome Statute on the Authorization of an investigation into the Situation in the Republic of Cote d'Ivoire, ICC-02/11-14, 3 October, 2011, para. 10.

West Africa is today bedeviled with a lot of challenges in its commitment towards the implementation of IHL. Some of these challenges are emergence of military regimes in Africa, emergence of non state actors, the lack of commitment on parts of some State to fully enforce IHL treaties and multiple alliances to different regional blocs.

10 Section 10: Summary of Findings and Suggested Areas for Further Studies

This study is able to establish that (a) laws and customs of warfare akin to IHL existed in among ancient West African Kingdoms. (b) Some of these customs and laws of warfare predated IHL. (c) This laws and customs were transformed as a result of contacts with the Islamic World and European powers. (d) There were acceptable and prohibited practices regarding these customs and tradition of warfare. (e) There were sanction regimes, and (f) Different kingdoms and communities had different customs and tradition regarding warfare.

However, this study is limited in that it only ended it analysis on laws of war among West African States at the capitalist stage; it could not extend Marxist stages of socialism and communalism. Also, this study could not be totally exempted from the challenge surrounding the historicity of the Marxist stages of historical development. Nevertheless, this study could inspired areas of further studies such as (a) appraisal of laws and customs on naval warfare among pre-colonial West African States, and (b) how Islam and colonialism influence laws and customs of warfare in pre-colonial West Africa.

Conclusion

As Sir Christopher Greenwood noted:

> There is no doubt that IHL has undergone a massive expansion in scope and complexity. Lieber's Code, which endeavoured to articulate the whole of the law of land warfare in 157 articles, was a masterpiece of brevity. The example which it set was followed in the other attempts to codify IHL in relation to land warfare adopted between the American Civil War and the outbreak of the First World War. Admirable as this may seem, these brief statements of the law left too many questions unanswered and too many subjects largely untouched. Modern IHL has followed a trend, noticeable in all law, of entering into far more detail.[1]

Sir Christopher's remarks bear further reflection. It has become increasingly clear that the history of IHL is polycentric. There is no one starting point – and the myth-building that surrounds the Lieber Code or the Battle of Solferino is one that should be critically questioned. Why the Lieber Code, but not the Mexican Code?[2] Why the Battle of Solferino (which triggered protection of civilians) but not the Conquest of New Spain (which triggered a paradigm shift in international law)? Why is there a need, 75 years after the last ratification of the Geneva Conventions, to try to ascribe the 'development' or 'crystallisation' of attempts to control warfare to one man, at one battlefield, in one European country? It seems too simplistic, too political, and perhaps too legalistic. It is more opaque (and perhaps near impossible) to try to determine when rules around warfare began, just as it is difficult to try to determine *what* constitutes a rule regulating warfare.

1 What Are Rules?

A clear friction emerging in this study is that exact question: what are rules? Kardon perhaps best captures the friction when looking at contemporary Law of the Sea issues:

1 Sir Christopher Greenwood, Human Rights and Humanitarian Law – Conflict or Convergance1 (2010) 43 Case Wester Reserve Journal of International Law 491, 495.

2 Tania Atilano, 'The 1871 Mexican Criminal Code as the missing piece in the history of criminalizing violations of the laws of war' (2022) 104 *International Review of the Red Cross* 1650–1683.

 | DOI:10.1163/9789004703094_009

> If a rule is an emergent property of patterned interactions among states whose behaviours are guided to greater or lesser degree by rules, norms and institutes, it has no conceptual boundaries and prescribes no object way to decide which state or states decide which rules are fundamental to a given order.[3]

To me, a rule is something that applies because it is internalised, either by fear of sanction or hope of reward. There is no need for explicit legal constructs, or case law. These 'rules' can exist in domestic law and international law, as they applied at the time. Once scholars begin to look for these rules across history – be it general public international law or the laws of war – they are clearly there. For this reason, the research methodology of *The Laws of Yesterday's Wars* is one that can be applied across a spectrum of international legal issues and case studies. It is one that a fellow co-author and I have recently applied to filling the gap in the legal frameworks around British colonial wars;[4] and one that can be applied to any instance of pre-colonial, colonial or even post-colonial studies.

As famously reasoned by Max Huber in the 1928 *Island of Palmas* (*or Miangas*) (*The Netherlands v the United States of America*) ('*Island of Palmas*') arbitration, judicial facts must be evaluated 'in the light of the law contemporary with it, and not of the law in force at the time when a dispute in regard to it arises or falls to be settled.'[5] This is arguably in line with the non-retroactive character of legal construction (*nova constitutio futuris formam imponere debet, non praeteritis*), as advanced by influential legal writers since at least Lord Coke (Chief Justice of the King's Bench from 1613–1616).[6] It is clear that

3 Isaac B. Kardon's *China's Law of the Sea: The New Rules of Maritime Order* (Yale University Press, 2024) 16.

4 Samuel White & Ihkwan Fazli, *Pax Britannica* (Brill, 2025).

5 *Island of Palmas* (*Netherlands v United States of America*) (*Award*) (*1928*) 2 RIAA 829, 845. See also: *Cameroon v Nigeria* (n 57) 404–5 [205]; Alexander Orakhelashvili, 'Treaties and Titles to Territory' (2003) 62(1) *Cambridge Law Journal* 9, 10.

6 Edward Coke, *The Second Part of the Institutes of the Laws of English* (Brooke, 1797) vol. 1, 292. See also: Elmer E Smead, 'The Rule Against Retroactive Legislation: A Basic Principle of Jurisprudence' (1936) 20(1) *Minnesota Law Review* 775, 776; Ben Juratowitch, *Retroactivity and the Common Law* (Hart Publishing, 2008) 29; Zhenni Li, 'International Intertemporal Law' (2018) 48(2) *California Western International Law Journal* 341, 388. See generally: B.S. Chimni, 'Customary International Law: A Third World Perspective' (2018) 112(1) *American Journal of International Law* 1, 1–46; J Patrick Kelly, 'Customary International Law in Historical Context: The Exercise of Power Without General Acceptance' in Brian D. Lepard (ed), *Reexamining Historical and Theoretical Perspectives on Customary International Law* (Cambridge University Press, 2017) 47, 47–85.

between the Imperial Period after the Conquest of New Spain, international law developed along separate Imperial lines (with separate Imperial powers holding separate concepts of international law).[7] These multiple sources of (European) international law increasingly converged until the 1899 *Hague Conventions*. Yet again, this is not to say that international law (and international humanitarian law) did not develop outside of Europe. It did.

1.1 *Whose Rules?*

It is clear that European notions and ideals hold a hegemonic position within international law. The Gramscian theory of hegemony is grounded in the concept of coercion, but rather in the exercise of 'effective leadership' by a ruling social group over other groups, resulting in their consent to such leadership.[8] Moreover, Gramsci refers to the aim of hegemony in being the constitution of a 'common sense' – a 'conception of the world' which fundamentally structures the actions of all participants within a particular society.[9] Through the creation of such a 'common sense', a particular social group achieves hegemonic social power 'to the degree that it [is] able to posit its own interests as "universal"'.[10] There is risk, then, in proclaiming rules in the Gramsci tradition.

Knox suggests that hegemony should be understood as a specific rhetorical strategy organised around universalism, and that this assists with explaining why international law, which 'takes abstract universality as one of its key starting points … proves so attractive for hegemonic claims.'[11] Koskenniemi, drawing on Laclau and Mouffe's further development of a Gramscian theory of hegemony,[12] similarly refers to international law as a site of hegemonic contestation, where the aim of the ruling group being 'to make their partial view … appear as the total view, their preference seem like the *universal preference*.'[13] Moreover, Rajagopal argues that such hegemonic ideas have become embedded

7 White & Fazli (above n 5) 17–30.

8 Antonio Gramsci, *Selections from the Prison Notebooks of Antonio Gramsci*, tr Quentin Hoare and Geoffrey Nowell Smith (Lawrence & Wishart, International Publishers, 1971) 58.

9 Ibid. 134, 327.

10 Robert Knox, 'Hegemony' in Jean d'Aspremont and Sahib Singh (eds), *Concepts for International Law: Contributions to Disciplinary Thought* (Edward Elgar Publishing) 328, 339 [2].

11 Ibid. 351 [4].

12 Ernesto Laclau and Chantal Mouffe, *Hegemony and Socialist Strategy: Towards a Radical Democratic Politics* (Verso, 2001).

13 Martti Koskenniemi, 'International Law and Hegemony: A Reconfiguration' (2004) 17(2) *Cambridge Review of International Affairs* 197, 199 [3] (emphasis in original).

within international institutions, and have therefore become internalised by non-Western states operating in international law.[14]

Locating this account of hegemony within existing socio-economic relations explains the universalism of Western approaches to international law.[15] Anghie refers to this dynamic as a 'self-sustaining' and 'endless' one, being 'a gap between two cultures, demarcating one as "universal" and civilised and the other as "particular" and uncivilised'.[16] This dynamic is reflected in, for example, the reference to 'countries which differ most widely from the normal type' in the *travaux* to the *PCIJ Statute*,[17] and the domination of Western European and Others Group states in the drafting and debates about the *ad hoc* role.[18] Linking this universalism to a consent-based theory of hegemony means that the ruling group (i.e. Western states) can present its interests as being congruent with everyone's interests (i.e. non-Western states).[19]

So, to counter that, it is clear that strict methodology needs to be applied, and strict legal/historical approaches taken. With more temporally disconnected case studies, however, authors are largely reliant upon a selection of texts and other forms of evidence that represent the lives of a small, albeit highly influential, cadre of society: those of the ruling class. The lives and values of the less privileged and illiterate majority are much harder to touch. It is difficult to be sure how representative our image of any historical society truly is,[20] particularly those without agency and power (such as slaves, minority religious sects, or women in most societies prior to the late modern era).[21] As Rory Cox so eloquently notes:

> Our evidence for thoughts about control of violence is often the product of authors looking to the past and writing about military events that took place potentially years, decades or even centuries earlier. In some cases, these "historical" events probably did not take place at all, being merely

14 Balakrishnan Rajagopal, *International Law from Below: Development, Social Movements, and Third World Resistance* (Cambridge University Press, 2003) 82.

15 Knox (n 171) 357 [3].

16 Antony Anghie, *Imperialism, Sovereignty and the Making of International Law* (Cambridge University Press, 2007) 4 [2].

17 *Procès-Verbaux of the Proceedings of the Committee (16 June–24 July 1920)* (n 5) 532 [2].

18 See Chapters III and IV.

19 Knox (n 171) 359.

20 Also noted by Carly L. Crouch, *War and Ethics in the Ancient Near East: Military Violence in Light of Cosmology and History* (Berlin and New York: Walter de Gruyter, 2009), 5.

21 Regarding the experience of women and war specifically, see the important treatment by Jean Bethke Elshtain, *Women and War* (Chicago, IL: University of Chicago Press, 1995).

> a literary invention of the scribe to serve an ideological, didactic or rhetorical purpose. Nor should we assume that ancient scribes – who were usually non-military elites – shared the same values or codes of conduct as soldiers.
>
> Any attempt to describe an ancient ethics of war will always require a degree of generalisation and speculation that undoubtedly goes beyond the ancient "reality" of that system of thought. As such, there is no way of knowing whether our descriptions of a culture would be "true" to the historical persons who constituted it.[22]

The difficulty is in the research and research methodology. The 'othering' within international law, or the 'exoticization' that has plagued international legal systems can occur from the onset of research. Helen Durham, who wrote the foreword for this Volume, offers a useful antidote:

> This process of storytelling and connection to traditional practices can be dangerous if it takes the universally positioned and secular sensibilities of IHL and reduces them to local and, in particular, transient elements. For every story, poem or traditional practice which highlights compatibility with the legal norms found in the Geneva Conventions and their Additional Protocols, there are examples which digress from the concept of limitations in warfare.
>
> It is neither intellectually rigorous nor useful to attempt to squeeze inconsistent examples together or 'cut and paste' cultural practices to suit themes. An honest approach, which makes comparisons with traditional cultures as a way of understanding principles found in an area of international law within a local framework, can be powerful.[23]

In a search for universality, past scholars have sought to find the points of connection (rather than difference). This Volume, as other Volumes of this series, does not. If such connections exist, they are not there for comparison to the Geneva Conventions. They are there to be compared to themselves.

Shabtai Rosenne cautions that societies facing similar problems may produce similar solutions, but still 'start from different underlying premises and

22 Rory Cox, *Origins of the Just War* (Princeton University Press, 2023) p. xxx.

23 Helen Durham, 'The laws of war and traditional cultures: A case study of the Pacific region' (2008) 34(4) *Commonwealth Law Bulletin* 833, 837.

different general philosophies'.[24] If these similarities are to be found – which they are[25] – then that is more supportive of a universal principle of IHL, than by their similarity to the Geneva Conventions. I believe, however, that violence and war are one of the most fundamental human states of affair that actually provide a similar underlying premise from which comparison can occur. When I use the term 'war', I re-confirm my acknowledgement of its genealogical baggage and refer readers to the Introduction of Volume II.[26] Being a fundamentally political concept, war must be seen within its historical construct. As Shadeen Ali highlighted in Volume 3, the Ottoman approached the world as an Empire-in-the-Making, based on Mongol concept of law. All were in a state of subjection, or rebellion. The Iban of current-day Malaysia and Indonesia had no concept of 'peace', only periods without fighting.[27] This Volume has highlighted similar tensions. For the Egyptian, being divinely-authorised, neighbours were merely in a state of rebellion. 'War' was through a lens of criminal retribution rather than international laws of war. The Hitties were the only culture to think of a peace/war divide – and this was one based on, I would argue, a sovereign respect for sovereign neighbours.

I tend to use 'war' in its Clausewitzian form: imposing one's will on an enemy. On this, it is conventional in war studies to dismiss international law in the words of Clausewitz himself:

> war is thus an act of force to compel our enemies to do our will ... Attached to force are certain self-imposed, imperceptible limitations hardly worth mentioning known as international law and custom, but they scarcely weaken it.[28]

Yet such quotations are either deliberately misleading, or highlight an inability to read to the end of the page. Clausewitz almost immediately contradicts this claim in contrasting the wars of different states:

---

24 Shabtai Rosenne, 'The Influence of Judaism on the Development of International Law', *Netherlands International Law Review* 5 (2) (1958): 121. See also *ILA*, 6; Jared L. Miller, *Studies in the Origins, Development and Interpretation of the Kizzuwatna Rituals* (Wiesbaden: Harrassowitz Verlag, 2004), 458–459.

25 Samuel White, 'Sharp War, Soft War' (2024) *International Review of the Red Cross* (forthcoming).

26 Samuel White, 'Introduction' in *Laws of Yesterday's Wars: Volume III* (p. XX).

27 Angeline Lewis, 'Iban laws of war' in *Laws of Yesterday's Wars: Volume III* (p. XX).

28 *On War*, trans. Michael Howard and Peter Paret, New York, Everyman's Library, 1976, p. 83.

> If wars between civilized nations are far less cruel and destructive than war between savages, the reason lies in the social conditions of the states themselves and in their relationship to one another. These are the forces that give rise to war; the same forces circumscribe and moderate it.[29]

It is these social conditions that this paper has been focused upon, and illuminated to be found in all cultures so far surveyed in the *Laws of Yesterday's Wars* series. What the volumes reflect is the absolute impact the *environment* plays on social structures, and consequentially law. That which is valued is protected; and value is often placed on scarce resources. Earlier volumes have demonstrated as such. Within Ancient India, the value of cows (reflected in a still-current taboo on their killing) was reflected on the battlefield – those looking to surrender put grass in their mouth, claiming a linked sacrosanctity.[30] Within Papua New Guinea, traditional values incentivising the control of terraced-farming land subsequently shaped warfare to protect farmland and fertile areas.[31] We find this protection of fertile land across the Torah, Koran and Bible. The Mongols valued wealth; their social structure was based around wealth generation; and as such their laws of war revolved around ensuring trust in the political economy of the steppe.[32]

That the environment shapes society, and society in-turn shapes law is no great revelation. Yet it is important in continuing the trend of international law that Sir Christopher notes. The 21st century is currently grappling with an accelerating pace of technological development, which legal frameworks globally cannot keep pace with. With treaty law lagging, custom is developing. Contemporary practice I would suggest simply reflects past approaches to regulating warfare, captured in the *grundnorm* for IHL in the Martens Clause. What is valued today? Critical or sensitive infrastructure, including sensitive data (medical, personal, etc); hospitals; satellites & global navigation; power grids; supply chains, which despite nearly two decades of State capacity to target during conflict have remained conspicuously free from targeting. There is a line that States are not willing to cross in 21st century warfare, and that line would appear to be the permanent destruction of critical infrastructure. That which remains valued remains protected.

---

29 Ibid., p. 83.

30 Zuzana Spicova, 'Ancient Indian Laws of War' in Samuel White (ed.) *The Laws of Yesterday's Wars Volume II* (Brill Nijhoff, 2022) 5, 24.

31 Emily Defina, 'Papua New Guinean Laws of War' in Samuel White (ed.) *The Laws of Yesterday's Wars Volume III* (Brill Nijhoff, 2023) 1, 14.

32 Samuel White, 'Mongol Laws of War' in Samuel White (ed.) *The Laws of Yesterday's Wars Volume III* (Brill Nijhoff, 2023) 88.

Index

www.ingramcontent.com/pod-product-compliance
Lightning Source LLC
Chambersburg PA
CBHW051358240926
51852CB00001B/57
9789004703070